PENGUIN  CLASSICS

THOUGHTS FROM THE ICE-DRINKER'S STUDIO

LIANG QICHAO was born in southern China in 1873. He was heavily involved in the ultimately disastrous Hundred Days of Reform movement in 1898; following its brutal repression, he fled to Japan where he lived for fourteen years. His long exile, travels around the world and constant writing gave Liang a unique authority in the first years of the twentieth century. He introduced many key Western texts, penned fiction, edited newspapers and, above all, wrote essays. Liang then became a key figure in the politics of the Republic of China, founded when the Qing dynasty was overthrown in 1912; his attempts to foster parliamentary government failed, but he successfully opposed efforts to re-establish the monarchy and advocated China's participation in the First World War. He died in 1929.

PETER ZARROW is Professor of History at the University of Connecticut and Adjunct Research Fellow at the Institute of Modern History, Academia Sinica. He has held teaching and research positions in Australia and Taiwan, and he has published extensively in English and Chinese on the intellectual and cultural history of China in the nineteenth and twentieth centuries.

T0182354

LIANG QICHAO

Thoughts from
the Ice-Drinker's Studio

Essays on China and the World

Translated with an Introduction and Notes by
PETER ZARROW

PENGUIN BOOKS

PENGUIN CLASSICS

UK | USA | Canada | Ireland | Australia
India | New Zealand | South Africa

Penguin Books is part of the Penguin Random House group of companies
whose addresses can be found at global.penguinrandomhouse.com.

First published in Penguin Classics 2023
002

Set in 10.25/12.25pt Sabon LT Std
Typeset by Jouve (UK), Milton Keynes
Printed and bound in Great Britain by Clays Ltd, Elcograf S.p.A.

The authorized representative in the EEA is Penguin Random House Ireland,
Morrison Chambers, 32 Nassau Street, Dublin D02 YH68

A CIP catalogue record for this book is available from the British Library

ISBN: 978-0-241-56878-1

www.greenpenguin.co.uk

Contents

Introduction

Liang Qichao became China's pre-eminent public intellectual shortly after the turn of the twentieth century. He invented political journalism, promoted democratic reforms and introduced Western political theory to Chinese readers. He led China's break from tradition. Forced to flee China for political crimes at the age of twenty-five, he found a welcoming home in Japan, which also provided him with enormous intellectual stimulation. Shortly after Liang's arrival, he began writing a series of short essays that he called 'Notes on Liberty'. Often little more than reading notes and quick reflections – as Liang himself described them – their topics ranged from 'self-help', 'ideals and power' and 'revolution' to short biographies of various 'heroes'. They were bound together by Liang's belief that hope for the future lay in freedom of thought and disinterested pursuit of the truth.

In calling himself the 'Master of the Ice-Drinker's Studio', Liang cited a story from the *Zhuangzi*.[1] Namely, in about 500 BCE Duke Zigao of She had been designated the Chu kingdom's envoy to the Qi kingdom, meaning he had to deal with the irascible and stubborn rulers of that land. According to the *Zhuangzi*, Zigao was normally a man of equable temperament, but now he was consumed by anxiety and told Confucius, 'I only got my orders this morning, already I am drinking ice water this evening, and yet my insides are still on fire!'[2] Liang was not only saying that he identified with Zigao's anxiety and terror; in the following passage, which Liang did not quote, Confucius told Zigao to devote himself to his assigned task so wholeheartedly that he would forget his own existence and, not worrying about death, he could then carry out his orders successfully. Liang was perhaps also suggesting that he needed ice to cool down his hot-blooded ardor. The Master of the Ice-Drinker's Studio thus arrived in Japan announcing his wholehearted devotion to the renovation of China. Over his lifetime, Liang used many self-epithets – Mourning for the Times, A Patriot, A Youth of Youthful China, Master of the Studio of Liberty, A New Citizen of China – but he always returned to the Ice-Drinker's Studio.

Over the years, Liang was to change his mind on many issues. It is difficult to say precisely that Liang believed this or believed that without specifying which Liang we are talking about. In his own self-evaluation of 1920, he wrote, 'I care not if I criticize myself of yesterday with myself of today' and, fittingly enough, then criticized himself for having 'too few convictions' and getting 'carried away by events'.[3] Liang had a 'burning desire for knowledge' and, as he acquired new knowledge and as circumstances changed, he was happy to change his mind. Yet his fundamental intellectual commitments were of a piece, and even when his opinions changed, he continued to smuggle in many of his previous views. If, as Liang said, 'his conservative instincts and his progressive instincts frequently fought against each other within himself', one can often see the progressive in the conservative and the conservative in the progressive.

When Liang Qichao was born in 1873, the Qing dynasty had been sponsoring conservative reform projects for a little over a decade. Chinese people (the 'Han race') had accepted the legitimacy of the Qing, founded in 1644 by Manchu invaders, for two centuries by this time, although currents of anti-Manchuism were bubbling to the fore. The government was turning to reform as officials sought to import Western technology, especially armaments factories. But political and social elites remained conservative insofar as efforts to learn foreign languages, train modern engineers and send officials abroad remained deliberately limited. The commitment of elites to Confucian ethics of hierarchy and respect was, if anything, reinforced, but they recognized that some reforms were necessary because the government faced unprecedented threats from abroad and massive rebellions at home. Britain forced the Treaty of Nanjing on China at the end of the Opium War in 1842, which was the first of what became known as the 'unequal treaties' signed in the following years with France, the United States, Germany, Russia, Japan and other countries. In addition to paying large 'indemnities', which limited any reform programs that the Qing might have wanted to pursue, the Qing was forced to open Chinese cities to Westerners, who quickly built mini-colonies ('concessions'). Christian missionaries spread across the land, and the numbers of Western and Japanese diplomats and soldiers grew steadily.

Liang was born in a farming village in Guangdong Province in southeast China. His father ran a village school and farmed. Growing up, Liang had no contact with Western civilization, but he was not too far from the bustling international port of Guangzhou (Canton), where he moved to study in his teens. Liang was extremely precocious. He had soon mastered the Confucian curriculum of the Four Books and the Five Classics, and he passed the first level of the examination system at the age of eleven. The examination system was the key social and political institution in China for at least six hundred years. To pass its higher levels meant an official career beckoned, offering prestige and riches. At the extraordinarily young age of sixteen, Liang passed the second level. The chief examiner was so impressed that he gave his younger sister to Liang in marriage. She helped Liang learn the northern dialect necessary for official life. And about this time Liang met Kang Youwei (1858–1927). Kang taught that Confucius had been a prophet, a reformer and an institution-builder – in fact, a sage-king in his own right rather than a man who simply transmitted China's ancient cultural traditions. In other words, Kang was justifying his calls for radical change not as anti-Confucian but as representing the true spirit of Confucianism.[4] Equally stunning, Kang reinterpreted a key classical passage to argue that history proceeded through three ages from the Age of Chaos, through the Age of Approaching (or Lesser) Peace, and finally to the Age of Universal Peace (or Datong, utopia). The Datong foresaw a future of absolute equality of class, race and gender as people lived in a rich and democratic world without families, classes or nations.

Constitutions! Parliaments! This was heady stuff for Liang, barely in his twenties. He began to read translations of Western

thought as well as continuing to study the Confucian classics
and Buddhist texts. Along with a great many others, Liang was
shocked by China's loss to Japan in a war over which empire
would dominate Korea that was fought from late 1894 to early
1895. Qing troops were decisively defeated on land and its navy
destroyed at sea. It seemed that three decades of reform in China
had failed, while Japanese reforms since the Meiji Restoration of
1868 had succeeded. The treaty terms were harsh. Traveling to
Beijing for the highest-level exams, as it happened, Liang, along
with Kang, led a protest against the treaty which was ignored by
the government but contributed to their growing roles in China's
nascent public sphere. (Kang passed his exam; Liang failed his.)
Over the next three years the two men continued to advocate
radical reforms and organized study societies to further promote
their ideas. What Liang added to Kang's eccentric Confucianism
was a large dose of social Darwinism. Liang learned his social
Darwinism from Yan Fu (1854–1921), the great translator of
T. H. Huxley ('Darwin's bulldog') who in the following years
translated Herbert Spencer, Montesquieu, John Stuart Mill and
other mostly British social thinkers. Like Yan Fu, Liang interpreted the 'struggle for survival' at the level of the nation, and
although he saw a role for 'competition' among individuals, it
was the 'grouping' necessary for China's survival in a dangerous
world that he most valued.

At different times, Liang emotionally condemned the brutal-
ities of Western imperialism and regarded it as a wake-up call for
the Chinese. Adopting Western racial categories, he subsumed
the nation's struggle for survival into that of the race. At least for
a few years, Liang accepted the West's teaching that the world
consisted of five major races with Reds, Blacks and Browns at the
bottom, but he insisted that Yellows were the equal of Whites. He
further predicted a future White–Yellow struggle for global
supremacy; Yellows, or Chinese (the distinction was not always
clear), had advantages in terms of their numbers, their willing-
ness to work hard and their trading networks. At the same time,
Liang's admiration for the British sometimes seemed boundless;
he found the Anglo-Saxons to be superior to the other White
races, the Teutons and the Latins. Although Liang at least

sympathized with anti-Manchuism from the mid-1890s into the early 1900s, his racial thinking suggested that the differences between Han Chinese and Manchus were minor. This also opened the door – again, temporarily – to pan-Asianism on the grounds that tensions between China and Japan were within the 'same race'. However, Liang did not fundamentally remain a racial thinker. He primarily thought of citizenship – the language of democracy – as vital to China's survival. His strong nationalism was thus ultimately based on a vision of civic rather than ethnic identity. This brought him to a sharp critique of monarchism, which was not in itself as big a break with past political theory as it may sound. Indeed, in the mid- and late 1890s, Liang's activities were sponsored by high officials and his responsibilities included editorship of a reformist newspaper in Shanghai and teaching in a new-style academy in Hunan Province.

In 1898 Liang's life was forced onto a new track by the 'Hundred Days of Reform' which ended with Liang in exile with a price on his head. At the beginning of the 1890s, the Empress Dowager Cixi had begun stepping back from daily rule and the Emperor Guangxu, her nephew, assumed greater responsibilities. Cixi had maintained a strong grip on power by balancing conservatives and reformers at court and among provincial leaders. The cautious reforms of the 1870s and 1880s thus grew a little bolder in a few provinces. Then, in the summer of 1898, Guangxu, partly influenced by Kang Youwei's vision of strong reform leaders like Peter the Great and the Meiji Emperor, took a series of bold steps. Guangxu issued nearly two hundred broadly worded edicts to reorganize the government, modernize the military, encourage commerce, build a new school system and send more students abroad, and, perhaps most threatening to the powers-that-be, to streamline the bureaucracy. There was no hint in Guangxu's edicts of a constitution or parliament, but this was the nightmare that Cixi, Manchu aristocrats and conservative Chinese officials foresaw.

With the support of the leading (Han Chinese) military official, Yuan Shikai, Cixi shut the program down in September. She put the emperor under house arrest, which lasted the rest of his life. Leading reformers such as Kang and Liang fled; others stayed and were executed. A paranoid Cixi then promoted a reactionary resurgence that led the court to support the anti-foreign Boxer Uprising in northern China in 1900. Facing years of drought in the north China plains, the Boxers blamed Christians for disturbing the ancient gods of China, and the Qing court turned a peasant uprising into a war against the foreign powers (provincial leaders in other parts of China ignored Cixi's declaration of war – in itself a sign of the court's weakness). In north China the Western powers plus Japan responded with force, the court had to flee Beijing, and the Qing was forced to agree to horrendous terms before it could resume power – from the foreigners' perspective, a chastened and compliant Qing was better than any realistic alternative.

A new 'scramble for concessions' followed, provoking Chinese fears that their country would be 'sliced up like a melon' at the hands of the foreign powers and even that the Chinese race would be exterminated. A pro-republican and anti-Manchu revolutionary movement was fissiparous but gathered support, particularly among students. In 1901 Cixi promulgated 'New Policy' reforms very much along the lines of the Hundred Days reforms. As historical irony goes, the new reforms went even further than the 1898 proposals: in 1905 imperial edicts abolished the ancient exam system and promised a constitution. And although they were meant to be purely advisory, provincial parliaments were organized and even a national parliament began to meet in 1910.

Meanwhile, at the end of 1898 Liang had settled in Japan with the support of some of the leading members of the Meiji political elite. There he found an advanced country with universal schooling, railways and military conscription, as well as a constitution, a parliament and political parties – a country which was not occupied by foreigners. Liang founded a school and several journals, writing vociferously on a wide range of topics. Learning Japanese, he absorbed Western social and political thought through Japanese translations and studies. At this time, the first blush of Japanese liberal enchantment with Western democracy and individualism was fading, and Liang was also influenced by strains of 'statism'. The number of Chinese students in Japan was also growing steadily as part of the Qing's New Policy reforms – from a few hundred when Liang arrived to eight thousand by 1905. They were his first audience, but not his last. Although his writings were banned in China, in fact they circulated widely among students, the gentry class and even officialdom. Generally speaking, Liang spent the next fourteen years studying, writing and teaching before he was able to return to China. Another of his jobs was raising funds for the Protect the Emperor Society, which Kang Youwei had formed in the wake of the 1898 debacle in order to oppose Cixi in the name of Guangxu. Under its auspices, Liang visited Hawaii in 1899, Australia in 1900 and the United States in 1903.

Writings poured out of Liang during his Japanese exile. At first, these were brief reflections and synopses of his reading. He was also quick to publicize his version of the debacle of 1898, which served to delegitimize the Qing, or at least Cixi. But by, say, 1902, Liang was writing more reflective essays on the nature of Western imperialism, on civilization, on modernity and how concepts such as freedom, rights, equality and democracy could make the Chinese people better and China stronger. Liang's ideal was the 'new citizen' who would rid themselves of old evil habits and contribute to social progress. Although Liang came out against revolution, his ideas were truly radical. He had long emphasized the importance of education and school reform, including the education of women. And he had long been reshaping China's public sphere as an enthusiastic writer and editor. Now he also advocated journalism as a key source of knowledge for a developing people, for journalism would ultimately 'define and convey the will of the nation'.

Liang advanced radical approaches to history and literature as well. His self-proclaimed 'new historiography' insisted that the meaning of history lay in the progress of the nation. Quite unfairly, Liang criticized traditional Chinese historians for focusing only on the trivial doings of the imperial court, but he was truly radical in his insistence on linear progress and what we might call his view of the motor of history: competition among races and nations determined by the laws of social Darwinism. The alternative to progress was stagnation and ultimately extinction.

Put crudely, for Liang, history was a tool to strengthen the Chinese nation. Similarly, he argued that literature, especially fiction, could be a powerful force to remold the Chinese character. That literature had a didactic function was not a new idea, but Liang's esteem for prose fiction was new, as was his desire to reach the less educated with the goal of promoting political progress. His own unfinished novel of 1902, 'The Future of New China', was half political treatise, half utopian fantasy of a China that by 1962 had become a strong, wealthy and orderly constitutional monarchy – a power in the world. In the 1920s Liang's historical work and literary scholarship became considerably more sophisticated and less political, or at least less programmatic, but it was these earlier writings that proved the more influential.

During his Japanese sojourn, Liang had two enemies: Chinese conservatives and student revolutionaries. He had always been more concerned with the former, but after 1903 he began to criticize the latter. His trip to the United States seems to have led Liang to something of a 'conservative turn'. He reported disillusionment with the insularity and backwardness of Chinese communities in an America he otherwise found impressive. Was American civic culture so advanced that it would take China decades to get there? Was Chinese culture so decadent that even in America Chinese people remained bound by dysfunctional customs and prejudices?

Liang himself said he was discarding Rousseau and rejecting destruction (pohuai). Yet we should not exaggerate the change in Liang's fundamental views. His criticisms of the backwardness of some aspects of Chinese culture – self-criticisms in effect – were not entirely new, nor was his appreciation of personal moral virtues informed by Confucianism. His earlier emphasis on 'public morality' had not precluded personal morality, and if his later emphasis on personal morality was a way to criticize revolutionaries, it also remained rooted in his vision of the need to build a strong, coherent and integrated community. Liang thus argued that revolution would be too disruptive, and that attempts to overthrow the Qing were weakening China even as the foreign threats against it were growing. In principle, he supported republicanism, but he increasingly doubted China was ready for it.

Liang wrote less after 1903, but in addition to calling for a stronger state – even at one point promoting 'enlightened despotism' – he devoted more attention to concrete problems such as China's dire fiscal situation and foreign indebtedness, and he also studied economics and law. Through such studies he was preparing himself for a new political role once China was ready for him.

When the revolution came, it did so less as the result of a sustained revolutionary movement and more because the Qing had lost its legitimacy, even among China's political elites. Revolutionary propaganda and uprisings certainly chipped away at the Qing – and were themselves based on an ideology that combined Liang's constitutionalism with a large dose of racial anti-Manchuism. As well, the Qing fell due to widespread rebellion that took more traditional forms, a post-Cixi court that set its face firmly against compromise, and in the end the de facto military mutiny of its own generals. Once it appeared that the Qing was on the ropes by the end of 1911, many provincial elites and community leaders declared their new allegiance to revolution and republicanism. This was a class that had deeply imbibed Liang for the past decade or more, and that in effect had first treated Liang as a dangerous radical and then adopted him as a sensible guide for a period of tumultuous change. This class had gained a political voice through the late Qing reforms and now wanted power to go along with voice. The Qing abdicated in February 1912 after a military stalemate was broken when its top general – none other than Yuan Shikai – went over to the revolutionaries. And so the revolutionaries gave way to the old Qing military apparatus, accepting Yuan as president, though hoping that promised elections would give them power.

If Liang was a precocious but still somewhat callow twenty-five when he fled China, he was an intellectually mature thirty-nine when he returned in 1912, but even he may not have fully appreciated the problems left in the revolution's wake. Liang was initially optimistic about the prospects of the new republic and about his own prospects. He founded a new political party which opposed the revolutionaries, who were now organized into their own party, but which supported a bicameral legislature that would make all laws – there could be no law by presidential decree – based on limited suffrage. Such dreams soon turned into nightmares. Yuan Shikai quickly crushed the revolutionaries and made himself de facto military dictator, though of a central government whose powers were weakening by the day.

Still, Liang and Yuan attempted to work with each other. Liang, if he could not be prime minister, still fancied himself an advisor to whom Yuan might listen. Yuan, for his part, found Liang's support useful in shoring up his legitimacy as a modernizer. Yuan gave Liang a salary and supported his new political party. Liang briefly became minister of justice in Yuan's cabinet and then even more briefly director of the Bureau of Currency. In 1915 Liang was one of the leaders of Chinese resistance to Japanese demands for a larger role in the Chinese government. Later that year, Yuan began preparations to found a new dynasty with himself as emperor. He promised his would be a constitutional monarchy and his supporters pointed out to Liang that this was precisely what Liang had been calling for. But Liang would have nothing to do with the plan. He fled to Shanghai, helped organize military opposition and wrote a powerful condemnation of Yuan. Liang disputed the charge that he was being inconsistent by previously supporting a constitutional monarchy and now supporting republicanism. Rather, he insisted, he was consistent in his opposition to revolutionary change. Even if the overthrow of the Qing had been a mistake, China was now a republic, and whatever was wrong with it would not be fixed by monarchism or any other change in the basic form of the state.

Yuan died of illness (or humiliation) just as provincial armies began their moves against him, and his monarchy died with him. In the aftermath of this debacle, the Beijing government was further weakened and became a plaything of competing militarists. Notwithstanding the breakdown of the central government, Yuan's death was widely seen as legitimizing the principle of republicanism. The revolution was two-pronged: first, a nationalism that temporarily took on the form of anti-Manchuism; and second, a republicanism that was stymied but refused to die. Liang's nationalism was based on a vision of a strong state, strong precisely because of its citizens' republicanism. In the wake of the revolution, Chinese elites strove to create a multinational state closer to Liang's thinking than that of the revolutionaries. One could even say that the new school system, limited though it was, taught Liang-ist values in history, geography and civics classes. In the early years of the republic, Liang tried, with a certain degree of success, to carve out a political role for himself, but had little more to say on the theoretical issues that had so preoccupied him in the previous decade: democracy, nationalism, liberty and the like. He did, however, have more to say about Chinese culture and the ways to syncretize Western and Chinese values.

Liang had supported China's declaration of war against Germany in 1917 in the hopes that it would give China a place at the Paris Peace Conference. Yet the First World War was disillusioning for most Chinese, including Liang, on two grounds. First, China did not get a real place at the peace table and Germany's Chinese concessions were turned over to Japan. And second, more broadly, how could a civilization as advanced as Europe have decided to tear itself apart? Liang spent most of 1919 in Europe, witnessing the war's destruction, observing the peace conference and meeting with European intellectuals. Philosophers like Henri Bergson confirmed Liang's sense that Chinese civilization had much to contribute to the West, even as his faith in Western-style constitutionalism and democracy remained strong. Upon his return to China, Liang found a country in political ferment. The 'May Fourth' protests of 1919 against the Versailles Treaty had turned into a broad anti-imperialist revolutionary movement. Liang, however, was largely done with politics, though he did continue to urge 'gradual reform' or a middle way between conservatives and radicals. He also contributed to discussions of the 'May Thirtieth Incident': the killing of workers and demonstrators when British police opened fire on a crowd in Shanghai in 1925, which led to nationwide demonstrations, strikes and boycotts. He added his voice to the chorus of Chinese demanding revision of the unequal treaties. Appealing to Westerners directly, he claimed that the Chinese simply wanted the same political freedoms that Westerners took for granted, such as those enshrined in the French Declaration of the Rights of Man.

Yet on the whole Liang made few direct interventions in the new era's political debates. He spent most of the 1920s teaching in universities and conducting research on ancient Chinese thought and culture. He published extensively on these topics, which he regarded as relevant to the questions of the day but which inevitably had a flavor of antiquarianism. Yet if radical circles could dismiss Liang, he still retained great prestige – his opinions continued to be widely disseminated – in broader society and among the intelligentsia. He died of a possibly botched operation in 1929, leaving five sons and four daughters, most of whom became prominent in their own right, and his concubine or second wife (his first wife had died in 1924).

In sum, Liang was a quick study and a facile and voluminous writer, especially in the period from 1899 to 1903. Liang once remarked that whatever he had to say, he published. He wrote in a time of turmoil, even crisis. Much in his essays may strike the modern reader as crude, but it should be remembered that Liang's goal was never to sit back and think through new political theory *in toto*, but to enlighten his fellow Chinese and chivvy them to take action. Liang's writings of those four years alone arguably make him the father of Chinese nationalism as well as the father of Chinese liberalism. This was a civic rather than an ethnic nationalism, and a liberalism based as much on morality and duties as on rights. Liang shaped the development of journalism, education, historiography and literature in modern China. His influence was vast; even those who rejected his ideas learned from them – several generations of students starting from the turn of the twentieth century, including Mao Zedong, noted their indebtedness to Liang.

Indeed, Liang's influence was not limited to China, and included Korea and Vietnam as well. But are his writings of more than antiquarian interest today? This question can be answered on two levels. First, it may be impossible to understand China today without an appreciation of the role Liang's writings played in creating it. He helped to bring down a Confucian-bureaucratic empire and construct a new, deliberately modernizing nation-state. Second, it may be that Liang was not only an intellectual pioneer in what were then considered (by some) to be hopelessly conservative and backward countries, but also offers a model of how one should wrestle with new, foreign ideas. In ways both deliberate and unconscious, Liang reshaped Western concepts to make them useful and alive in China. He also reinterpreted Confucian doctrines, participating in a long hermeneutical tradition even as he started a new tradition by Sinifying Western political concepts – and, indeed, combining various strands of the two traditions into one. That ideals of democracy, liberty and rights are today as Chinese as they are Western is due in considerable part to Liang Qichao.

NOTES

1. *Zhuangzi* was a miscellaneous collection of texts central to the Daoist tradition, credited to Zhuang Zhou (*c.* fourth century BCE) and compiled in its present form around the third century BCE. A theme of the *Zhuangzi* that may have appealed to Liang can be summarized as freedom, though more in the sense of transcending conventional constraints and prejudices than in the modern sense of political liberty. Liang Qichao, 'Yinbingshi ziyou shu' 飲冰室自由書 [Notes on Liberty from the Ice-Drinker's Studio], *Qingyi bao* 清議報, no. 25 (Guangxu 25-7-21) (August 1899). Liang was also participating in a long tradition wherein literati chose different names for themselves to highlight some feature of their character or their changing circumstances.

2. Cf. *Zhuangzi: The Essential Writings*, translated by Brook Ziporyn (Indianapolis: Hackett Publishing Co., 2009), pp. 27–8.

3. Liang Ch'i-ch'ao, *Intellectual Trends in the Ch'ing Period*, translated by Immanuel C. Y. Hsü (Cambridge, MA: Harvard University Press, 1970), pp. 102–7.

4. Kang Youwei was heir to the 'New Text' school of Confucianism that relied on slightly different versions of the Classics than those of the dominant 'Old Text' Confucianism. Kang's textual interpretations were arguably eccentric and arbitrary, and were vehemently criticized at the time, but they were also part of a larger movement promoting change. The standard biography of Kang and his thought remains Kung-ch'uan Hsiao, *A Modern China and a New World: K'ang Yu-wei, Reformer and Utopian, 1858–1927* (Seattle: University of Washington Press, 1975).

Bibliography

Angle, Stephen C. 'Should We All Be More English? Liang Qichao, Rudolf von Jhering and Rights', *Journal of the History of Ideas*, vol. 61, no. 2 (2000): 241–61.

Chan, Sin-wai. *Buddhism in Late Ch'ing Political Thought* (Hong Kong: The Chinese University Press, 1985).

Chang, Hao. *Liang Ch'i-ch'ao and Intellectual Transition in China, 1890–1907* (Cambridge, MA: Harvard University Press, 1971).

Dong Fangkui. *Liang Qichao yu lixian zhengzhi* [Liang Qichao and constitutional politics] (Wuhan: Huazhong shifan daxue chubanshe, 2011).

Fogel, Joshua A. (ed.). *The Role of Japan in Liang Qichao's Introduction of Modern Western Civilization to China* (Berkeley: Institute of East Asian Studies, University of California, 2004).

Hazama Naoki. *Ryō Keichō: Higashi Ajia bunmeishi no tenkan* [Liang Qichao: The transformation of the history of East Asian civilization] (Tokyo: Iwanami shoten, 2016).

Hazama Naoki (ed.). *Kyōdō kenkyū Ryō Keichō: Seiyō kindai shisō juyō to Meiji Nihon* [Joint research on Liang Qichao: The reception of modern Western thought and Meiji Japan] (Tokyo: Misuzu shobō, 1999).

Huang Kewu [Max Ko-wu Huang]. *Yige beifangqi de xuanze: Liang Qichao tiaoshi sixiang zhi yanjiu* [The rejected path: A study of Liang Qichao's accommodative thinking] (Taibei: Zhongyang yanjiuyuan jindaishi yanjiusuo, 1994).

Huang, Philip C. *Liang Ch'i-ch'ao and Modern Chinese Liberalism* (Seattle: University of Washington Press, 1972).

Huters, Theodore. *Bringing the World Home: Appropriating the West in Late Qing and Early Republican China* (Honolulu: University of Hawai'i Press, 2005).

Lee, Theresa Man Ling. 'Liang Qichao and the Meaning of Citizenship: Then and Now', *History of Political Thought*, vol. 28, no. 2 (2007): 305–27.

Levenson, Joseph. *Liang Ch'i-ch'ao and the Mind of Modern China* (Berkeley: University of California Press, 1970).

Makeham, John (ed.). *Transforming Consciousness: Yogācāra Thought in Modern China* (Oxford: Oxford University Press, 2014).

Meng Xiangcai. *Liang Qichao zhuan* [The life of Liang Qichao] (Beijing: Beijing chubanshe, 1980).

Tang, Xiaobing. *Global Space and the Nationalist Discourse of Modernity: The Historical Thinking of Liang Qichao* (Stanford: Stanford University Press, 1996).

Xia Xiaohong. *Yuedu Liang Qichao* [Reading Liang Qichao], 3 vols (Beijing: Dongfang chubanshe, 2019).

Zhang Pengyuan [P'eng-yuan Chang]. *Liang Qichao yu minguo zhengzhi* [Liang Qichao and the politics of the Republic] (Taibei: Zhongyang yanjiuyuan jindaishi yanjiusuo, 1978).

Zhang Pengyuan [P'eng-yuan Chang]. *Liang Qichao yu Qingji geming* [Liang Qichao and the Qing revolution] (Taibei: Zhongyang yanjiuyuan jindaishi yanjiusuo, 1964).

Zhang Pengyuan [P'eng-yuan Chang]. *Lixianpai yu xinhai geming* [Constitutionalists and the 1911 Revolution] (Taibei: Zhongyang yanjiuyuan jindaishi yanjiusuo, 1969).

Translator's Note

Out of Liang's extensive writings I have chosen essays that deal with fundamental questions about how to organize society and state, foster citizenship and national identity, reconcile rights and obligations, raise the level of the culture and become better persons, fight imperialism and make China strong, and adapt certain ideals derived from the West such as democracy and liberty to China's conditions. I have also tried, to a more limited degree, to select essays that represent some of Liang's central concerns at different junctures in his life. His writings reflect his participation in three great traditions: Confucianism, Buddhism and Western Enlightenment thinking. Thanks to Liang – and, of course, many other thinkers and activists as well – all three traditions became part of modern China's social and political discourse. The essays in this volume focus on Liang's efforts to assimilate what he considered essentially Western thought; this did not mean, as readers will see, that he rejected either Confucianism or Buddhism.[1] He rejected *aspects* of those traditions (and aspects of Western traditions as well).

With one exception, I have also chosen essays that do not require a huge scaffolding of footnotes to explain Liang's references (the exception is his 1904 essay on 'Personal Morality'). Nonetheless, Liang seldom went long without citing a historical case or quoting from the Classics. I provide brief footnotes for Liang's historical references and his explicit citations of classical texts, but generally not for his unattributed phrase-borrowing or allusions to the Classics, though I have consulted the original texts and standard translations. In some cases, Liang's unacknowledged classical references would have been understood to his readers at the time but are too abbreviated to make sense in translation; in those cases, I have translated more text from the original to clarify Liang's point. When Liang cites 'a Western philosopher', I have in some cases been able to track down his source.

A brief volume such as this cannot do justice to the range of Liang's thought. Liang's more scholarly writings will not be found here, nor have I translated those essays that were largely based on (or plagiarized from) Japanese sources – though they did express his own thinking at the time. Similarly, I have not translated his numerous essays describing Western historical figures and philosophers. Other Liangs than the Liang found here include the educator, the institution-builder, the journalist-publisher, the politician and economist, the historian and philosopher, and the cultural critic. The Liang in these pages is the political thinker and public intellectual.

I have translated key terms according to context. Liang uses *guo* and *guojia*, for example, in ways variously closest to *country*, *state* and *nation*; conversely there were several different ways in Chinese to express the loose notion of *democracy*. The same applies to the words 'people', 'race', 'citizen', 'national', 'sovereignty', 'liberty', 'rights' – and a host of other terms and concepts. Terms used to express Western political concepts were still in flux during Liang's lifetime. When Liang speaks of democracy, he is not referring to universal suffrage but some kind of more or less extensive popular participation in the political realm.

Many of his readers loved Liang's innovative writing style; others despised it. To simplify, Liang wrote in classical Chinese (*guwen*), historically the grammar of all serious writing, but quite distinct from everyday vernacular Chinese. In Liang's own third-person description, however: 'He would often interlard his writing with colloquialisms, rhyme and foreign expressions, letting his pen flow freely and without restraint.' Not the least of the translator's headaches is the impossibility of conveying the flavor of Liang's use of the Chinese language's infinitely varied colloquialisms, which have none of the childish flavor of their English cousins and which Liang often altered from their standard form to gain greater effect. Liang was writing at a moment of great linguistic change – not only were a great number of neologisms being invented to capture Western concepts, but there were also a great many debates over which genres and forms of writing were best suited to the times. Over the course of the 1910s and 1920s vernacular forms of writing (*baihua*), which their proponents regarded as closer to spoken Chinese and easier for less-educated people to understand, came to dominate. Liang wrote the last three essays translated in this volume in the vernacular. Where possible, I have tried to preserve the structure of Liang's sentences as the best way to convey his thought processes. Probably the biggest change from the original texts is that I have given Liang the gift of paragraphing.

My translations are based on both the text as originally published and the collected works of Liang that were published in the 1930s in the *Collected Works from the Ice-Drinker's Studio* (*Yinbingshi heji*). There are a few mostly minor differences between the two, and in those cases I have followed the version that I believe best expresses Liang's thinking. All the endnotes are mine, not Liang's. He used long parenthetical remarks, translated as such here, where we might use footnotes today. I use Hanyu Pinyin to romanize Chinese names and terms; Chinese names are given family name first. This volume offers the first English translation of a set of Liang's essays.[2] Existing translations of Liang's writings include the following (original Chinese publication date in parentheses).

1. On political and social questions

'On Women's Education' (1897), in Lydia H. Liu, Rebecca E. Karl and Dorothy Ko (eds). *The Birth of Chinese Feminism: Essential Texts in Transnational Theory* (New York: Columbia University Press, 2013), pp. 187–203.

Excerpts from *The New Citizen* (1902–3), in Wm. Theodore de Bary and Richard Lufrano (eds). *Sources of Chinese Tradition*, Volume 2: *From 1600 through the Twentieth Century* (New York: Columbia University Press, 2010), pp. 287–302.

'On Rights Consciousness', abridged (1902), in Stephen C. Angle and Marina Svensson (eds). *The Chinese Human Rights*

Reader: Documents and Commentary, 1900–2000 (Armonk, NY: M. E. Sharpe, 2001), pp. 5–14.

'Notes from a Journey to the New Continent', excerpts (1904), in R. David Arkush and Leo O. Lee (eds). *Land without Ghosts: Chinese Impressions of America from the Mid-Nineteenth Century to the Present* (Berkeley: University of California, 1989), pp. 81–95.

2. On literature

'Foreword to the Publication of Political Novels in Translation' (1898), translated by Gek Nai Cheng, in Kirk A. Denton (ed.). *Modern Chinese Literary Thought: Writings on Literature, 1893–1945* (Stanford: Stanford University Press, 1996), pp. 71–3.

'On the Relationship between Fiction and the Government of the People' (1902), translated by Gek Nai Cheng, in Denton (ed.), *Modern Chinese Literary Thought: Writings on Literature, 1893–1945*, pp. 74–81.

3. Historical scholarship

Intellectual Trends in the Ch'ing Period (1920), translated by Immanuel C. Y. Hsü (Cambridge, MA: Harvard University Press, 1959).

History of Chinese Political Thought during the early Tsin Period (1922), translated by Li-t'ing Chen (New York: Harcourt, Brace, 1930).

Archaeology in China (1926). (Peking: Peking Leader Press, 1926).

4. Autobiography

'My Autobiographical Account at Thirty' (1902), in Li Yu-ning (ed.). *Two Self-Portraits: Liang Ch'i-Ch'ao and Hu Shih* (Bronxville: Outer Sky Press, 1992), pp. 1–31.

NOTES

1. Nor is this to say that Liang essentialized 'Western' thought. He understood that both the West and China were homes to enormous intellectual diversity. Liang also rejected the briefly popular view that Western concepts such as liberty and equality had actually originated in ancient China before somehow traveling to Europe, although he did not deny the existence of correspondences between aspects of Western and Chinese thought.

2. A one-volume Japanese translation of selected essays is *Ryō Keichō bunshū*, translated by Okamoto Takashi, Ishikawa Yoshihiro and Takashima Kō (Tokyo: Iwanami shoten, 2020). There is also a French translation of Liang's history of Qin political thought: *La Conception de la loi et les théories des légistes a la vielle des Ts'in*, translated by Jean Escarra and Robert Germain (Pekin: China Booksellers, 1926).

PART ONE
EARLY REFORMIST
THOUGHT: FOUNDATIONS,
1896–1898

In 1896 Liang wrote a series of essays under the title *General Discussion of Institutional Reform*. They covered various topics, but mostly revolved around education: Liang criticized the examination system, called for a modern school system and girls' education and urged greater use of the vernacular as opposed to writing in classical Chinese. These essays brought him to national attention. Liang's two essays from this period translated here include the 'Preface to the *General Discussion of Institutional Reform*', and an essay on what he called 'grouping' – a concept closely related to community, society and nation. At this time, Liang was also calling for the equalization of the legal status of Han and Manchus, and an end to footbinding.

While Liang did not call publicly for the adoption of a constitution or establishment of a parliament, he spoke privately on these topics with his students and even expressed a certain amount of anti-Manchu sentiment. But his public proposals were radical enough. Above all, Liang's call for 'institutional' reform was a challenge to the traditional promise of emperors to never change the system handed down by their ancestor, the dynastic founder. Liang's proposed reforms were all designed to push China toward greater social and political cohesion – this was what he fundamentally meant by 'grouping'. Liang's 'Essay on Grouping' was an early effort to link the processes that would create a stronger Chinese polity to cosmic or at least natural or biological laws based on evolutionary principles. He was increasingly skeptical of monarchism, which he regarded as a recipe for stagnation and the inability to 'group', and he associated dynamism and progress with more 'civilized' forms of government.

At this time, Liang understood himself to be operating within the Confucian tradition, which could be strengthened, rather than threatened, by knowledge of Western science and institutions. In various writings from this period, Liang reflected a view of history (which he took from Kang Youwei) as moving from the Age of Chaos, or primitive tribalism and barbarism, to the Age of Lesser Peace, or monarchism, much like China at the time; and finally to the Great Peace (Taiping, or Datong), or democracy. This was perhaps a reassuring vision, except that progress was not guaranteed and the alternative was racial extinction.

I

Preface to the *General Discussion*
of Institutional Reform[1]

Liang's main argument for institutional reform was that China's
military and technological reforms to date were insufficient to
save the nation. Rather, the basic political and social institutions
of the Qing dynasty needed to be rethought. First published in
Shiwubao, *August 1896.*

Why is it necessary to change our institutions? Everything in
the world changes. Day and night alternate, making a full day;
winter and summer alternate, making a full year. When the
Earth first formed, it consisted of flowing magma, and the constant activity of volcanos and glaciers changed the planet into
our Earth. Seaweeds and conches, giant trees and great birds,
flying fish and flying lizards, marsupials and vertebrates, appeared
and disappeared, changing through generation after generation
to form our world. Dark blood and red blood circulated inside
bodies to continuously carry out carbon dioxide and bring in
oxygen, and after endless changes human beings were formed.
Without change, the world and humanity would cease to
exist. Thus 'change' has been a universal principle operating
across all time. The ancient harvest tax changed into the grain-
corvée-textile tax, which changed into the summer-fall tax,
which changed into the single-whip cash payment.[2] Local
militia became garrison militia, which became the capital
guard, which became the imperial army. The ancient academic
selection system became the recommendation system, which
became the Nine Ranks system, which became the examination
system.[3] For millennia, there has never been a time without

change, nor an institution without change. Universal principles work on their own, independent of human actions.

Those who oppose change constantly proclaim, 'Preserve tradition! Preserve tradition!' How can they not know that since the most ancient times, antiquity, the Middle Ages, and the modern period, through to today – changes have been too numerous to comprehend. How vastly different are what we consider to be our traditional institutions – institutions we try to preserve – from those of the ancients!

Today's natural changes are the Way of Heaven, and some are for good and some for evil, while the Way of Humanity is amenable to the judgment of the wise. The *Analects* states: 'The knowledgeable progress upwards while the ignorant regress downwards.'[4] And the same applies to governance. If we fail to attend to events, not taking responsibility for change, then affairs will gradually go downhill. But if we rally to rectify events and deliberate with flexibility, then affairs will gradually improve.

According to my studies of antiquity, once a new dynasty comes to power, its founder establishes new laws and institutions; after several generations the laws and institutions that the later generations follow are certainly different from the founder's, but these later emperors and their subjects audaciously claim to be following the founder. A dynasty that rules with the institutions that it used to establish the empire, merely preserving them, purely keeping to routine, declining slowly and neglecting affairs, is finally exhausted beyond resuscitation. Then the next dynasty examines the previous dynasty's faults and changes them, and thus renews the kingship. But if the imperial descendants understand this principle, they will examine their faults and change; this is called a restoration. This describes the Han Restoration and the Tang Restoration.[5] *The Book of Odes* states: 'Although Zhou was an old country, it received a new Mandate.'[6] This is to say that to govern an old country, one must use new institutions. This task is self-evident and its principle is clear: there are opportunities to carry it out, there are precedents to follow, there is only one path forward and there is no time to waste.

Those who oppose change still proclaim, 'Preserve tradition! Preserve tradition!' With perfect indifference, they sit and watch the country stagnate and decline. Alas! Is this not completely incomprehensible? *The Book of Changes* states: 'When a series of changes has run its full course, another change ensues. When it obtains free course, it will continue for a long time.'[7] Yi Yin said, 'Use that which is new and remove that which is old.'[8] That way, the illness is cured. Without bright candles, the night is dark. Without fur coats, the winter is cold. It is dangerous to cross a river in a carriage. And it is deadly to use the old prescriptions when the symptoms change.

I am raising this critical issue here with extreme urgency. I follow the old royal advisors and risk scorn for speaking out, but I cannot be blamed for speaking out to awaken my readers. There follow sixty chapters in twelve sections. I will accept whatever praise or criticism comes my way.

2

Essay on Grouping[1]

'Grouping' for Liang means something like 'community', if community were a powerful verb as well as a noun. It refers to people coming together in a natural process to form associations that are increasingly integrated and cohesive. The key concept here is 'natural' – Liang links chemical, biological and politico-social processes; he flavors the theory of linear progress through the Three Ages (as proposed by Kang Youwei) with a large dash of social Darwinism. For Liang, the problem was not that the Chinese were incapable of forming associations, but that they had little sense of national identity; in other words, their grouping was not yet highly developed. Although at the time he wrote this essay Liang still foresaw the emergence of a truly global grouping in the future (the final stage of the Three Ages), he was soon to abandon this idea, believing, rather, that the nation-state was the final form of grouping. Liang originally intended that his 'Essay on Grouping' would include a series of chapters on the subject, but he abandoned the project. Still, he continued to discuss grouping in the following years, as several of the other essays translated below show. The Preface was first published in Shiwubao *in May 1897; the Preface and Part One were published together in* Zhixinbao *the following week.*

Preface

I asked Kang Youwei about the Way of governing the world. Kang replied, 'With grouping as the foundation and with change as the means. As long as these two principles are established, the world can be governed even for eons.' Having recounted what I heard, and written *A General Discussion of Reform*, I wished to further develop the meaning of 'grouping'. The concept is very abstruse and subtle, and I could not get anywhere, but after reading Yan Fu's *On Evolution* and Tan Sitong's *On Benevolence*, my ideas were clarified.[2] Alas! Persons of resolution can scarcely hear mention of Kang Youwei's writings or catch sight of the great works by the two aforementioned gentlemen. Even if any of them happen to see or hear of the works of Kang, or Yan, or Tan, they cannot understand or believe them. Here, then, I elaborate on the words of my teacher, Kang Youwei, backed up by the two works mentioned above, to write ten essays 'On Grouping' in one hundred and twenty chapters in simple prose backed with facts.[3] My work is not even worth one-tenth of the works of Kang Youwei or the masterpieces of Yan and Tan. Only in considering my ideas on reform can I say that I have made some contribution.

The Book of Rites states, 'He who can unite a group can be called a ruler.'[4] Those who ruled in ancient times distinguished themselves from the group, calling themselves 'The Solitary', 'The One of Small Virtue' or 'I the One Man'.[5] Such delusion! 'Solitary' and 'Small Virtue' through the ages were used to describe those with no one to turn to, but then people took delight in using these terms to refer to the ruler. The Classics, when they wish to defile the name of a deceased king, call him the 'Autocrat' or the 'Alone'. There are none who hear such words without knowing that these are vile names. I am confounded as to how the exegetical sense of the term 'I the One Man' is different from 'Autocrat'.

Today, a thousand people or ten thousand people group together to form a country, and millions and millions of people group together to form the whole world. So are not these countries and the whole world defined by their ability to form groups? To govern through methods of grouping, the group coalesces; to govern through methods of autocracy, the group fails to coalesce. The failure of one's own group is to the advantage of another group. What is meant by 'methods of autocracy'? Everyone knows of their own existence and does not know of the existence of the whole world. The ruler hoards his palace, the official hoards his noble rank, the farmer hoards his land, the worker hoards his craft, the merchant hoards his profit, the individual hoards his advantages, the household hoards its wealth, the lineage hoards its clans, the clans hoard their families, the township hoards its land, the district hoards its villages, the teacher hoards his doctrine, and the scholar hoards his learning. Thus to have 400 million people of China means to have 400 million countries, which is to say there is really no country at all.

Those who are skilled at governing a country know that in relation to the people the ruler is but another individual of the group. With knowledge of the operating principle of grouping and its workings, they will keep the group united and not divided, coalesced and not in disarray, and this is called 'methods of grouping'. The division of the world into separate countries is due to the differentiating of one's own group from other groups. In the Age of Chaos groups are governed through autocracy, while in the Age of Great Peace groups are governed through grouping.[6] When autocracy encounters autocracy, they will both survive, but when autocracy encounters grouping, we can count on it to collapse in an instant. The perfection of the West's methods of grouping has taken place within just the last hundred years, and so its rise followed. Now, if we follow others to practice grouping while our nature remains inclined to autocracy, this would be like Xi Shi's knit brow, or stretching a tiger's skin over a sheep.[7] Innumerable changes would result, all improper. Moreover, I have heard of national grouping and of world grouping. As for Western governance, it can be practiced at the level of national grouping but not at the level of world grouping.

The Book of Changes states: 'To see a flock of dragons without a head is an auspicious occurrence.' *The Spring and Autumn Annals* states: 'In the Age of Great Peace, the world is unified regardless of the sizes and distances of states.'[8] *The Book of Rites* states: 'When the Great Way prevailed, the empire was held in common. They chose men of virtue and ability [to rule]. They did not love their parents only, nor treat as children only their own sons. They hated to throw objects away, but nor did they keep them for themselves. They hated not to work hard, but nor did they work for themselves. This was called the Great Harmony.' This is precisely what a world grouping is!

The Principle of Grouping, Part One

If there were just one Earth in space, and one person on Earth, and one nature shared by all humanity, then it would be permissible not to advocate the learning of grouping. Grouping is a universal principle of the universe. The Earth groups with other planets, and the sun groups with other stars in patterns of mutual attraction that never fall apart. If there were only centrifugal forces, then the universe would collapse. The sixty-four chemical elements mix and react with one another and, in the unlimited changes in their proportions and combinations, give rise to all things.[9]

If none of the elements possessed the force of attraction, then they would constitute the only sixty-four creations on the entire Earth, and there would be no way for the world to emerge. A plant has stamens and pollen to propagate, an ovary to germinate the seed, a cotyledon to sprout, roots to absorb the Earth's nutrients, a stem to grow upright, and branches and leaves to soak up air and water and light. Each part of the plant stores up its energy and contributes its labor to the whole: this is the 'grouping' of a living thing. If any part is missing or if the parts do not respond to one another, it will soon wither. A human body has ears for hearing, eyes for seeing, a mouth for speaking, hands and feet for moving, bones for supporting the body, tendons for connecting its muscles, lungs for breathing, a stomach for digesting food, a heart for pumping blood, blood vessels for circulating the blood and a brain for processing sensations. Each part of the body stores up its energy and contributes its labor to the whole: this is the 'grouping' of the human body. If any part is missing or if the parts do not respond to one another, it will soon die.

Therefore, in regard to all things, compounds are nobler than elements, and complex compounds are nobler than simple compounds.[10] And therefore, dead things are the basest, plants are above them, and animals are the noblest. The nature of all things is to honor the principle of grouping. In regard to animals, the simpler their physical organization, the stupider they are, while the more complex their physical organization, the smarter they are. Therefore, plants are the stupidest, mollusks are above them and vertebrates are the smartest. Physical organization honors the principle of grouping. In regard to humans, the more complex their nervous system is, the more intelligent they are, while the simpler their nervous system is, the stupider they are. The more social contact people have, the more open-minded they are; and the less contact, the more close-minded. The more people study, the greater their knowledge; and the less they study, the greater their ignorance. This is why Africans are inferior to Europeans and Asians, country folk are inferior to urbanites and the ancients are inferior to the moderns: the development of knowledge honors the principle of grouping. Therefore, throughout space and time, beyond accounting and beyond ending, things that have a physical existence and consciousness can only exist and endure through the principle of grouping.

Grouping is the inherent nature of all things, which they know without learning and can achieve without thinking. But there are those that disintegrate and perish due to their inability to group, such as heavenly bodies that fall from their orbits, gases that diffuse, plants that wither, and humans and animals that die. Why is this? There are two forces in the universe: attraction and repulsion. These two forces as a whole never increase or decrease, but they do change in inverse ratio to one another. Their relationship alternates so that when one increases, the other decreases. In this way, if there are people who can group, then there will be people who cannot group; if there are people whose grouping is strong, then there will be people whose grouping is weak. And so the people who cannot group will certainly be destroyed by the people who can group, and the people whose grouping is weak will certainly be conquered by the people whose grouping is strong. For example, when needles are placed on a plate, they will be attracted to the plate, forming a group with it.[11] But when a magnet is used to attract the needles, they will be separated from the plate to group with the magnet. This is because the grouping strength between magnets and needles is greater than that between needles and the plate.

Since the beginning of life on Earth, there has always been a vast variety of species all of which constantly change. If we thoroughly study the principles of progress and renewal, it is clear that the groups that emerge later gradually prevail and the earlier groups gradually decline. The advocates of evolutionism in the West describe this process as survival of the fittest. Before the Floods, the tracks of animals and birds crisscrossed all China, but it was the Duke of Zhou's great enterprise to expel the dangerous beasts, and to this day there are virtually no traces of tigers, leopards, rhinoceroses or elephants in China. This is because grouping of animals could not withstand the grouping of humans. The Americas, Africa and Australia were all populated by aboriginals, but when peoples from other continents settled in their territories, the aboriginal populations were steadily wiped out. The grouping of barbarian peoples cannot withstand the grouping of civilized peoples. The more the world progresses, the more grouping develops. If a group cannot keep developing, it will face extinction. This is terrifying!

It is inevitable that the struggle for survival depends on grouping. The struggles of groups are especially sharp when they are close to one another in strength and also in proximity. The groupings of plants, fishes, birds or animals – none can withstand the groupings of humans. Why, then, is it only animals that have been destroyed? Humans and animals come into conflict because they live in proximity to one another. The reason why the fishes can survive in the water, the birds can survive in the sky and the plants can survive on the ground is because they do not pose problems for humans or come into conflict with them. As for those creatures that are still able to survive, even in close proximity to humans – such as bees, locusts, ants, mosquitoes and horseflies – they must have grouping abilities comparable to those of humans. Therefore, they have never been wiped out. Let me compare this to the peoples who live in places like the central African desert or the frozen Arctic Ocean – they can survive even though they are completely incapable of grouping, because like the fishes, birds and plants, their territories are not worth fighting over. As for weak and small countries like Denmark, Holland, Belgium and Switzerland, they can survive even though they are surrounded by stronger European powers, because their own grouping abilities are comparable to those of the great nations. If a country located in a strategic area does not have the grouping abilities it needs to preserve itself, then it will be gradually weakened to the point that its race will die out. This is the fate of the Muslims of Turkey, the Brown race of India, and the Indians of America.

How is matter composed? By grouping. How does matter decompose? By breaking down grouping. If one wants to create water, one combines two parts hydrogen with one part oxygen into a group, and so water is composed. If one wants to break down water, one passes an electrical current from a voltaic pile through water, which separates into bubbles of hydrogen and oxygen, and so water is decomposed. This principle universally applies to all things. So if we wish to destroy a family, we should destroy its grouping. If brothers are feuding and fathers and sons are killing each other, even a family of great wealth will soon decline. If we wish to destroy a country, we should destroy its grouping. If its upper and lower classes are divided and lack any sympathy for each other, then even a land of abundance will soon perish. When a tree is parasitized by another plant, it will wither while the parasitic plant flourishes. The wood of trees such as the pagoda, mulberry and willow is soft, and parasitical plants can take root in them, while the pine, cypress and camphor do not suffer from this problem because their grain is hard.

The internal organs and the diaphragm and the muscle tissues of old and sick people become loose and pathogenic influences will dwell in them and the heat and cold will invade them, while sturdy youth do not suffer from this problem because they are fit and tough.[12] How could ruling states be any different? 'If Emperor Shun dwelt in a place for a year, he built a town and in three years a metropolis,' and 'King Wu of the Zhou had three thousand retainers who were one in their loyalty.'[13] This is grouping. *The Spring and Autumn Annals* stated, 'The kingdom of Liang was destroyed', and the *Gongyang zhuan* added, 'like a fish that rots and perishes'.[14] Whoever refers to the destruction of a state speaks of 'downfall' and 'disintegration' – this is the breakdown of grouping.

PART TWO
RADICALISM: EXILE 1, 1899–1903

The essays translated here from this brief but extremely productive period of Liang's life form the bulk of this volume. They include the first six chapters of the series of essays Liang called *The New Citizen*, two later chapters from the same series, and three more essays. By 1902 Liang had been reading steadily and deeply in Western political writers such as Rousseau, Montesquieu, Spencer, Mill, Bentham and even Kant, and such Japanese writers as Katō Hiroyuki, Inoue Enryō, Fukuzawa Yukichi and Nakamura Masanao. Liang's nationalism assumed a sharper form. He rethought the nature of modern imperialism, in effect concluding that it was not a crime but an advanced form of political organization. Liang distinguished between pre-modern forms of rule and imperialist aggrandizement on the one hand, and 'national imperialism' or the imperialism of 'citizenries' on the other, an idea he borrowed from the Japanese legal scholar and politician Katō Hiroyuki. The lesson? China had better become a nation of citizens if it was going to survive.

During these four or five years, Liang was an indefatigable explorer of new terrains of modern political thought, and he toyed with thoughts of revolution. Although in the end he turned against revolution, his ideas were revolutionary enough in the Chinese context. The essays translated here show Liang discussing a wide range of basic political concepts: democracy, liberty, the state and sovereignty, the relationship between individual and state, the differences between personal morality and public morality, and, inevitably, racial and national competition. Liang was vaguely sympathetic to socialism; indeed, his journal *Xinmin congbao* (New People's Miscellany) was a major conduit of Western and Japanese socialist thought into Chinese. But on the whole Liang was not much interested in socialist thought, which seemed to him to better apply to conditions in the West than in China.

Liang promoted – and perhaps proposed to exemplify – the 'new citizen' who would think for themselves but remain devoted to the public good, who would be independent but a full member of their nation, who would have rights but be required to assert those rights for themselves, and who would be both ruler and ruled. The new citizen recognized that personal liberty and the liberty of the nation were not in contradiction but went hand in hand. It was no coincidence that Liang adopted the term 'new citizen' (*xinmin*) from the classic Confucian text *The Great Learning*.[1] Long central to the Confucian curriculum, there the term referred to 'renewing' the people by spreading practices of self-cultivation. Liang freely referred to Confucian (and Buddhist) ideas during this period, but did not promote Confucianism as such. Indeed, Liang's historical thinking turned to the problem of why China had failed to progress as it 'should' have. Looking back to ancient China, Liang rejected the idea that the ancients had discovered anything like modern democracy or equality, but he did find much to admire. As for China's failure, he basically had two answers. First, the stagnation imposed by despotic rule. Liang now emphasized the fecundity of ancient Chinese thought and institutions, but said that their development was blocked by the unification of the realm and the 'one family' rule imposed by Qin Shihuang's conquest of 221 BCE. Second, China's very position as the largest, strongest and wealthiest nation surrounded by lesser tribes. Liang said that without competition, China naturally stagnated, since progress came from the kinds of competition that Liang thought were best explained by social Darwinism.

During those early years in Japan, without ever directly disavowing traditional thought *in toto* – indeed, recognizing that there was no such thing – Liang freed himself to think in new ways. He spoke no more of New Text prophecy or the Datong ideal that he had earlier imbibed from Kang Youwei. Indeed, he ridiculed longing for a global utopia as inimical to the reality of struggling nation-states. Liang declared: 'I love Confucius, but I love the truth more. I love my elders, but I love my country more. I love my friends, but I love liberty more.'[2] That said, Liang was trained as a classical scholar. On the one hand, he saw that classical learning and the imperial state were virtually two sides of the same coin. The one could not survive without the other, and the classical fetters had to be broken. On the other hand, the byways of classical learning remained worth exploring for their own insights. They could lead to prophetic thinking such as Kang Youwei's, or to revolutionary ideas via the ancient non-canonical (non-Confucian) thinkers or Mencius, or – for Liang – to moral insights that had lost none of their power.

3

The Similarities and Differences in the State Structures of China and Europe[1]

Are there intrinsic differences between China and the West? How does one explain China's relative backwardness? Is progress a universal law? Liang here asks these questions based on historical units of states, races, clans and tribes. By 'class', Liang essentially means hereditary status. First published in Qingyibao, *September 1899.*

Asia was home to the world's first civilizations, and China was the most prominent of these civilizations. Today, the civilizations of China and Europe are vastly different, and when we compare their histories over the last several millennia, we can see how and why they grew apart. When we examine the causes for this, we can see how the current situation came to be. And when we examine current trends, we can predict what the future will bring. Therefore, I have chosen this topic for the consideration of those who are concerned with contemporary trends.

Chapter One: Similarities between China and Europe

1. *The clan era and the tribal era*

Although we cannot completely believe the most ancient histories, there were no differences between East and West in terms of the origins of the human race and of the first states. When the human race first appeared, there were no forms of transportation like boats or carts, and people were divided into small groups by

mountains and rivers. As Laozi said, 'In ancient times neighboring states were within sight of each other, and they could hear
the sounds of the others' fowls and dogs, but their people never
came into contact.'[2] At that time all these states were divided
by 'race'; the number of 'races' was limitless and the number of
states was also limitless. The 'nine emperors and sixty-four
peoples' that Dong Zhongshu referred to were all states based
on clans.[3]

Subsequently, these states gradually swallowed each other,
the strongest emerging to conquer the others, annexing them to
their own states. This was the tribal era. War at the time arose
from 'racial' differences, the strong preying on the weak. In the
first stage, the Gonggong clan was the strongest and occupied
the Nine Provinces, and then the clans of Chiyou and the
Yellow Emperor fought on the fields of Banquan.[4] In the second
stage, the most numerous and fiercest clan was the Miao, who
were the indigenous people. In the third stage, the descendants
of the Yellow Emperor conquered the Central Plains and then
moved into the San-Miao territory and occupied it.[5] After this,
the so-called Three Dynasties were founded by the descendants
of the Yellow Emperor.[6] All this 'racial' competition was like
the struggles among the Aryans, Semites and Hamites, the later
ones always defeating the previous ones. The stages of progress
in China were exactly the same as in Europe. Although the Xia
and Shang dynasties are called monarchies, actually they were
the unions of various 'racial' tribes. Yu the Great met with the
assembled lords at Mount Tu, accepting the jades and silks
offered by the myriad states – which were actually all tribal
clans.[7] The Xia and Shang were nothing more than leaders of
tribal alliances. However, the Xia and Shang were not the only
powers in the Territory of Yu during that millennium; such
clans as Youqiong, Kunwu, Dapeng and Shiwei all tried to
replace them as alliance leader.[8] They were basically like Egypt,
Babylonia, Armenia and Persia in the West, each of which
dominated in turn, and all of which took the form of a great
state, as distinct from small 'races' attacking one another.

2. *The feudal era and aristocratic government*

The political structures of China's Zhou dynasty and Europe's Greece shared many similarities as they both had a feudal era and aristocratic governments.[9] They were both assemblies of states, and although they differed in terms of their original state formation, they were the same in terms of gradually perfecting the institutions of the state and gradually developing civilization. The Zhou dynasty was purely an aristocratic government. The Zhou state thus included the dukes of Zhou, Zhao, Dan and Liu; the feoffment of Qi had Guo and Gao; the feoffment of Lu had the three Huans; the feoffment of Zheng had the seven Mus; the feoffment of Jin had Luan, Xi, Xu, Yuan, Fan and Xun; and the feoffment of Chu had Zhao, Qu and Jing – each holding power in their own state.[10] The political structure that Europeans call a 'minority republic' was simply an aristocracy. Their governments (aristocracy) held enormous power, surpassing that of the king. The decision to crown a king or dethrone him was in their hands. They could keep the king's actions in check. In China, similarly, when King Li of Zhou behaved tyrannically, the people banished him to Zhi and the Gonghe Regency took power.[11] Likewise, when Duke Wen of Teng wished to observe mourning for three years, his family's senior members and his ministers did not agree to this.[12]

To compare this to the Greek states, China's political structure was closest to that of Sparta, where power was neither in the hands of the king nor the people, but in the hands of an oligarchy. The power of this oligarchy was truly awesome. However, it was also close to the people. Thus the people were also integral to the state and sometimes could offer their opinions on major state affairs. (For example, Cao Mo went alone to the military conference of the Duke of Lu at the Battle of Changshao. The merchant Xian Gao of the state of Zheng repulsed the Qin forces with a gift of oxen. Han Qi of the state of Jin was refused by the ruler of Zheng when he sought to obtain a jade ring from a Zheng merchant, a story that describes the alliance between governments and merchants, demonstrating that at certain times governments and merchants treated each other as equals.[13] There are many more examples that I could cite.) Thus this era of aristocratic government also saw a modest growth in democracy.

Various states emerged without being unified (at that time the Zhou house was merely one state among the others, powerless to unify them), but often leaders arose who could forge alliances among the states. The states of Jin and Chu fought for hegemony, alternating leadership of the other states, rather like the way Athens and Sparta at the center of the Greek world alternately seized command. It followed that because of this competition, every state had to promote men of ability in order to strengthen itself. The states thus gave their peoples freedom of speech and thought, and so this time became a golden age of philosophy and humanities that offered unlimited wisdom and unlimited possibilities to the future world. These trends were all due to the states' powers. This was the greatest commonality between ancient China and ancient Greece.

After the Spring and Autumn and the Warring States periods, Qin Shihuang suddenly seized power and then, with the unification of the Han dynasty, China entered the Lesser Peace.[14] After the Greek era, Alexander the Great rose to power, followed by the Roman unification, and Europe entered the Lesser Peace. In terms of structure, China and Europe shared a good deal, but in substance they were very different. Please let me explain in the next chapter.

Chapter Two: Differences between China and Europe and Their Causes and Influences

1. Post-Roman Europe divided into various states, post-Han China remained unified

Before the Spring and Autumn period (which European historians call antiquity), the state forms of China and Europe were basically the same. After the Spring and Autumn period, they became entirely different. There is much evidence for this, but two points stand out. In this section I discuss the first point. The evolution from tribal competition to state competition inevitably followed from the natural development of humanity. This trend has persisted unceasingly to the present day and is constantly intensifying not only in Europe but also in Asia. India thirty years ago and Japan fifty years ago both consisted of countless small states. For millennia, except for the Roman period, Europe has always consisted of competing states. Only China has been different. After the Qin abolished feudalism and instituted the system of commanderies and counties, China followed this system for two millennia without change. Although there were feudal practices – the Han enfeoffed imperial kin as princes and meritorious officials as dukes; the Jin had 'eight princes'; and the Ming had the Princes of Yan and Ning and so forth – they were all quickly abolished and never formed their own states.[15] Regional governors of the late Han and the frontier commanders of the Tang all held their own territory and favored their own kin, but although they were swollen with arrogance, they could create only a little trouble and were never able to form states. Throughout Chinese history, the Three Kingdoms, the Southern and Northern dynasties, and the Song facing the Liao and Jin could be considered periods of competing states.[16] However, competition was not severe since there were only a few rivals; the country was soon reunified, and in sum such competition exerted little influence on Chinese history. Even less influential were the Sixteen Kingdoms of the Jin or the Ten Kingdoms at the end of the Tang period.[17] Thus the whole period from the Qin and Han to today can be considered an era of unity. This is the first major difference between the state forms of China and Europe.

What are the reasons for this difference? Division into different states is generally based on differences in religion and race. The states of Germany were able to federate because their race and religion were compatible, but Greece and Serbia split away from Turkey due to incompatibility of race and religion. Since Emperor Wu of the Han dynasty promoted the Confucian Six Arts and dismissed the Hundred Schools, China has unified its religion.[18] Although Buddhism entered China, since its teaching was transcendental and detached from the secular world, China could still be said to uphold just one teaching: Confucianism. Yet within Europe, countries are divided between Christianity and

Islam, and Christianity itself is divided among the Orthodox, Protestants and Catholics. This is the first reason for this difference between China and Europe.

As for racial amalgamation, this is rather difficult to trace. From before the Xia and Shang dynasties through to the Zhou, tribes competed with one another. Except for the Central Plains, which was enfeoffed among meritorious officials and kin, surrounding tribes such as the Qin, Chu, Wu and Yue were regarded as barbarians, and all were foreign to the Central Plains. All kinds of races lived together in the interior, such as the Xirong, Lairong, Luhunrong, Jiangrong, Huaiyi, Chidi, Baidi, Changdi and so forth.[19] This was clearly the case through the Spring and Autumn period, so how did racial distinctions suddenly disappear after the Han dynasty? All of the people in the Central Plains thought of themselves as compatriots. This change came incomprehensibly fast. Examining the reasons for this, at that time the theory that men and women of the same clan could not propagate was widespread. The rulers and nobles of every state married persons from states of different clans (that is, foreign races), and commoners imitated them. Thus, after the Spring and Autumn and Warring States periods, the people of every clan were already intermarried, and they gradually lost their differences. As state territories merged, their peoples united as one body. In Europe, however, the races of every state were constantly dividing into new races that developed different customs and practiced ingroup marriage. This is the second reason for this difference between China and Europe.

Due to these two reasons, the various states of Europe were generally separate while the whole territory of China was generally unified. However, what was the effect of this? Rival states inevitably struggle with one another, causing the destruction of innocent people. And power-holders in feudal aristocratic states inevitably become arrogant and despise their people, and their peoples are devastated. Thus, in terms of government that gives peace to the people, there is no doubt that state unity is better than division. However, since rival states inevitably struggle with one another, their governments must strengthen themselves to promote national progress, striving to compete with other states and not fall behind. Consequently, their governance improves. Since their people are often in contact with other countries and frequently go to war, they invariably develop hatred for their enemies and form an indomitable will. Consequently, the popular spirit is strengthened. As governance improves and the popular spirit strengthens, the civilization and the happiness of the people also continually advances. This is the result of a system of rival states. Since China remained unified through dozens of dynasties, its rulers became so arrogant and so ignorant that they no longer understood global conditions; they were only covering up their mistakes, living on stolen time and oppressing their people to prevent rebellion, until the government was corrupted and weakened beyond repair. As the people have been oppressed for so long, their hatred of enemies has been depleted and their spirit of independence has been exhausted, to the point they have become indifferent to the world around them. This is the result of two thousand years of the unification of the state.

2. Europe was divided by classes, which China lacked

Since the beginning of this century in Europe, scientific principles have flourished, and natural rights and the equality of citizens have spread across the entire continent. The division of people into classes then gradually diminished. Yet over the past several millennia, while everyone deplored it, even a man of great knowledge like Aristotle maintained that slavery was a natural law. In the civilizations of Greece and Rome, the lower social classes were endlessly abused, while those who were showered with the blessings of civilization were but a small minority. As for America, it even went to war over slavery in the nineteenth century. France is a republic, but its aristocracy still retains power. Among Asian countries, the Indian caste system is unchanged to this day, and the Japanese class designations of *hinin* and *eta* were abolished only after the Meiji Restoration. One can thus say class systems are nearly universal. Only in China has a class system never really flourished;

and, after the Han, it disappeared entirely. Bu Shi was a shep-
herd who became a Court Gentleman, and Gongsun Hong was
a commoner who became a Grand Councillor.[20]

From that point on, great ministers of commoner origins
became a typical sight. As long as they were talented and had
the right qualifications, regardless of their family background
and occupation, they could govern the people. At one point,
the Jin dynasty established the Nine Ranks system to select officials, whose abuses led to the view that the upper ranks had no
commoners and the lower ranks no aristocrats, although this
was not the original intention of the system and it was soon
abolished. And it goes without saying that from the Tang dynasty on, the examination system has allowed commoners to
rise smoothly to high rank. The Han dynasty often issued edicts
against slavery and although bond-servants and slaves still
exist in the modern period and cannot become officials, their
numbers are very small and they cannot be considered a class.
It can therefore be said that China has no aristocracy and its
people are not divided into classes. This is another difference
between the state forms of China and Europe.

What are the reasons for this difference? Struggle among states
reached its height in China during the Warring States period,
leading them all to focus on promoting the talented and expanding their powers. Their bold and fierce leaders knew that they
could not take control of the empire with only their aristocra-
cies. Thus they treated eremites with great respect and recruited
ministers from other states. Men like Zou Yan, Chunyu Kun, Su
Qin and Zhang Yi all used their eloquence to become high-
ranking ministers of state, and the barriers protecting aristocratic
officialdom were destroyed.[21] At that time sages like Confucius
and Mozi ardently promoted the principle of equality.[22] Confucius criticized the nobility and Mozi valued men of talent. Most
of their disciples were low-born but became renowned in their
time and thus changed the empire. (Zizhang had been a rude
merchant; Yan Zhuoju had been a bandit – they studied under
Confucius. Qin Huali had also been a bandit – he studied under
Mozi.) This was greatly different from Aristotle's advocacy of
slavery. Han Gaozu rose out of the backwoods to become

emperor.[23] His close associates, such as Xiao He, Cao Can, Han Xin and Peng Yue, all rose out of the lower classes of clerks, traders and menials to reach high positions. Since the rulers and their ministers all rose this way, it was not a coincidence that China could sweep away the abuses of the class systems that had risen naturally since the beginning of humanity. In Europe, however, the aristocrats were generally intelligent and strong, while the lower classes were generally stupid and weak, and so it makes sense that it was not possible to break down these barriers for thousands of years.

What has been the result? A nation without class divisions generally enjoys happiness, and this is certainly a proof of an evolved civilization. However, evolution stems from competition, while competition stems from violent struggle. Europe divided people into classes, and the aristocratic minority unconscionably abused the commoner majority, which caused frequent struggles between the people and the officials. The people's spirit increased more and more, and the people's intelligence developed further and further, and the people could then abolish such longstanding abuses and in one leap attain a world of peace and humaneness. As for China, the people are not victims of direct tyranny, but are often the victims of indirect oppression. Although the natural rights of the people have not been entirely eliminated, they are generally not complete. Their rights are often secretly violated by tyrants without their knowing. Thus their resentment is weak, and they barely struggle to defend themselves. Moreover, when the ruled suddenly become rulers, if they are ruthless and violent, they will betray their principles to practice favoritism and use petty regulations to become rich and powerful. Then the people's sentiments cannot cohere and the people's spirit cannot be roused. This is what Song Taizu meant when he said that all the heroes of the empire were under his command, and shows how the strategy used by Chinese rulers and ministers throughout the ages was superior to that in Europe.[24] Alas! This is precisely why it is so difficult to foster democracy in China. How pitiful!

Chapter Three: Conclusion

Although there were various differences between the state structures of China and Europe, in my opinion these two are the
biggest differences, which encompass all the others. According
to the laws of civilization, when the struggles among various
states are compared to the unification of a state, the unified state
is better. And when a people divided by classes is compared to a
people lacking classes, the latter is better. This view is accepted
by the whole world. Yet Chinese progress precedes that of the
Europeans by two thousand years, while today the civilizations
of China and Europe are as far apart as Heaven and Earth. Why
is this? From before the Spring and Autumn period (antiquity in
Western history), conditions in China and Europe were about
the same; and after the Han, the Chinese made great progress
while the Europeans stagnated. But in this century, the Europeans have made great progress while the Chinese stagnated. The
progress made by China over the past two thousand years is now
being lost. Why is this? Now I have one more thesis to present.

Europe has adopted the parliamentary political form since the
days of Greece and Rome, while it is unknown in China. This is
the ultimate difference, and also the ultimate curiosity. Why is it
that China never developed this political form? It is because the
people never demanded their rights. Why did the people never
demand their rights? Because their unified state was closed off
from the world and they never knew that other peoples possessed
rights. Therefore, they did not demand their rights. Because they
were content in a classless society, they did not know they had
lost their rights and therefore they did not demand their rights.
Thus I still incorporate this difference into the previous two differences. Alas! We never knew that by following the laws of
civilization, China would in reality obstruct the progress of its
civilization. Yet I maintain that the laws of civilization are not an
obstruction but have simply not been carried out in full. Alas!
The past cannot be changed. But today the world is shrinking.
China is now a neighbor to all the countries of the world, and the
country that has been unified for thousands of years is now

suddenly one among many. World economic competition is rapidly changing; today China has become its target, and the social change coming to China will be unimaginable. The classless society of thousands of years will suddenly have classes. During two thousand years of stagnation, China failed to progress, but now it can progress beyond this stagnation. Perhaps the day may still arrive when China will rise up.

4

The General Trend of Struggles of Citizenries in
Recent Times and the Future of China[1]

*In focusing on the nature of imperialism, Liang discusses the
state in this essay, using the term* guojia, *which depending on
context can equally refer to country or nation; the term also
includes the character for 'family', with connotations of the
state as the family writ large (connotations of no use to Liang).
Liang speaks of citizens and citizenry using the term* guomin,
*which can also refer to a national, a people, or the people, but
here for Liang it is tied to the notion of popular sovereignty.
The term translated here as 'struggle'* (jingzheng) *also refers to
competition. First published in* Qingyibao, *October 1899.*

1. The difference between the citizenry
and the traditional state

The Chinese are ignorant of citizenship. For thousands of years,
in the common parlance there was only the term 'state', while no
one used the term 'citizen'. What is a state? What is a citizen?
The traditional state refers to a land that is the private property
of a single family. In ancient times, states originated solely from
clans. If a clan head proved to be strong and took command of
his clan to struggle with other clans, in time he turned his clan
into a state, its powers were unlimited, it enslaved and suppressed all the clans, and it subjected the whole state to its savage
rule. But if the clan lost power, another would replace it, one
tyranny replacing another endlessly: this is what has been meant
by the state. Citizenship refers to a land that is the common

property of all the people. The state is formed by the assemblage of all the people, and there is no state outside the people. Should the people govern a state, legislate its laws, pursue its interests and protect it from any threats, then they cannot be humiliated and the state cannot be destroyed. This is what is meant by citizenry.

2. The difference between the struggles of citizenries and the struggles of traditional states

There is the struggle of traditional states and the struggle of citizenries. When traditional states struggle, their rulers cruelly exploit their people in order to struggle with other states. When citizenries struggle, all the people struggle with other states to protect their own lives and property. Confucius said, 'there are no righteous wars'; Mozi issued his 'condemnation of offensive war'; and Mencius said, 'for those who turn the land into killing fields, death is not enough for such a crime' – all were referring to the struggles of states.[2] A modern European thinker once said, 'Struggle is the mother of evolution; warfare is the carrier of civilization' – he was referring to the struggles of citizenries. The ability of traditional states to struggle is weak, while the ability of citizenries to struggle is strong; and the struggles between traditional states are brief, while the struggles between citizenries are prolonged.

Qin Shihuang, Alexander the Great, Chinggis Khan and Napoleon are all considered to be the men of the greatest military accomplishments in Eastern and Western history from ancient to modern times. But they went to war purely for their own ambitions to tyrannize, brutalize, conquer and rule over the whole world. Their ravenous ambitions out of control, they never hesitated to force their people to die for them. Their wars were wars for the sake of one individual, not wars for the nation. Since they were wars for the sake of one individual, people were conscripted into the army with no choice in the matter. They hoped against hope for a reprieve that would save them, and so morale tended to crumble and courage to collapse. Therefore, I say that the ability of traditional states to struggle is

weak. Since their wars were for the sake of one individual, once
that individual was defeated and died, their wars simply evap-
orated leaving no trace. So I say that the struggles between
traditional states are brief. But the struggles between citizenries
are the opposite. When a nation is facing foreign aggression,
those in charge must decide whether their enemy is a traditional
state or a citizenry, and then decide which strategies to employ
accordingly.

3. Struggle in the modern world and its evolution

Alas! The struggle to dominate the world has become extreme.
Its original impulse came from Europe, and it has spread in a
flash like a whirlwind to quickly claim dominion over the world.
If we open the map, we see that the White race has already taken
five of the six continents, excluding only Asia. And of Asia, half
of its territory and 40 percent of its people are already in the
hands of the Whites. The whole territory extending from Central
Asia to North Asia is occupied by Russians, and the Caspian Sea
is virtually a Russian inland lake. In central-south Asia, India has
been entirely enslaved by the British, and Afghanistan and Ba-
luchistan to the west of India are also British protectorates
governed under their authority. Just forty years ago France
started meddling in Southeast Asia. In 1862 they occupied Jiaozhi
and seized Cambodia; in 1884 they seized Annan; and in 1893
they defeated Siam and took a third of its territory.[3] In 1885 the
British took Myanmar and captured its king. Persia manages to
linger on as Britain and Russia maintain a balance of power
there. Korea survives for the time being, thanks to an agreement
between Russia and Japan. When we calculate what the Europeans struggled for, aside from their four continents, their territorial
gains in Asia are as follows:

	Area (Japanese *ri*)[4]	Population
Asia total	2,880,000 square *ri*	835,000,000
Russian possessions	1,100,000 square *ri*	20,000,000
British possessions	330,000 square *ri*	300,000,000
French possessions	44,700 square *ri*	22,000,000
Portuguese possessions	1,300 square *ri*	1,000,000
Total European possessions	1,476,000 square *ri*	343,000,000

Such is the ferociousness of European struggle, which led to these vast achievements. Now they are bringing their wars eastward, deploying massive armies in China.

From the beginning of the last century, learning has flourished unceasingly, machinery has been invented unceasingly, capital has increased unceasingly, manufacturing has prospered unceasingly in Europe, which has led to the problem of over-production that forced them to find new places to sell their merchandise. When Columbus first discovered the Americas, they were called the New World and were said to be able to absorb Europe's expansion. Over the last several centuries, however, the Americas themselves have become a center of production, and these lands once colonized by the Europeans now intend to colonize other places. Moreover, Europeans are doing what they can to turn places like India and Australia into markets for their goods. However, in just a few decades, not only will they be unable to absorb Europe's products, but they will be anxiously trying to find other places to sell the goods made in their own territories. Thus the Europeans are so hard-pressed that they are being forced to carve up Africa in such a frenzy that now every grain of sand in the Sahara is subject to their sovereignty claims. However, although Europeans want to find customers in Africa for their industry and commerce, it will take up to a century to yield a result even if they expend all their efforts to open up the market. Thus the problem of over-production still haunts the Europeans, and they are ever more hard-pressed. Anxiously looking all around the vast globe, they turn their eagle eyes to China with savage greed in their hearts, full of ruthless tricks to devour our ancestral land of four thousand years of civilization, 200 million square *li* of fertility and abundance.[5]

4. *Struggles in the world today are struggles of citizenries*

From this perspective, the struggles that Western nations engage in today are not like those of Qin Shihuang, Alexander the Great, Chinggis Khan or Napoleon, which were simply to fulfill their ambitions to engage in self-aggrandizing wars of aggression. Nor are they like those struggles of feudal states, which were led by tyrants who acted out of their personal hatred or for their personal gain. Rather, the original impulse behind the rivalrous wars of Western nations is their citizens' struggle for survival. Given the laws of evolution, there is no stopping natural selection and survival of the fittest – even if we wanted to. Thus the current struggles of the Western nations are not a matter of the state, but of the people as a whole; not a matter of the ruler, but of the populace; not a matter of politics, but of economics (or to use the current Japanese translation, means of subsistence). Struggles in the past were a matter of the state, the ruler or politics, and were not necessarily in accord with the people's wishes, but today's struggles are constituted by the people fighting in complete unity for their lives and property. Once their time was up, those struggles in the past that were a matter of the state, the ruler or politics truly ended. But now people are constantly fighting for their lives and their property, in struggles that never end. Alas! The danger is upon us! How can we defend ourselves in the face of such threats?

5. *China's future*

I, mourner of the times, exclaim: Alas![6] China knows nothing of citizenship. And precisely because we know nothing of citizenship, we mistake the struggles between citizenries for the struggles between traditional states. Therefore, we do not understand how to deal with them and end up overpowered. How should we deal with them? I would say that when a traditional state attacks, we can resist with the power of our traditional state, but when a citizenry attacks, we must resist with the power of our citizenry. In any struggle, the power of citizenries is the strongest and most resolute. The European citizenries developed their power in just a hundred-odd years, but with their power the Europeans have been able to reach every corner of the Earth, easily extending their dominance and overcoming any resistance. However, the countries that they can dominate are precisely those that lack citizenries of their own.

If the Europeans ever encountered the power of the citizenry of a nation, their momentum would be blunted and they would be forced to change course. Where is the proof? In times past, vanishingly few countries outside those of the Whites possessed this kind of power of the citizenry. But thirty years ago, they encountered Japan; more recently they have encountered the Philippines, and now they have encountered the Transvaal (that is, the Republic of South Africa, which recently discussed going to war with Britain). Comparing the Japan of thirty years ago and the Philippines and Transvaal of today with the great Western powers, the difference in their strength is still enormous. But then why was the West's momentum blunted, forcing it to change course? Because the right strategy will yield good results, specifically to resist the attacks of the citizenries of other nations with the power of one's own citizenry.

Today, the land of China is the private possession of one family; foreign affairs (that is, diplomacy) are the private affairs of one family; the national calamity is the private calamity of one family; and the national humiliation is the private humiliation of one family. The Chinese people do not know they have a state, and our state does not know it has a people. It might have been able to survive in the earlier world of struggles between traditional states, but how can it survive in today's era of fierce struggles between citizenries? Since the Europeans are aware of our fundamental weakness, they savagely attack the Chinese state while they deviously attack the Chinese people. Why are they savagely attacking our state? Because they know that our state lacks the strength necessary to resist them and that our people – lacking patriotism since they are not allowed to participate in national affairs – will not become angry even if their state is ravaged and humiliated. Why are Europeans deviously attacking the Chinese people? Because they know that since the government does not love the people, it will not be disturbed even if they attack the people. The Europeans' only fear is that once the Chinese people realize they are being attacked, they will unleash their power and can no longer be suppressed. This is why the Europeans use devious and conciliatory strategies to placate the people. Alas! Are not their rights in China to build railroads, dig mines, collect tariffs, develop concessions and engage in Christian proselytizing all devious strategies?[7] By making the best use of such devious strategies, they concentrate on making the government and provincial officials suppress the people for them, and thus the Chinese people never awaken and unleash their power. In this way the Europeans can treat China as a kind of colony and never worry again about their so-called over-production and their anxious struggle for survival. This is their goal.

Alas! Do any of my fellow Chinese know what is happening? If not, I want them to learn about it. If so, I want them to think about how to deal with it. What is the only way to deal with it? The answer simply lies in the power of our citizens. How can our citizens gain power? Power is not something that others can give us but what we ourselves have and develop, and what we ourselves seek and obtain. Europeans were able to obtain power because uncountable numbers of their citizens shed their blood and sacrificed their lives in exchange for it. My fellow citizens! My fellow citizens! If we do have the will for the struggle to survive, will we be in any way inferior to the Philippines and the Transvaal?

5

Preface to *The New Citizen*[1]
(*The New Citizen*, chapter 1)

*Liang published most of the series of essays that he put in the
'new citizen' category during 1902 and early 1903. In these
essays he offered reflections on the nation and the state, how
states interacted with one another and how they should be
constituted. Liang's key term* xinmin *('new citizen') equally
refers to a process ('renewing the people'). First published in*
Xinmin congbao, *February 1902.*

Ever since the appearance of human beings on Earth, there have
been countless numbers of countries. But when we inquire how
many remain standing today with their own color on world
maps, the answer is: only a hundred-odd. And how many of
these hundred-odd countries can rise up with the power to
master the world and become the fittest in the struggle for survival? The answer is: just four or five. With the same sun and
moon, the same mountains and rivers, the same round heads
and square feet, why is it that some countries rise and some fall,
and some are weak and some are strong?[2] Some people claim it
is due to favorable geography, but America today has the same
territory as before, so how is it that it was the Anglo-Saxon
people (that is, the English race) who built its glory? Ancient
Rome had the same territory as today's Rome, so how is it that
the Latin people lost their glory? Some people claim it is due to
great men, but there was Alexander the Great, so how is it that
Macedonia has turned to dust? And there was Chinggis Khan,
so how is it that Mongolia is near collapse?

Alas! Alas! I know the reasons for this. A state is formed by gathering people together. People are to a country as the four limbs, five organs, blood vessels and corpuscles are to a body. There is no way the body can survive if the four limbs are broken, the five organs damaged, the blood vessels injured or the corpuscles dried up. Similarly, there is no way the country can survive if the people are ignorant, cowardly, lax or muddled. Therefore, if we are to seek a long and healthy life, then we must understand how to promote good health. If we are to make a country stable, prosperous and glorious, then we must understand the Way of renewing the people.

6

Renewing the People is China's Most Urgent Task Today[1]
(*The New Citizen*, chapter 2)

First published in Xinmin congbao, *February 1902*.

I now wish to emphasize that the 'new citizen' is our most pressing concern. My argument deals with two fundamental issues. First, domestic governance. Second, foreign affairs.

What do I mean by domestic governance? There are many political theorists who constantly claim that Person A is ruining the country or Person B is harming the people, or in some matters the government blundered or in some institutions the officials neglect their duties. I certainly cannot say they are completely wrong. However, how is the government formed? Where do its officials come from? Do they not come from the people? And are Person A and Person B not members of the nation themselves? We can never produce a Li Lou by assembling blind people together.[2] We can never produce a Shi Kuang by assembling deaf people together.[3] We can never produce a Wu Huo by assembling cowards together.[4] With this kind of people, you get this kind of official. That is, precisely, 'You harvest what you sow.' Why is this?

Western philosophers often say that the people are to the government as the air is to a thermometer. The level of the mercury necessarily corresponds to the temperature of the room, and there is no room for error. When the cultural level of a people is low, even if government is in the hands of brilliant rulers and wise ministers, once they die, their government is at an end. This is like placing a thermometer in boiling water during a harsh winter, which will quickly raise its temperature,

but when the water cools off, it will return to its original temperature. When the cultural level of a people is high, even if
cruel tyrants and corrupt officials wreak devastation for a time,
the people can recover on their own and rectify the situation.
This is like placing a thermometer on a block of ice during a
blazing hot summer, which will quickly lower its temperature,
but when the ice melts, it will return to its original temperature.
Therefore, as long as we renew the people, there is no need to
worry that institutions, the government and country will not be
renewed. Otherwise, even if we change a law today, or replace
a person tomorrow, merely chasing reforms around the edges
and slavishly imitating others, none of this will do any good, in
my view. China has been talking about reform for decades, but
why have there been no results? Because we have failed to
attend to the Way of renewing the people.

Those who worry about the fate of the nation today often
live alone deeply pondering, sighing and hoping, 'Can we not
find worthy rulers and ministers to save us?' I do not know
what precise qualifications they have in mind for these worthy
rulers and ministers. But given the state of today's popular
morality, popular intelligence and popular strength, I do know
that, even with worthy rulers and ministers, it would be impossible to solve our problems. Now, even Napoleon, a brilliant
general, could not fight against the Black barbarians if he was
leading our useless Green Standard troops.[5] Columbus, a great
mariner, could not cross a small stream if he was taking out a
failing boat with a rotten hull. Rulers and ministers cannot rule
by themselves. They must deploy officials across the land; these
officials must rely on provincial intendants; provincial intendants must rely on local magistrates; and local magistrates must
rely on village functionaries. Even if half the officials in all these
ranks are good, as long as half are bad, they cannot provide
good government. Not to mention if only one out of a hundred
is any good!

Those who advocate these ideas today no doubt understand
the virtues of Western governance and want China to copy
them. But can it be the case as, according to their logic, Western
governance is created by the rulers and ministers alone? If we

tour the cities of Britain, America, Germany and France, we can observe the nature of the people's self-government and the relationship between the people and the government. When we observe a province there, its governance operates like that of the country. When we observe a town or a village, its governance operates like that of the country. When we observe an association or a company or a school, their governance operates like that of the country. And even at the level of individuals, their self-governance also operates like that of the country. This is like the salinity of salt. When salt is piled up into a mountain, its salinity increases, but when this salt mountain is divided into piculs, and the piculs into pecks, and the pecks into quarts, and the quarts into grains of salt, and the grains of salt into atoms – every one of them is saline and thus together they amount to great salinity. If we try to get salt by gathering sand and grinding it up, even a mountain of this stuff higher than Mount Tai will be useless. Thus the people in Western countries do not really need worthy rulers and ministers to achieve good government. As for their rulers, it matters not if a Yao or Shun is reigning, or if a mere child sits on the throne.[6] As for their officials, it matters not if they only follow their predecessor's policies, or if they let affairs run themselves. Why is this? It is due to the people. Thus it is the rulers and ministers who depend on the people, not the people who depend on the rulers and ministers. Since this is true for small countries, it is even more true for China with its large territory, too large for just a few people to really control.

I will now compare the country to the family. If the son and his wife and brothers all have their own work and their own skills, and in addition they uphold sincerity, respect, diligence and resourcefulness, then the family must prosper. But if they abandon their responsibilities and only rely on the head of the family, and that head of the family is not worthy, then the whole family will certainly starve. Even if the head of the family is worthy, how well can he support his family? Even if he can support them, the children are a burden to him, causing him to work anxiously the whole year from dawn to dusk. Not only are their consciences troubled, but in the end they remain a burden on the family. Today, those who are always looking to the government and worthy rulers and ministers – what is unforgivable there? What is not intelligent there? Englishmen often say, *'That's your mistake. I couldn't help you.'* Although this seems to be a vulgar statement expressing egoism, it is actually an aphorism encouraging people to practice self-governance and self-help. Therefore, although I constantly long for wise rulers and ministers, I am afraid that even if such wise rulers and ministers did exist, they could not help us no matter how much they wanted to. Why is this? Because the more people expect from their rulers and ministers, the less they expect from themselves. This bad habit of looking to others and not to oneself is the fundamental reason why China has been unable to reform. As long as everyone is looking to everyone else and not to themselves, and the 400 million Chinese all shift their responsibilities to others, then who will establish the country? Renewing the people does not mean that every new citizen is renewed by another new citizen, but rather that every person renews themselves. Mencius said, 'If you practice this diligently, you will renew your kingdom.'[7] Self-renewal refers to the new citizen.

What do I mean by foreign affairs? Since the sixteenth century (about three hundred years ago), the reason why Europe has risen and the world has advanced lies entirely in the extraordinary upsurge of 'nationalism'. What is nationalism? It is each people of the same race, language, religion and customs who come to see each other as people of the same country; they pursue independence and self-rule and organize a perfect government to seek the public good and defend themselves from outside peoples. This doctrine flourished until the last two or three decades of the late nineteenth century, when it grew into 'national imperialism'. What is national imperialism? As the strength of a nation grows, it inevitably overflows its borders and unceasingly expands its power over other lands and absorbs them. Regardless of the methods used – military, commercial, industrial or religious – national imperialism always controls and administers these lands. Recent cases include Russia's takeovers of Siberia and Turkey, Germany's takeovers of Asia Minor and Africa, Britain's war on the Boers and America's annexation of Hawaii, plunder of Cuba and seizure of the Philippines. All these countries could not but follow this new doctrine. And today on the Eastern continent lies the largest country with the most fertile land, the most corrupt government and the weakest people. Once the foreigners became aware of its domestic conditions, they dispatched their national imperialists to gather there, like an army of ants attracted to rank meat or thousands of arrows reaching their target. Russians in Manchuria, Germans in Shandong, British in the Yangzi River valley, French in Guangdong and Guangxi, and Japanese in Fujian – they all cannot but follow this new doctrine.

This national imperialism is different from the past imperialism. In the past, the likes of Alexander the Great, Charlemagne, Chinggis Khan and Napoleon all possessed great ambition, made farsighted plans, aimed to crush the world and swallowed up weaker countries. However, past imperialism all stemmed from personal ambition, whereas national imperialism results from the rising power of a nation. The former was driven by powerful rulers, whereas the latter follows the trends of our times. Therefore, the former's invasions lasted but a little while, like a violent squall that is over by noon, whereas the latter's advances look to endure, ever expanding, ever deepening.

Unfortunately, China is trapped in the middle of this vortex. What can it do? If the threat stemmed from just one or two men of ambition, we could resist them with one or two heroes of our own. But facing nations that are following the inexorable trends of the times, there is no way we can resist them without unifying the whole nation. If this were but a quick attack, we could raise an army of braves to respond quickly. But faced with the gradual penetration of nations possessing farsighted strategies, there is no way we can survive without establishing a great hundred-year plan. Have you ever seen water in a bottle? When it is half full, more water can be poured in. But if the bottle itself is already full, then there is no room to add more water. Therefore, to resist the national imperialism of the foreign powers today, prevent calamity and rescue the people, the only course for us is to promote nationalism. And to promote nationalism, the only course is to renew the people.

Today, the whole world worries about foreign threats. Yet if foreigners present a threat, worrying certainly will not solve the problem. In the face of such fierce and aggressive assaults by the forces of national imperialism, we are still discussing whether foreigners really constitute a danger. How stupid! I believe whether they are a danger depends on us, not on the foreigners. Now, given that all countries practice national imperialism, why do the Russians not overpower the British, the British not overpower the Germans, the Germans not overpower the Americans, or the Western powers not overpower the Japanese? This is simply due to whether there is 'room' for them.

All people are vulnerable to the six seasonal diseases.[8] Yet will people who are vigorous and healthy have any problems even if they encounter snowstorms, droughts, miasmas and tsunamis? On the other hand, if they only complain about the snowstorms, droughts, miasmas and tsunamis instead of taking care of themselves, anyone, even foreigners, will fall ill, much less the Chinese, who are so good at complaining. For today's China, there is no way we can merely rely on the rulers and ministers to resist foreign threats or rely on a few heroes to emerge from the people to do so. Only by elevating the morality, intelligence and strength of the 400 million Chinese people to the level of the foreigners can they be stopped. Then what would there be to fear? And yet this task cannot be accomplished overnight – as Mencius said, 'When you seek mugwort for three years to cure a seven years' sickness, if it was not already stored, the patient may never get it.'[9] Today, there is no alternative to this approach. Do we really want to waste more years before we realize that the opportunity we have today will never return? Ah! How can we Chinese not be anxious? How can we not spur ourselves on?

7

The Definition of the New Citizen[1]
(*The New Citizen*, chapter 3)

The key term in this essay is guomin, *which Liang uses both in the sense of a 'national' (that is, a person who is a member of a nation and identifies as such) and particularly in the sense of a 'citizen' (that is, a person who actively participates in the political affairs of their community). Liang does not distinguish between 'national' and 'citizen', but he does distinguish* guomin *from 'the people' (*renmin*) who are mere passive subjects (as, for example, subjects of the ruler). First published in* Xinmin congbao, *February* 1902.

The ideal of the 'new citizen' does not mean we have to discard all our old ways to follow other people. The meaning of 'new' has two aspects: first, honing what we already have in order to renew ourselves; and second, adopting what we lack in order to renew ourselves. If either aspect is missing, our efforts to renew ourselves will fail. When the former sages established their Teachings, the two courses they adopted were to teach students according to their existing qualities and to transform their characters. This is precisely what I mean by honing what we have and adopting what we do not have. What applies to the individual also applies to the people as a whole.

Any country that can stand up in the world must have a people who possess a unique character. From morality and law down to customs and habits, literature and art: all display a unique spirit. Their genius is passed down from ancestors to descendants, and thus the group is formed and the state is established. This is truly the fountainhead of nationalism. That we Chinese

could establish a state on the Asian continent is certainly due to
our unique character – a character that is glorious, noble and
flawless, and clearly distinct from other nations – a character
that we should preserve from loss. To preserve our character
does not mean that we simply let it be while we proclaim, 'We
are preserving it! We are preserving it!' Take a tree: if a tree does
not produce new buds every year, it will soon wither away. Or
take a well: if it is not fed constantly by new springs, it will soon
dry up. How can these new buds and new springs possibly be
coming from the outside? Though old, they are renewed, for it is
precisely through daily renewal that they are preserved. When
we clean and polish the old, its radiance shines forth; when we
forge and temper the old, its structure is formed; and when we
cultivate and clean up the old, its inherent nature is strengthened. It thus continues to grow and mature over time, and the
spirit of the people is preserved and developed. Our era may
regard 'preserving the old' as an extremely detestable term. But
how can this be right? Our problem does not lie in preserving the
old but in our inability to properly preserve the old. What is
properly preserving the old? It is nothing more than what I called
honing what we already have.

Will it be enough to merely hone what we already have? No,
because today's world is not the world of the past, and today's
people are not the people of the past. In the past, there were only
tribal people in China, not citizens. This was not because China
could not produce citizens, but simply reflected the conditions of
the time. Since China has always majestically dominated the
Orient, surrounded by small barbarian tribes and lacking contact with other major states, its people always regarded it as the
whole world. Everything that they saw and heard, everything
that influenced their thinking, everything that the sages taught,
everything that the ancestors passed down – all were meant to
give the people the ability to act as individuals, or family members, or villagers or clan members, or cosmopolitans, but were
never meant to give people the ability to act as citizens of a state.
The ability to act as citizens is not necessarily to be superior to
the ability to act as individuals, family members, villagers or clan
members, or cosmopolitans. But without this ability, there is no

way that we will be able to establish our independence in today's world of contending states in which the strong crush the weak and only the fittest survive.

Therefore, if today we do not want to strengthen our country, that's one thing; but if we do want to strengthen it, then we must study extensively how various nations have established their independence, and then select and adopt their strong points to compensate for what we lack. Everyone who discusses politics, learning and technology today understands that we must adopt their strong points to compensate for our shortcomings, but they fail to understand that popular morality, popular intelligence and popular strength are the true foundations of politics, learning and technology. To neglect popular morality, popular intelligence and popular strength while focusing on politics, learning and technology is to confuse the structure for its foundations. How is this different from seeing a luxuriant tree and wanting to graft its branches onto your own withered tree? Or seeing a bountiful well and wanting to divert its flow to your own dry well? Therefore, to renew the people, we must carefully consider what to adopt to compensate for what we lack.

Everything that happens in the world is based on two basic principles: the conservative and the progressive. When it comes to these two principles, people may tend to the one or to the other; or, if both are adopted, they may either conflict or merge together. Neither pure conservatism nor pure progressivism can work by itself. Out of conflict comes merging, for conflict is the precursor of merging. The peoples who are good at merging conservatism and progressivism are great nations such as the Anglo-Saxon race. When you walk, you need to keep one foot on the ground. When you pick up objects, you need one hand to hold fast and the other to take. Therefore, the 'new citizen' that I define here is absolutely not like those who are enchanted by the Westerners' ways and reject their own millennia-old morality, learning and customs in order to join with the West. In addition, the new citizen is absolutely not like those who slavishly follow the old traditions and say that it is enough only to hold onto their millennia-old morality, learning and customs to stand fast in this world.

8

The New Citizen as Vindicated by the Law of the Survival of the Fittest, with a Discussion on How to Renew the People[1]
(*The New Citizen*, chapter 4)

In this essay Liang does not draw fine distinctions between the categories of race, nation, ethnicity and language groups. Again, he uses the term xinmin *as both a noun ('new citizen') and a verb ('renew the people'). First published in* Xinmin congbao, *February 1902.*

In today's world, where states are founded on nationalism, it is inevitably the case that if the people are weak, the state is weak, and if the people are strong, the state is strong, just as a shadow follows a person and an echo follows a sound. Here I present the general structure of the world's races in a chart to discuss the reasons for their rise and fall.

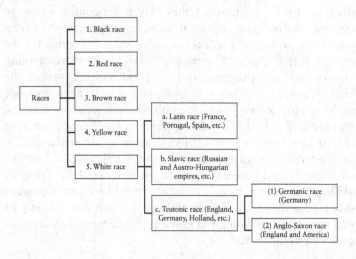

Basically, there are five major races in the world. Which of them is the strongest today? The strongest race is the Whites, who are divided into three major races. (The Whites include more than these three races, and the Teutons include more than just two races. I am simply listing the major ones – this essay is not an analysis of race, and such details need not detain us.) Of the White races, which is the strongest today? It is the Teutons, who are divided into two major groups. Which of these two groups is the strongest today? It is the Anglo-Saxons.

When people began to settle in separate valleys and never came across one another, every single group could build up its strength unmolested in its own territory. However, once the law of natural selection pushed people into making contact, communicating and struggling with one another, it was immediately clear that some would rise and some would fall. Have you watched fighting crickets? When a hundred fighting crickets are all in their own cages, each is its own commander. But when they are put together in one cage, on the first day sixteen or seventeen will die, on the second day another eighteen or nineteen will die, and by the third day only a few will remain. Those who remain are certainly the strongest, while the slightly weaker ones are in grave danger.

As everyone knows, when Black, Red and Brown peoples meet with Whites, they can be instantly destroyed like pouring boiling water on snow. And now, too, when Yellow people meet with Whites, they are no match either. Looking into the struggles among the Whites themselves, we see that the Slavic race was often under the autocratic rule of the Ottomans and the yoke of the Romanov and Hapsburg Teutonic dynasties. To this day, they have rarely achieved autonomy. Although the Latin race flourished during the Middle Ages, when they met with the Teutons, they were lost. From the collapse of the Roman Empire until today, there has been no European state that was not established by the Teutons; for example, the Visigoths in Spain, the Suebi in Portugal, the Lombards in Italy, the Franks in France and Belgium, the Anglo-Saxons in England, the Scandinavians in Denmark, Sweden and Norway, and the Germanic peoples in Germany, Switzerland and Austria. These peoples became the motive force behind all the world's modern states, which were all established by Teutonic peoples. The Teutons are nothing less than the masters of the whole world. And of the Teutons, the master of the masters and the strongest of the strong are the Anglo-Saxons. Over a quarter of the world's territories are held by them today, and over a quarter of the world's population is under their rule. And still their power continues to spread unceasingly across the five continents.

By charting the changes in the numbers of people speaking each national language over the last hundred years, we see the astounding progress of the Anglo-Saxon nation:

1801

Language	Speakers	Percentage
French	31,450,000	19.4
Russian	30,770,000	19.0
German	30,320,000	18.7
Spanish	26,190,000	16.2
English	20,520,000	12.7
Italian	15,070,000	9.3
Portuguese	7,480,000	4.7

1890

Language	Speakers	Percentage
English	111,100,000	27.7
German	75,200,000	18.8
Russian	75,090,000	18.7
French	51,200,000	12.7
Spanish	42,800,000	10.7
Italian	33,000,000	8.3
Portuguese	13,000,000	3.2

By comparing these two charts, we see the leap of English from fifth place to first place in just ninety years – from 20,520,000 speakers, constituting some 12 percent of Europe's population, to 111,100,000 speakers, over 27 percent. The Anglo-Saxons appear to have quickly swept across the whole world. Who could resist their superiority?

We can thus see which nation has proved to be the fittest for survival in today's world. Of the five races, the Whites are the fittest. Of the Whites, the Teutons are the fittest. Of the Teutons, the Anglo-Saxons are the fittest. I am not saying this to fawn on them, but this is just the reality of the inescapable law of evolution. If the Germanic race could renew itself to surpass the Anglo-Saxons, they might replace the Anglo-Saxons one day. If the Slavic and Latin races could renew themselves to surpass the Teutonic race, and if the Yellow race could renew itself to surpass the White race, they could achieve a similar result. In sum, the current standing of each nation in terms of its fitness for survival is precisely as described above. However, when I call for the study of how various nations rise, so that we can learn their strong points to compensate for our weak points, it seems we must learn from the Whites. Of the Whites, we must learn from the Teutons. And of the Teutons, we must learn from the Anglo-Saxons.

Wherein lies the superiority of Whites over other races? Other races prefer tranquility, while Whites prefer action. Other races are content with peace, while Whites never cease struggling. Other races are conservative, while Whites are progressive. Therefore, other races are only able to foster civilization, while Whites are able to spread their civilization. Those who foster civilization rely on natural development, while those who spread their civilization rely on human action. As we can see, the core of Western civilization has shifted from Assyria and Egypt to Greece, from Greece to Rome, and from Rome to the nations along the Atlantic Ocean, then across the continent, and then over to the Americas. Now they are looking to the Orient, never stopping for a moment. How does their bravery, their determination, their liveliness and their splendor compare with that of the Indians? Or with that of the Chinese? There is no need to speak of the smaller countries. Thus the reason that the White race soars above the whole world is not due to providence but because it is the fittest race in the struggle for survival.

Wherein lies the superiority of the Teutons over the other Whites? The Teutons have political abilities that other people cannot match. For example, although the Greeks and Slavs were able to establish local self-government systems, they could not expand them beyond the tiny communities that their political abilities could manage. Both state organs above the level of the community and individual rights below it remained beyond the scope of their political abilities. This system thus displayed three faults. First, the people's rights were incomplete. Second, their communities remained separate from one another. And third, they lacked the ability to resist foreign aggression. Therefore, the Greeks were oppressed for thousands of years, first brought under the yoke of Rome, then under the yoke of the Ottomans and then under the yoke of the Teutons. And the Slavs today are still groaning under cruel despotism without end. As for the Celts (the pre-Roman Gauls and today's highlanders of Ireland and Scotland belong to this race), they were most courageous people at the time, but their political thought was so weak that they revered just a few muscular heroes, and their people were unable to unify. They could establish innumerable fiefdoms, but they had no way to unify them. They could establish a major religion, but they could not form a large state.

As for the Latin people, they are far superior to the Celts, as they could establish the great Roman Empire and unify the European continent. They were able to perfect Roman civil law and pass this model down for a thousand years. However, their political thought was too ambitious to be put into practice. They constantly aimed to rule the world but ended up destroying their local self-government system and suppressing individual rights. Focused on expanding state power but not on nurturing individual character, the Latin people thus became notoriously corrupt and base in the last years of the Roman Empire. Even today they are unable to eliminate their inherited character traits, and they are vainglorious and impractical. Sometimes they tend toward conservatism, maintaining outworn practices with no desire to change them. But at other times they rush to extremes, pushing change haphazardly. A good example is the French, as they changed their political system six times and their constitution fourteen times within a hundred years. To this day, they claim to be a democracy, but have been completely unable to deepen either local self-government or individual rights. In this way the Latin people are falling behind in the evolutionary race for survival.

Originally the Teutons were barbarian tribes in the German forests who displayed a spirit of individual strength and freedom which was passed down through the generations without loss; then, after they were molded by Roman culture, the result of this fusion was a unique race. Subsequently, they organized a 'nation-state', established a parliamentary system, gave all the people political rights, turned the people's will into the public will and merged the people's power into the nation's power. Furthermore, they set limits on the powers of the group and the individual, and on the powers of the central government and local self-government, so that neither violated the other. The whole nation was thus able to develop in accord with the needs of the times. Therefore, the Teutons' superiority in the world today is not due to providence but because it is the fittest nation in the struggle for survival.

Wherein lies the even greater superiority of the Anglo-Saxons over other Teutons? Their culture of independence and self-sufficiency is the strongest. In their youth, within the family and at school, their parents and teachers do not treat them as dependents but teach them practical skills so that they grow up to be independent and do not rely on others. As they deeply believe in discipline and order and are devoted to *common sense*, they hardly ever engage in reckless action. As they also deeply believe in rights, they regard those rights as important as life itself and are never willing to give them up. As they are physically strong, they can tackle any danger. As they are resolute by nature, they never yield in the face of adversity. As they mainly engage in commerce, they do not seek vainglory. They all have employment and treat every profession equally, while indolent officials and politicians are disdained. They do their utmost to preserve these characteristics, while they can generally change with the times and learn from outsiders to further develop their original characteristics. It is for these reasons that the Anglo-Saxons of three tiny, isolated islands in the far north were able to extend their race across the two continents of North America and Australia, to plant their flag wherever the sun can reach and to consolidate their power over the choke points of the five continents and the four seas. No one in the world can rival them. The reason the Anglo-Saxons are the hegemonic power of the nineteenth century is not due to providence but because they are the fittest race in the struggle for survival.

It is thus clear from whom we should learn. By examining how one race weakens and declines, while another strengthens and rises, we can reflect on ourselves. What are the differences and similarities between the character of the Chinese and that of a declining race? And that of a rising race? What are our major shortcomings? What are our minor weaknesses? We must investigate these issues one by one, examine them one by one, change them one by one and resolve them one by one. Then we can create the new citizen. I will outline and analyze in detail the major and minor steps that our citizens should take to renew themselves in the next chapter.

9

Public Morality[1]
(*The New Citizen*, chapter 5)

Liang's term 'public morality' (gongde) could equally well – and perhaps more naturally – be translated as 'civic virtue', or in some contexts as 'social ethics'. However, Liang is explicitly contrasting the public (gong) with the private or personal (si), and his later essay 'Personal Morality' (translated below) was in some ways a refutation of this essay. First published in Xinmin congbao, *March 1902.*

What the Chinese people are most in want of is public morality. What is public morality? It is by relying on this morality that human groups can be formed and states can be established. Humans are a species that is good at forming groups (as noted by the Western scholar Aristotle). But if humans fail to group, how are they any different from animals? We cannot achieve grouping simply by speechifying, 'Group together! Let's group together!' But in reality the group can be created only when there is something that can focus and connect it – that is, public morality.

In essence, there is only one body of morality. In practice, though, there is public morality and there is personal morality. People who cultivate their own virtue are practicing personal morality. People who aim to help each other are practicing public morality. Both are necessary to human life. Without personal morality, a person cannot be steadfast. It is impossible to create a state with despicable, hypocritical, cruel and cowardly people alone. Without public morality, people cannot form a group. It is impossible to create a state even with countless self-disciplined, honest and kindly people. The development

of morality in China certainly came early, but it emphasized
personal morality while neglecting public morality. We see that
the orthodox sources of morality for the Chinese are the *Analects* and *Mencius*, 90 percent of which teach personal morality
while less than 10 percent teach public morality. For example:

- the nine virtues of 'The Counsels of Gao Yao';[2]
- or the three virtues of the 'Hongfan'; [3]
- or the *Analects'* 'gentle, kind, courteous, temperate
  and amiable', 'discipline the self and return to ritual',
  'speaking honestly, behaving respectfully', 'speaking
  nothing blameworthy, doing nothing regrettable',
  'steadfast and plain spoken' and 'knowing the
  ordinances of Heaven and knowing how to judge the
  meaning behind words';
- or *The Great Learning's* 'knowing when to stop and
  vigilance in solitude' and 'to avoid self-deception and
  seek to be modest';[4]
- or *The Doctrine of the Mean's* 'loving learning,
  practicing vigorously, knowing shame', 'careful at all
  times not to make mistakes' and 'meticulous
  observation';[5]
- or Mencius's 'preserve one's heart-and-mind and
  nourish one's good nature' and 'self-examination and
  vigorous reciprocity'.

All these precepts thoroughly depict personal morality and
provide an exemplary guide for the cultivation of the 'private
person' (private person, as opposed to public person, refers to
times when one lacks social intercourse with others). Yet can such
a 'private person' be considered a complete person? Certainly
not. If we compare China's old ethics with the West's new ethics,
the categories used in the old ethics are the five cardinal human
relationships: ruler–minister, parents–children, elder–younger
siblings, husband–wife and friends, while the categories used in
new ethical relations are: family ethics, social ethics (that is,
human grouping) and state ethics. What the old ethics emphasizes is the relations between one private person and another

private person. (The cultivation of virtue by private persons of course falls within the sphere of private morality, while the moral principles of social intercourse among private persons also fall within the sphere of private morality. This can be verified by the legal concepts of public law and private law.)

What the new ethics emphasizes is the relations between the private person and the group. (Mapping the old ethics' five relationships onto the new ethics' categories, then 'family ethics' includes the relationships of parents–children, elder–younger siblings and husband–wife; 'social ethics' includes that of friends; and 'state ethics' includes that of ruler–minister. However, the old relationship of friends cannot represent the entirety of the new social ethics, and still less can the old relationship of ruler–minister represent the entirety of the new state ethics. Why is this? The duties of people to society are not limited to those that friends have to one another. And even if people have absolutely no social intercourse with others, they still have inescapable responsibilities to society. As for the state, it is even clearer that it cannot be reduced to the relationship of ruler–minister. If we only speak of the righteousness between ruler and minister – 'A ruler should employ his minister according to ritual, and ministers should serve their ruler with loyalty' – this refers only to the bond of gratitude and service between two private persons and has nothing to do with the larger society. And do the upright eremites who 'do not serve their kings or their lords' not fall outside this relationship? All people must fulfill the duties imposed by these three new ethics to become a complete person. China's five cardinal relationships virtually map onto 'family ethics' but say little about 'social ethics' or 'state ethics'. We must fix this deficiency, which entirely stems from emphasizing private morality over public morality.)

Needless to say, both when the private person is alone and when they deal with others, they always act on the basis of morality – yet this just a part of morality, not the whole, which requires a combination of public and personal morality. Personal morality and public morality can be implemented together with no contradiction. However, as moralists have their own preferences, personal and public morality end up in conflict.

Obviously, heterodox men with little learning, like Weisheng
Mu, who criticized Confucius for his smooth talk, and Gongsun Chou, who thought Mencius was argumentative, were all
ignorant of public morality.[6] Even the great sages were not
aware of it. I am not trying to take the random comments of
the ancients out of context for the sake of denouncing them.
But, in brief, for thousands of years China has followed the
doctrine of self-restraint, which was truly the core of our moral
education. As the limits of moral concern became more and
more restricted, anyone who went beyond those limits in word
or deed to devote themselves to the benefit of their group or
their state was always criticized and persecuted by vulgar
scholars on the fallacious principle that 'one should not meddle
in affairs above one's station'. As such fallacious views became
widely accepted at the expense of correct views, the people
became even more ignorant of what public morality is.

Nowadays, as people live in groups and enjoy the rights of
belonging to the group, they must fulfill their obligations to the
group. Otherwise, they are nothing but parasites. The people
who abide by the doctrine of self-restraint imagine that
although they offer no benefit to the group, neither are they
harming it. But they do not realize that providing no benefit to
the group is the same as harming it. Why is this? When the
group benefits the individual, but the individual does not benefit the group, then the individual is in debt to the group. In
personal morality, to leave a debt unpaid among private persons is definitely wrong, because it will harm others. Yet those
who are in debt to the group come off as good people. Why is
this? If all its members were in debt to their group, how much
of its original capital would remain? How can any group survive countless debtors sucking the group dry, carving it up and
taking without repaying? A group will be dragged down by its
debtors just as a private individual will. This is inevitable. What
can account for China's decline but that the country is full of
'good people' who practice the doctrine of self-restraint, enjoying rights without fulfilling their obligations? Everyone simply
disregards their debts to the group. In spite of how numerous
the Chinese are, no one can contribute to the group, but, on the

contrary, all are a burden on the group. How can China not continue to decline?

Parents give birth to their children, raise them, protect them and teach them. Therefore, children have the obligation to repay their parents' kindness. If everyone fulfills their obligations, parents' lives become easier and clans more prosperous the more children they produce; otherwise children become a burden on the family. Therefore, if children fail to repay their parents' kindness, they are called unfilial. This is the first principle of personal morality, as everyone knows.

The kindness of the group to its members and the state to its citizens is the same as kindness of parents to their children. Without groups and states, there can be no security for our lives and property, nor any way to nurture our wisdom and abilities, and we would not be able to survive for a single day. The obligation to repay the kindness of one's group and one's state is upheld by all upright people. When people fail to uphold this obligation – regardless of whether they are good or evil in terms of their personal morality – they are all despicable traitors to their group or state. For example, take a family with ten sons, one of whom is a monk and another a gambler and drunkard. Even though one is good, seeking enlightenment, and the other is bad, a scoundrel, they nonetheless both betray the doctrines of Confucianism by failing to fulfill their obligations to their parents. When we understand this principle, we see that those who are content to cultivate their own virtue are in fact in the same category as the unfilial. If they were prosecuted for violating public morality, then a verdict of guilty of heinous treason against their group would be just.

There is an old fable about an official who died and was being judged for his sins by the Lord of the Underworld. His spirit said, 'I am without sin. I was an incorruptible official.' But the Lord of the Underworld said, 'In your place wouldn't a wooden statue that didn't require food and drink have been better? You did nothing noteworthy except avoid corruption. That was your sin.' The Lord of the Underworld then bound him to a burning-hot pillar. Whoever takes self-restraint as the only virtue fails to realize that they cannot be excused for their obsession. The maxim that officials all worship today is 'honesty, circumspection and diligence'. But aren't these simply the highest virtues of personal morality? Officials who have been entrusted by the group to govern it must fulfill their duties to the group as well as to individual members of the group. How can the maxim 'honesty, circumspection and diligence' excuse them from negligence toward both these two grave duties? This is all because they understand personal morality but not public morality, which entirely explains our political stagnation and national decline. If officials in public life are like this, we scarcely need to mention ordinary people in private life. Not a single Chinese person regards state affairs as their own affairs. All of this is due to the failure to elucidate the great principle of public morality.

And do those who advocate personal morality even understand the origins of morality? Morality is established to benefit the group. Therefore, the morality that is suitable for different groups generally differs according to how civilized they are. Essentially, its purpose lies in consolidating the group, perfecting the group and advancing the group. According to the British constitution, violating the monarch is treason (this is true of all monarchies). According to the French constitution, plotting to restore the monarchy is treason. According to the American constitution, accepting titles of nobility is treason (any violation of the constitution is treason). In form, these moral propositions are opposed to one another, but in spirit they are the same. In what sense are they the same? Simply in that they all seek the general benefit of the group. Ancient barbarian tribes sometimes regarded sharing women as public property to be moral. (That is, the women in the group are all shared by the men in the group without a marriage system – ancient Sparta never abandoned this custom.) Or they regarded treating slaves as non-human to be moral. (That is, they regarded slaves as less than human. The ancient philosophers Plato and Aristotle both saw nothing wrong here. Until the American Civil War, Westerners never regarded slavery as immoral.) Furthermore, contemporary philosophers still cannot consider these practices as immoral, because they were the best practices that would benefit the group given the conditions of the time. After all, the spirit of morality arises from nothing but seeking the benefit of the group. If this spirit is violated, even perfect virtue may turn out to be absolute evil. (For example, freedom is perfect for modern society but would be evil in a primitive barbarian society, while autocracy was perfect for ancient societies, but would be evil in an advanced civilized society. These are the proofs.)

Therefore, public morality is the source of all virtues. That which benefits the group is good, and that which does not benefit the group is evil. (That which does not benefit the group but actually harms it is a great evil; that which neither harms the group nor benefits it is a small evil.) This principle is applicable everywhere and will stay true for hundreds of generations. The form of morality varies in proportion to the civilizational level of the group. Since the civilizational levels of groups differ, that which will benefit them differs, and accordingly that which forms their morality differs. Morality itself is not unalterable. (This might sound shocking, but such is the application, though not the essence, of morality. The essence of morality is unchanging since time immemorial. Please do not mistake my meaning. Then what is this essence of morality? It is simply what benefits the group.) Morality is not something that could be established by people thousands of years ago as the sole standard to be followed everywhere and forever. (The norms of personal morality seldom change, but those of public morality often change.) Since we are born in this group at this time, we should take into account world trends to determine what is suitable for our race and thus develop a new morality that will consolidate our group, perfect our group and advance our group. We should not let the limited views of the former kings and sages confine us and fail to dare to advance beyond them. When we understand public morality, a new morality will emerge and then the new citizen will come forth.

(The scholars advocating reform today dare to claim they can reform everything, but there is not a word about new morality. This is because the slavishness of scholarly circles is not yet eradicated, and their faith in love of group, love of country and love of truth is not yet sincere. Assuming morality to be unchanging, as eternal as the sun and the moon and as natural as the rivers running through the land, the ancient sages revealed all its profound principles to admonish later generations – how could they conceive of any distinction between old and new morality? But what they did not realize is that 'morality' is itself half natural and half a human construct; it develops and progresses, completely following the laws of evolution. As the former sages were not born in today's world, how could they formulate morality that completely conforms to the conditions of today? It is clear that if Confucius and Mencius returned today, they would have to adjust their ideas. In this transitional period, as the old world is dying while the new world is yet to be born, the profound principles of the ancient sages appear to be fading into obscurity while the simple morality that prevails across society cannot regulate public mores anymore. Furthermore, there will be those who would abolish everything that they detest as outmoded. This is justifiable; however, if morality is abolished altogether, there will be no end of disasters. Already signs of this trend are visible today, and so, filled with anxiety, the older generation of scholars is trying to restore the old theories of the Song and Yuan periods to suppress it.[7] But do they not know that the law of the survival of the fittest is inescapable? You can't dam a river with a handful of dirt or put out a fire with a cup of water. Thus, even if we exhaust all our strength, we still cannot stop it. If we do not immediately develop and promote a new morality that takes into account both the ancients and the moderns, and both the Chinese and the foreign, then I am afraid that from now on, as our intellectual education improves, our moral education will decline. Then, if the material civilization of the West spreads across China, the 400 million Chinese would all turn into beasts. Alas! I know that the theory of moral revolution will be denounced all over China, and I detest my inability to pull it off. Even if I have to fight the whole society, I will have no fear and I will never quit. Are there any persons who wholeheartedly love their group, love their country and love truth in this world? I would like to join them to investigate this issue!)

Since the main purpose of public morality is to benefit the group, its thousands of applications all stem from this. 'Benefitting the group' will be the core of all of my later chapters. Thus this chapter of *The New Citizen* has focused only on the urgency of public morality, and I will later take up the question of how to practice public morality.

10

State Consciousness[1]
(*The New Citizen*, chapter 6)

In English, the distinctions between 'state', 'nation' and 'coun-try' can be slippery. The Chinese guojia *can mean any or all of these concepts; here, Liang uses* guojia *mostly in the sense of 'state' – that is, a political structure that is distinct, at least to a degree, from the people (nation). Liang's term* sixiang *means 'thought', but here it refers more specifically to a kind of aware-ness or 'consciousness' of the state. Still, the title of this essay, 'Guojia sixiang', might also be translated simply as 'National-ism'. First published in* Xinmin congbao, *March 1902.*

The first stage of social grouping consists of tribes, not citizen-ries. Tribes evolve into citizenries, which marks the distinction between barbarism and civilization. What is the difference between a tribe and a citizenry? A tribe is built by grouping clans together, which create their own customs, while a citi-zenry is built from having state consciousness, which is able to establish its own governance. It has never been possible to establish a state without citizens.

What is state consciousness? First, recognition that the state exists in relation to the individual; second, recognition that the state exists in relation to the imperial court; third, recognition that the state exists in relation to foreigners; and fourth, recog-nition that the state exists in relation to the world.

First, what does it mean to say that the state exists in relation to the individual? The reason that humans are superior to other animals lies in their ability to create groups. Since people are unable to fly like the birds or run like the beasts, if everyone had lived a solitary life, humanity would have disappeared long ago. Therefore, during times of peace, people within a group cooperate and divide up their tasks to help one another and make life easier, for it is certainly impossible for any single individual to have all the necessary skills. And during times of grave threats from outside the group, people defend their territory and resist invasion through their collective wisdom and concerted efforts, for it is even more impossible for a single individual to defend their own life alone. Thus did states arise.

The establishment of states was inevitable; that is, people realized that it is not possible to survive alone, but rather that they needed to unify in order to help each other, defend each other and benefit each other. If people were to unify to help, defend and benefit each other permanently, they needed to understand that there was a bigger and greater social grouping above the individual. Every thought, every proposal, every decision must take this so-called social group into account. (This is the doctrine of 'universal love'. It is also acceptable to call this the doctrine of 'self-benefit', because unless you benefit the group, you cannot benefit yourself.[2] This is a universal law.) Otherwise, the group can never be established, and then humanity may come close to extinction. This is the first principle of state consciousness.

Second, what does it mean to say that the state exists in relation to the imperial court? A state is like a company with the imperial court as its head office and the emperor as its chief executive officer. A state is also like a town with the imperial court as the town council and the emperor as its chairman. Is the head office established for the company, or is the company established for the head office? Is the town council established for the town, or is the town established for the town council? The answer is all too clear. They are fundamentally different insofar as one is greater than the other and neither can overstep its bounds. Therefore, the statement of Louis XIV, 'L'état c'est moi', is still considered heinous treason to this day. In Europe and America, even children all curse him when they hear this, but when it comes to China, no one bats an eyelid. Yet, for example, if the head of a company said, 'I am the company', or a council chairman said, 'I am the town', can you imagine how the company stockholders or the town residents would react?

Now, it is certain that the state cannot do without the imperial court. Therefore, we extend love of country to love of the court, as captured in the saying 'Love for a person extends to their house and even to the crows on its roof'. So if we take the crows to represent the house, and the house to represent the person, then loving the crows and the house is to love the person. But gradually people grow accustomed to loving the crows and forget the house, or grow accustomed to loving the house and forget the person. We can only call this a kind of insanity. In this way, people with state consciousness generally love the court, but people who love the court do not necessarily possess state consciousness. If the court is established on a legitimate basis, then it represents the state, and to love the court is to love the country. But if the court is not established on a legitimate basis, then the court is an enemy of the country. Therefore, to establish the court on a legitimate basis is to love one's country. This is the second principle of state consciousness.

Third, what does it mean to say that the state exists in relation to foreigners? The term 'state' is used to distinguish one's own state from foreign states. If there were only one state in the world, then the idea of the 'state' could not be conceived. It is thus from standing next to someone else that you recognize yourself. It is from living next to other families that you recognize your own family. It is from confronting other states that you recognize your own state. Over millions of years, humanity has spread all over the Earth, each people developing independently, different in substance and spirit – from language and customs to thought and institutions – each inevitably creating its own state. In accordance with the law of natural selection, people could not but come into conflict, and states could not but come into conflict. And thus the idea of the 'state' was created in response to other groups.

Even if a foreign country was led by wise and saintly philosophers, true patriots would never submit themselves to their rule. True patriots would rather fight to the death without a single survivor than yield a single iota of their rights to another people. If they were to yield, then the foundations of the state are already lost. For example, even if a family possesses nothing in their humble dwelling, they still do not want strangers to enter it. I recognize myself, therefore I exist. This is the third principle of state consciousness.

And fourth, what does it mean to say that the state exists in relation to the world? Religious doctrines are full of ideas about Heaven, the Great Harmony and all sentient creatures.[3] Don't the doctrines of universal love and one-worldism reflect perfect virtue and profound humaneness? Yet can we expect these doctrines to ever evolve from fantasy to reality? We cannot know whether this would take millions of years, or if it might happen today. Now, competition is the mother of civilization; if competition ever ceased, then the progress of civilization would instantly stop. The competition between individuals leads to the formation of families; the competition between families leads to the formation of clans; and the competition between clans leads to the formation of states – while the state itself is the ultimate 'grouping', and states mark the highest level of competition. Let us say that states, regardless of how unlikely it would be, abolished their boundaries. Then competition would cease – and with it, civilization. Moreover, it is human nature to be competitive. Even after humans have attained the Great Harmony and reached Heaven, they will instantly start to compete again for some reason or another, at which point they will revert to tribal competition, not national competition. Thus humanity is brought back to the stage of barbarism.

Modern scholars all know the beauty of these doctrines, but this is a beauty found in the mind, not a beauty found in history. This is why we insist that the state, rather than the entire world, is the ultimate 'grouping'. However, it is reasonable for those who promote universal love to sacrifice their own interests to love their families. It is reasonable for people to sacrifice their family's interests to love their clan. It is reasonable for people to sacrifice their own interests, their family's interests and their clan's interests to love their state. The state is the foundation of personal love, and it is the ultimate form of universal love. Falling short of the state is barbarism, while going beyond the state is also barbarism. Why is this? Because either course leads to tribes rather than citizens. This is the fourth principle of state consciousness.

*

How pathetic that the Chinese people lack state consciousness! Vulgar people only care whether they and their families are prosperous. High-minded types speak loftily of philosophical principles that have no practical application. The malicious turn to the foreigners and become their servants. The wise follow an autocrat and become his running dogs.

In terms of the first principle of the relationship between the state and the individual, how many of today's 400 million Chinese can see beyond themselves? Is there anyone who has ever been able to resist every chance to pursue any possible gain even if it meant betraying the whole nation? The supposedly superior people are those who cultivate their own virtue and care for their reputation, which is what I call failing their obligations to repay the group (see chapter 5).[4] Although those who cultivate their own virtue are different from those who pursue private gain, they are the same insofar as they lead the state to its destruction.

In terms of the second principle of the relationship between the state and the imperial court, the unalterable virtues passed down the generations that we respect above all are loyalty and filial piety. However, while it is correct to speak of loyalty to the country, it is perverse to speak of loyalty to the monarch. Why is this? The two virtues of loyalty and filial piety are the most important elements of a person's moral character. If either is lacking, a person is not considered human. But if loyalty is only directed toward monarchs, then monarchs have no one to be loyal to. Would they not regret their lack of moral character their whole lives? Are peoples like today's Americans or French, who have no monarchs to be loyal to, forever to be deprived of this morality and no longer considered human? In my view, the virtue of loyalty that monarchs must repay to their country is greater than that of citizens in democracies. Without parents, no one can be born; without a country, no one can survive. To be filial to one's parents and loyal to one's country – these are the righteous way to repay a debt of gratitude, which is beyond the capacity of slaves or the running dogs of kings. The Chinese even conceive the relationship between master and servant in terms of 'loyalty'. How absurd! (The loyalty laid on monarchs is heavier than that laid on the people. Why is that? For the people, loyalty lies only in their duty of service to the country. For monarchs, loyalty extends further to their duty to be worthy of the trust of the people – how can there be a limit to the monarch's virtue of loyalty? Filial piety lies in the responsibility that children have toward their parents, but parents must also hold to the virtue of filial piety. And if parents must be filial, how can monarchs be disloyal? Those who only advocate loyalty to the monarch cannot, I think, justify their views.)

In terms of the third principle of the relationship between the state and foreigners, I cannot bear to speak of the immense humiliations China has experienced in our history. From the end of the Han dynasty to today, the whole Chinese territory has been occupied by foreign races for a total of 358 years and the territory north of the Yellow River for 759 years. These foreign races and their corresponding periods are listed here:

Dynastic state	Founder	Race	Capital	Present-day site	Dates (Western calendar)
Han	Liu Yuan	Xiongnu	Pingyang	Pingyangfu, Shanxi	304–329
Cheng	Li Xiong	Ba Di	Chengdu	Chengdufu, Sichuan	304–347
Later Zhao	Shi Le	Jie	Ye	Xundefu, Zhili	318–351
Yan	Murong Huang	Xianbei	Ye	Xundefu, Zhili	337–370
Dai	Tuoba Yilu	Xianbei	Shengle	Datongfu, Shanxi	309–376

Qin	Fu Jian	Di	Chang'an	Xi'anfu, Shaanxi	351-394
Later Yan	Murong Chui	Xianbei	Zhongshan	Dingzhou, Zhili	383-408
Later Qin	Yao Chang	Qiang	Chang'an	Xi'anfu, Shaanxi	384-417
Western Yan	Murong Chong	Xianbei	Changzi	Luzhoufu, Shanxi	384-394
Western Qin	Qifu Qianggui	Xianbei	Yuanchuan	Gongchangfu, Gansu	385-431
Later Liang	Lü Guang	Di	Guzang	Liangzhoufu, Gansu	386-403
Southern Yan	Murong De	Xianbei	Guanggu	Qingzhoufu, Shandong	398-410
Southern Liang	Tufa Rutan	Xianbei	Lianchuan	Xiningfu, Gansu	402-414
Northern Liang	Juqu Mengxun	Xiongnu	Zhangye	Ganzhoufu, Gansu	402-439
Daxia	Helian Bobo	Xiongnu	Tongwan	Ningxiafu, Gansu	407-431
Later Wei	Tuoba Gui	Xianbei	Pingcheng	Datongfu, Shanxi	386-564
Khitan	The Sixteen Prefectures of Yan and Yun, Five Dynasties period				
Jin	Wanyan Aguda	Jurchen	Bian	Kaifengfu, Henan	1126-1234
Yuan	Chinggis Khan	Mongol	Beijing	Shuntianfu, Zhili	1277-1367
...	...	...	...	...	...[5]

Alas! So often has China, the domain inherited by the divine descendants of the Yellow Emperor, been seized by outsiders.[6] Yet too many of these so-called descendants of the Yellow Emperor welcomed foreigners with offerings of wine, kowtowed to the

foreigners, enslaved themselves to the foreigners and cannibal-
ized their own people to aid the foreigners. In Chen Baisha's
poem on visiting Mount Ya, we find the line 'Zhang Hongfan,
who carved a record of his defeat of the Song in wondrous rocks,
was not a barbarian himself but a Han.'[7] Alas! There have been
innumerable Han since the Jin–Song period whose achievements
were as glorious as those of Zhang Hongfan. Chen Baisha's
understanding of the state in its relationship to foreigners was
too narrow – such was the extent of the bankruptcy of state
consciousness.[8]

In terms of the fourth principle of the relationship between the
state and the world, Chinese Confucians are always speaking of
pacifying all-under-Heaven and governing all-under-Heaven.
Their most idealistic expressions, such as Dong Zhongshu's
Luxuriant Dew of the Spring and Autumn Annals and Zhang
Zai's 'Western Inscription', took the state to be an insignificant
trifle not worth their consideration.[9] But if we thoroughly study
their ideas, has their so-called all-under-Heaven above the state
been improved by their splendid empty words? Indeed, the state
has further declined. This being the case, the Chinese people
truly lack state consciousness. How dangerous! How tragic!
That the Chinese people's lack of state consciousness has reached
such an extreme!

Looking into the matter, I have found two reasons for this.
First, people know of all-under-Heaven but do not know of the
state. And second, people know of the self but do not know of
the state.

There are two reasons for mistaking the state to be all-under-
Heaven. The first is based on geography. Because Europe is
crisscrossed with mountains and rivers, and its terrain is divided,
it tends to be politically divided. Because the Chinese terrain
consists of vast plains with strategic transportation and commu-
nication, China tends to be unified. Therefore, in over two
thousand years since the Qin dynasty, China was only partially
divided during the three hundred years of the Three Dynasties
and the Northern and Southern dynasties. Other than that,
China has always been one family within the four seas. Even
though there have occasionally been separatist regimes, China

soon reunified. There were countless barbarian tribes surrounding China, but their territories, populations and cultures have never been a match for China's. Although civilized countries like Persia, India, Greece and Rome lay beyond the Pamir Mountains, China and these countries had no contact or knowledge of one another. Therefore, China regarded itself as all-under-Heaven, not because of arrogance but because of geography. All countries are only formed in relationship to other countries. It was thus inevitable that it would be harder for the Chinese to develop state consciousness than for the Europeans to do so.

The second reason why Chinese mistook the state to be all-under-Heaven is found in the theories of its philosophers. Geographically, China remained divided up to the Warring States period.[10] The great lords struggled against one another and statism was at its height.[11] As for the evils of the day, there were no limits to the battles for land and cities, the number of corpses filling the fields and the suffering of the people. Virtuous philosophers worried so much over the situation that they over-corrected in trying to turn it around. Confucius wrote *The Spring and Autumn Annals* to abolish the boundaries of the states and return to the One King, thus achieving the Great Peace through civil institutions. When Mencius was asked, 'How can all-under-Heaven be set in order?' he replied, 'Under one rule.'[12] The philosophies of other pre-Qin masters such as Mozi, Song Keng, Laozi and Guan Yin all differed from one another, but with regard to political strategy, their first principle was the unification of the states. For there was no other way to rectify the evils of the day.

Popular exhaustion with conflict became extreme, and so ruthless hegemons like Qin Shihuang and Liu Bang arose, the one following the other.[13] The teachings of the pre-Qin philosophers suddenly became a basis for the centralization of power under the emperors, and thus the empire was consolidated. Yet the emperor, still anxious about his control of the empire, burned the works of the philosophers and banned the arts of necromancy and the like; he deliberately selected those ideas of the philosophers that were of use to him, promoting them to shape the age. Thus statism was lost. This loss may be traced

to the spread of the theories of Confucius, Mozi and other philosophers. However, this cannot all be blamed on the philosophers.
Their theories were common sense at the time, but then people
manipulated those theories for their own interests, reflecting an
unavoidable human weakness. The Buddha speaks of dharma to
save sentient beings, but attachment to dharmas is a source of
delusion. Later people adapted to the ideal of unity, forgetting
love of country. How could this have been the intention of the
former sages? It is human nature that when people make contact
with one another, there must be a 'boundary' between the self
and others. Yet if the boundaries between states are abolished,
then the boundaries between clans and between families will
become stronger. The Qin's abolishment of a dozen great states
gave rise to thousands and thousands of petty states, to the point
that our 400 million people constitute 400 million states. This
has truly characterized China for the last two thousand years.
Lacking consciousness of the state, the people see the emperor
not as their representative, but as the representative of Heaven.
That people are unmoved by the frequent change of dynasties is
not due to indifference. Rather, as dynasties rise and fall, and
emperors come and go, none of this has anything to do with the
lives of ordinary commoners. Given, first, the effects of China's
geography and, second, the influence of the theories of the philosophers, it is no wonder that the Chinese people lack state
consciousness!

Although people know of all-under-Heaven but do not know
of the state, this is merely a temporary error. When the times
change, this erroneous view will simply disappear. First, as for
geography, in today's interconnected world with the foreign
powers at our door, China's old, isolated unity is bankrupt, so
we know there is no use worrying about it. And second, as for
the theories of the philosophers, as the New Learning today
enters China, it tempers our ancient doctrines and gives rise to
comprehensive theories of reform suitable to the people, so we
know that there are alternatives to kings and hegemons.

The most difficult problem to solve is that people know of
the self but do not know of the state – this erroneous view is
deeply rooted in people's minds. People who cultivate their

own virtue and care for their own reputations fear that the affairs of state will become a burden and avoid them. The slaves and running dogs of kings boast of their loyalty to pursue rank and emolument, and they chase power and profit like ants running after honey, all while concocting a kind of morality to disguise their evil deeds and beautify their reputations.

China has had no contact with any great, civilized states for two thousand years, but are these barbarians surrounding it not also considered states? How can we say that the Chinese did not know there were other states? When we look into Chinese history since Liu Yuan and Shi Le, has there been a single foreign race that conquered China without the help and leadership of Han Chinese?[14] For example, Ji Shao was born under the Wei dynasty, but the Jin dynasty usurped the Wei throne and killed Ji Shao's father.[15] Yet Ji Shao brazenly served the Jin dynasty, the enemy which had doubly wronged him, and even died for the Jin out of his sense of loyalty. Later some witless historians actually praised his loyalty!

I am tormented that the perfect and noble virtue of loyalty will be lost by such people defiling it. This is all simply because people know of the self and not the state. 'Whoever can grant me wealth, I will suck their pus-filled sores. Whoever can grant me rank, I will kowtow to. Who cares who they are?' In such cases, this perversity has nothing to do with geography or with philosophical theories. No matter how geography and theories may change, the slavish nature of the Chinese can never change. Alas! What can I do? Do you not remember how everyone hoisted flags of submission on every house when Eight-Nation armies occupied Beijing in 1900?[16] And how thousands of officials publicly praised the virtuous government of the foreigners by offering them a myriad-persons umbrella signed by those very same officials?[17] What torment! When I speak of this, I can no longer summon any anger but simply tremble with fear and disgust. Ah! What is loyalty? The Chinese are only loyal to power and profit. Though we do not know the future, we can look to the past, and in the future wherever we find the world's power and profit is where we will find 400 million loyal subjects. This being the case, I simply do not know for whom a state should be built.

Alas! I do not want to waste any more time on this. I dare not hope that my compatriots will eliminate their belief in self-interest. I only hope that they will expand and strengthen this belief to seek their true self-interest and preserve their self-interest forever – which can only be achieved by fostering state consciousness. My dear compatriots! Do not say that we can depend on our large territory. The territory of the Roman Empire at its height was no less than ours is today. Do not say that we can depend on our large population. The population of India certainly reaches 200 million. Do not say that we can depend on our civilization. When ancient Athens was an independent state, its civilization led the whole world, but once it had submitted to another tribe, it was too dispirited to ever rise again. And the Chinese literati all learned Mongolian during the barbarian Mongol era (for details, see *Notes on the Twenty-Two Histories*).[18] Chinese literature virtually died out.

Only our state is like our father and mother. Without our father, on whom can we rely? Without our mother, on whom can we rely? *Isolated, sorrowful, to whom can we turn? If we miss the chance, we will be doomed; but reflect, reflect, for today is not yet the end.*

11

Limiting the Powers of the
Government and the People[1]

Liang Qichao wrestled often with the 'boundaries' between the individual, the collective people and the state. Key terms in this essay include the 'public good' as well as 'grouping', still a deep concern (see Liang's 1897 essay above), meaning something like 'political community'. Liang signed the essay 'A New Citizen of China' but it was not part of his New Citizen *series. First published in* Xinmin congbao, *March 1902.*

Across the world there is no state without a people; likewise, there is no state without a government. The government and the people are both essential to the construction of a state. Therefore, we cannot say that the government is the property of the people, nor that the people is in any way the property of government. Rather, the state with its own 'personality' stands above the government and the people to unite and lead them (the definition of 'personality' frequently appears in my other essays). The state alone possesses the highest sovereignty, while the government and the people exist under it. Those who emphasize the role of people claim that the state is nothing more than an assemblage of the people and that state sovereignty resides in the individual ('individual' means a person). At its extreme, this claim would give the people unlimited power, and its flaw is that the state would collapse into anarchy, leading the people back to barbarism. Those who emphasize the role of the government claim that the government is the representative of the state, embodying the will of the state to carry out its functions, and thus that state sovereignty resides in the government. At its extreme, this claim would give the government unlimited power, and its flaw is that the state would sink into autocracy, forever hindering the people from becoming civilized. Therefore, to construct a perfect state our top priority must be to clarify the powers of the government and the people.

At certain points in the modern history of the West, the unlimited powers of the people have harmed the state, such as during the early stages of the German revolutions at the end of the eighteenth century. Yet this has been very rare, and an overview of the past several thousand years of history suggests that 80 or 90 percent of the time it is governments that abuse their powers and violate their people, resulting in complete turmoil. This is particularly true of China. The argument of this essay thus focuses on the government's powers over the people while having less to say about the people's powers over the government.

Through what principle is government established? The principle of the social contract. (The theory of the social contract was espoused by the great French scholar Rousseau. Recent scholars have all criticized its errors, but while we can say this theory is mistaken with regard to the historical origins of the state, we cannot say it is mistaken with regard to the principle of the establishment of the state. Even those who despise Rousseau cannot criticize this point.) If people do not group, they cannot develop their nation. If people do not group, they cannot compete with foreigners. Therefore, on the one hand people are self-supporting individuals, and on the other hand they are part of a group based on mutual cooperation. (Some might say that the notion of the evolution from self-supporting individuals to cooperative groups is theoretically flawed. Yet humans are a cooperative species whose innate natures have inclined them to grouping from the earliest times. They did not need the establishment of the state to start cooperating with each other. After people learned to cooperate with each other, they often remained self-supporting individuals, and their autonomy remained intact. The reason that humans are superior to all other living creatures is because they can act as both individuals and as groups interchangeably.) This is the inevitable result of the universal law of evolution. It is certain that once people form groups, they must share responsibility for the group's work. However, when everyone is expending their time and labor on the group's business, there are inevitably limits on their ability to remain self-supporting. Then people say to one another: I am a farmer, I am a worker, I am a merchant, I am a scholar – I have neither the time nor the energy to spend on the group's business – I would rather pick some people from the group and entrust them with its business. Such is the principle of government. Government is that which represents the people in carrying out the governance of the group. Therefore, we must use this principle to determine the legitimate obligations and rights of the government.

And what is the goal of the government? It is the public good. There are different ways of achieving the public good, but it comes down to developing the nation and competing with foreigners. Thus, whatever people cannot accomplish in their individual capacity, the government will undertake; and if an individual's action interferes with others, the government will suppress them. Although the government's responsibilities are innumerable, they can be summarized in two principles. First, to help with what is beyond the capacity of the self-supporting individual. And second, to prevent any violation of people's liberty rights. As long as the government follows and sustains these two principles, it will be honored. Otherwise, having a government would be the same as not having a government. Or even worse, for if the government not only could not help with what is beyond the capacity of self-supporting individuals but actually obstructed them, and if it not only could not protect the people's liberty rights but actually violated them, then having a government might be even worse than not having a government. For thousands of years, this is why people faced many hardships and why governments could not endure.

If the goal of the government never changes, its powers will nonetheless change, depending on whether the people are more civilized or more barbaric, a change that should accord with the goal of the time. For example, the goal of the head of a family is to raise their children to become virtuous persons. When their children are small, the powers of the head of the family are great, and they strictly discipline their children's every word and deed, even down to their table manners. This is because otherwise they cannot raise their children to adulthood. But as their children's intelligence, morality and talents develop with age, the discipline imposed by the head of the family decreases accordingly. If the children have grown into adulthood, but their parents still treat them like babies on the teat, controlling every aspect of their lives, then their futures will be gravely harmed.

We know this is true for individuals; it is also true for nations. During the early stages of grouping, the people lack the capacity to be self-supporting. Without supervision, they would be without order and discipline, and the means of improving their lives would remain undeveloped. The people lack the virtue necessary to practice self-governance. Without restraints imposed on them, they would violate each other's rights, and endless horrors of intimidation, oppression, murder and robbery would follow. At this time, the government's powers must be great. But when a society comes out of the Age of Chaos and enters the Age of Approaching Peace, the people are able to support themselves and practice self-governance.[2] If, however, a government then still resorts to the powers it held during the period of barbarism to control the people, there are two possible outcomes. Either – in the case of a militant population – the people will be provoked into rebellion against the government, putting it in grave danger. Or – in the case of a submissive population – the people will be suppressed, leaving them so demoralized that foreign nations will take advantage of the situation to seize its powers, take its land and enslave its people, and thus the government will follow them to extinction. Therefore, the government's powers are in inverse proportion to the progress of the people. As the people progress, the government's powers decrease, yet precisely as its powers decrease, its strength increases. Why is this? The government depends on the people's wealth for its wealth; it depends on the people's strength for its strength; it depends on the people's gains for its gains; and it depends on the people's power for its power. Although the governments of civilized states consistently yielded power to the people, compared to the governments of barbarian states they have a million times more authority and glory.

In the world today, aside from the Brown, Black and Red

barbarian races, most peoples are civilized. But to what extent should their governments exercise their powers? The answer is that whenever people commit deeds that violate the liberty rights of others, the government interferes; otherwise, all the liberties of the people should be unimpeded by the government. There are two kinds of violations of liberty. First, violations of the liberties of individuals. Second, violations of liberties of the people. Violations of the liberties of individuals are punished according to private law; violations of the liberties of the people are punished according to public law. Private law and public law are both derived from the sovereignty of the state (sovereignty may reside in the ruler, or in the people, or in both together, as determined by the state's particular form). Yet it is the government that executes these laws. The most civilized citizenries can make and abide by their own laws; since there are so few cases of violations of people's liberties, there is less need for government prosecutions. The histories speak of the 'actionless rule' of Yao and Shun, just as the governments of today's constitutional states are truly examples of 'actionless rule'.[3] Otherwise, if a government prohibits the people from violating each other's liberties but is itself violating the people's liberties, the government is committing the greatest of crimes. (Western philosophers often say that no crime is greater than violating the people's liberty rights.) And if governments violate the people's liberties, how can they command the people? When people violate each other's liberties, punishment follows, but when the government violates people's liberties, there is no one to punish it. Then the people's crimes can be expected to constantly decrease, while the government's crimes will constantly increase. Therefore, limiting the government's powers not only benefits the people but truly benefits the government as well.

In his *On Liberty*, the British scholar John Stuart Mill said:

When we survey the histories of Greece, Rome and England, we see that the people often fought the government for their rights. Their rulers assumed the power of government either by inheritance or conquest. In their rule, not only did they not follow the wishes of the people, but they also oppressed and cruelly exploited the people. When the people could no longer tolerate it, righteous patriots rose up to blame the suffering of the people on the unlimited powers of the ruler. Thus did the principle of liberty begin to flourish. The people preserved their liberty in two ways. First, the people limited the ruling powers by making an agreement with the ruler, who guaranteed that if he broke the agreement, he was in violation of it and failing to fulfill his duties, and thus it would not be considered rebellion if the people joined forces against him. Second, all the people possessed freedom of speech, which could be expressed in public discussion and written into law in order to protect the interests of the whole people. The first method has been practiced in European nations for a long time. The second method has developed only recently and is starting to sweep across the world.

We might say that in the past, when autocracies dominated, since the rulers only considered themselves and not the people, they could not but limit the people's powers. But today, as democracy is spreading, all heads of state are chosen by the people through public elections, which means they want what the people want, and they take as their interests the people's interests (NB: 'head of state' refers to either the king in a monarchy or the president in a democracy – Liang[4]). Thus there is no cause for tyranny. However, can we not set any limits on the people's powers? We must still set limits, because even in a democracy, if the people's powers are not limited, they will never obtain liberty. Why is this? Because actually the idea that democracy means that everyone practices self-governance without being governed by other people is a total misunderstanding. It is not possible for everyone in a state to exercise executive powers: there is always a distinction between rulers and ruled. Although government decrees are meant to accord with what the people want, 'what the people want' cannot be what everyone in the whole state wants but rather merely what the majority wants. (NB: Democratic states always have political parties; when a party wins a majority in parliament, it forms the government, and so governing is actually based on what the majority want. In the past, political thinkers said that the goal of governing lies in seeking the happiness of the whole people, but starting with the great philosopher Jeremy Bentham, they said instead that the goal of governing lies in seeking the greatest happiness of the greatest number. According to the trends of the day, it could only be thus – Liang.) If there are no limits to their power, the majority will certainly oppress the minority, and then this vulnerable minority will lose their liberty. The abuses of the dictatorship of the majority are sometimes even worse than those of the dictatorship of monarchs. Therefore, regardless of the state's form of government, the powers of the government and the people must always be clearly defined.[5]

From Mill we can see that even in the most democratic of states, the powers of the individual are limited, not to mention those states where democracy has not yet developed. Did the *Rites* not say: 'Heaven gave birth to the people and established a ruler to govern them, but could it allow one person to wantonly abuse their power over the people?'[6] Therefore, in civilized states, there is no one who may wantonly abuse their power – this includes the people, the rulers, the minority and the majority. Why is this? It is because all persons have their own power, but all power has its limits. To limit power is the way to prevent people from abusing their liberties. When people abuse their liberties, they violate the liberties of others, which is barbarian liberty. But when no one can abuse their liberties, then everyone preserves their liberties, which is civilized liberty. Until civilized liberty is attained, the state cannot be established.

The ancient sages of China spoke of humane government, while the modern philosophers of the West promote liberty. The two are the same in substance but differ in spirit. Although they differ in spirit, they still share the same goal. Why is this? Humane government emphasizes protecting the people and governing the people. But the powers of those who took command of governing and protecting the people were unlimited, and thus the advocates of humane government could only speak of what it should be while they lacked any means to achieve it. Even such perfect sages as Confucius and Mencius, who endlessly preached humane government, could not prevent cruel tyrants and evil ministers from continuously emerging over the following two thousand years to oppress and exploit the people. Why was this? Because the rulers had all the power while the ruled had no power. Rulers who pursued humane government frequently worried that their policies would not reach the people, or existed in name only, or would soon end up a dead letter. Rulers who pursued tyrannical government were utterly vicious and, with no limits on their powers, one after the other they poisoned the whole state for hundreds of years.

Since sage rulers and wise ministers have not been seen for thousands of years, there have been few periods of order, but many of chaos. As in promoting liberty by limiting power, the responsibility for affairs of state cannot be monopolized by just one or two people, but governmental functions must be separated and thus easy to fulfill. The whole state is thus governed well and would-be tyrants are constantly contained, not only because they do not dare to make a move but because they simply cannot. Once order is established, chaos cannot return. Therefore, those who advocate limits on the powers of the government and the people insist that the government and people should reach agreement on those limits from a position of equality. They do not mean that the government bestows powers on the people. (One must have something oneself before one can give it to others – the people's powers are not something the government has itself, so how can it bestow them on the people? Mencius said, 'The emperor cannot give the realm to another.'[7] This, too, is because the realm is not something the emperor can possess.) Those whom Zhao Meng ennobles he can make humble again.[8] If the government can bestow powers on the people, it can take them away again. This is what I mean by saying the two are similar in substance but different in spirit. But then, are the teachings of our ancient sages and wise ones really inferior to some remarks made by Westerners? Yes and no – their times were different. As I said above, the government's powers should be in inverse proportion to the people's level of civilization.

Two thousand years ago, human grouping was in its first stage of development, like a child just learning to walk who is totally dependent on the care of the family elders. Therefore, based on how governments under the conditions of the day should exercise power and fulfill their responsibilities, Confucius and Mencius inevitably made humane government their first principle of politics. The goal of governing lies in the public good. Governing today regards liberty as the foundation of public good, while governing in the past regarded humane government as the gateway to public good. This is what I mean by saying they differ in spirit but share the same goal of the public good. For those of us born in this present generation, after two thousand years of progress we have left behind childish ways to become adults and abandoned barbarian customs to reach civilization. How can we still act like infants crying for their nanny to feed them instead of finding ways to cultivate ourselves and govern ourselves? And how can those who possess the powers of government still treat the people like little children? Ah! To limit power is the foundation of the state and the Great Peace![9] Without limits on power, how can we get there?

12

Liberty[1]
(*The New Citizen*, chapter 9)

Liang Qichao is sometimes regarded as the founder of modern Chinese liberalism. In traditional Chinese thought, the term 'liberty' (ziyou) referred to 'acting as one wishes', rather than denoting more or less specific freedoms from restriction or being defined politically as the opposite of slavery or despotism. An organic conception of the state remained central for Liang; liberty and nationalism went hand in hand. First published in Xinmin congbao, *May 1902.*

'Give me liberty or give me death.' This statement is the foundation on which the people of Europe and America established their nations in the eighteenth and nineteenth centuries. Can the idea of liberty be carried out in China today? I say, liberty is a universal principle critical to humanity which can be carried out anywhere. However, there is true liberty and false liberty, full liberty and partial liberty, and civilized liberty and barbarian liberty. 'Liberty!' 'Liberty!' This cry is on the lips of all our youth. But I believe that if our people want to enjoy the happiness of full, civilized and true liberty, we must first understand what liberty actually means. Allow me to discuss liberty.

Liberty is the opposite of slavery. Generally speaking, the struggle for liberty in the West developed in four spheres: the political, the religious, the national and the economic. Political liberty is the liberty that the people maintain vis-à-vis the government. Religious liberty is the liberty that believers maintain vis-à-vis the Church. National liberty is the liberty that one's state maintains vis-à-vis foreign states. Economic liberty is the liberty that labor and capital maintain vis-à-vis one another. In addition, there are three realms of political liberty. First, the liberty that commoners maintain vis-à-vis the aristocracy. Second, the liberty that the whole people maintain vis-à-vis the government. And third, the liberty that colonies maintain vis-à-vis the mother country.

These are precisely the four spheres in which liberty is put into practice. In pursuit of liberty, the Europeans achieved six outcomes.

First, the equality of the four classes.[2] Within the country, no one may possess special privileges (that is, special rights distinct from those of the ordinary people). This is the liberty that commoners struggled against the aristocracy to achieve.

Second, political participation. Everyone living in a country who is of age and possesses the qualifications of citizenship may participate in the governance of that state. This is the liberty that the whole people struggled against the government to achieve.

Third, colonists' self-government. The people who have colonized a territory may establish a government enjoying the same rights as in the mother country. This is the liberty that colonial settlers struggled against their mother countries to achieve.

Fourth, religious freedom. The people may worship the religion of their choice, which the government may not restrict even if there is a state-sanctioned religion. This is the liberty that believers struggled against the Church to achieve.

Fifth, the nation-state. The people of a state assemble together to claim their independence and establish self-government, and do not permit foreign states or foreign peoples to seize their sovereignty, interfere in the slightest with their domestic governance or take an iota of their territory. This is the liberty that the people of the state struggled against foreigners to achieve.

Sixth, workers' associations (the Japanese call this the labor question or the social question). All workers support themselves with their labor, and neither landowners nor capitalists may enslave them. This is the liberty that the poor struggled against the wealthy to achieve.

When we look over the history of the last three or four

centuries, we see that the wise talked themselves hoarse in the imperial court while the brave risked their lives in the wild. If one fell, the banner was taken up by another. They never lost heart and never gave up. The liberty that they struggled for lay in the spheres of the political, the religious, the national and the economic. And the outcomes that they achieved lay in equality, political participation, colonists' self-government, religious freedom, the nation-state and workers' associations. I offer a rough outline of these developments below.

The earliest governments in Greece and Rome built all their institutions for the common people, and their systems of republican self-government were unparalleled in the ancient world. However, the Greek political system was purely aristocratic. Its so-called citizens were merely a small fraction of the population, while the rest of the population – farmers, workers, merchants and slaves – were not treated equally. In Rome, the so-called citizens only included the members of the Latin tribes in the city of Rome itself, while the colonies they conquered were not treated equally. Therefore, although political liberty originated in Greece and Rome, violations of liberty continued throughout ancient times in the aristocracy's treatment of commoners, the mother country's treatment of colonies, the nation's treatment of foreigners and the landowners' treatment of workers. With the rise of Christianity and the founding of the Roman Empire, religious autocracy and political autocracy began to flourish. Needless to say, at the beginning of the Middle Ages, barbarian tribes ran amok and culture was devastated. In the end, the Roman emperor took command of the bodies of the Europeans while the Pope took command of their souls, leaving no escape from their power. Thus the Middle Ages were truly the West's dark ages.

After the fourteenth and fifteenth centuries, Martin Luther rose up, breaking free of Roman Catholicism. The gateway to intellectual freedom was opened, and a new world emerged into the light. Then, over the next two or three centuries, war and rebellion spread across Europe. Corpses covered the fields, blood filled the valleys, the sky and sun were obscured and the gods and ghosts were dismayed – all because of religion. This was the era of the struggle for religious liberty. In the seventeenth century, Cromwell arose in England; in the eighteenth century, Washington arose in America; soon the French Revolution broke out and a furious storm swept across all Europe. As other countries followed suit, this storm of political change affected countries from the Mediterranean westward to the eastern coast of the Pacific, all of which became constitutional states. Colonies such as Canada and Australia all established their own self-government. This trend has not come to an end even today. This is the era of the struggle for political liberty.

From the sixteenth century, the Dutch fought for over forty years to free themselves from the Spanish yoke. Subsequently, other countries followed in their footsteps, and by the nineteenth century nationalism was flourishing around the world. Italians and Hungarians were fighting for freedom from Austria, the Irish from England, the Polish from Russia, Prussia and Austria, the nations of the Balkans from Turkey, and today the Boers are fighting for freedom from the British and the Filipinos from the Americans. One after the other, patriots came forth to willingly sacrifice their lives in the belief that 'Whoever is not of my race cannot claim sovereignty in my country'. Whether or not they achieved their objective, they all exhibited the same spirit. This is the era of the struggle for national liberty (national liberty largely derives from political struggle, so political liberty and national liberty are often confused).

Since the previous (nineteenth) century, America has abolished slavery and Russia has abolished serfdom, which greatly affected the economic sphere. In the last twenty or thirty years, in addition, general strikes have frequently occurred and factory regulations have been repeatedly issued. From today onwards, this will become the biggest issue facing the entire world. This is the era of the struggle for economic liberty.

These four spheres of liberty – the political, the religious, the national and the economic – represent the major reforms in the West over the last four centuries. The goal was to abolish 80 or 90 percent of the old society. Ah! What inspired them? It was the slogan 'give me liberty or give me death' that raised people from Earth to Heaven, reborn to new life. Ah! How resplendent the flower of liberty! How majestic the god of liberty!

The main events in the struggle for liberty in modern history are listed below:

1532	Conclusion of a treaty between Catholicism and Protestantism permitting religious freedom	Religious liberty
1524	Alliance of Protestant Swiss republican cities	Religious liberty
1536	Danish parliament establishes Protestantism	Religious liberty
1570	Truce in the French civil wars, Protestants obtain religious liberty	Religious liberty
1598	French Protestants given political rights	Religious liberty
1648	The Netherlands achieves independence from Spain after forty years of harsh war	National liberty; also religious causes
1618–1648	Agreement on equal rights for Protestants and Catholics after continuous warfare among Spain, France, Sweden, German states and Denmark	Religious liberty
1649	The English execute Charles I and establish a republic	Political liberty
1776	American declaration of independence	Political liberty (colony vis-à-vis mother country)
1789	French Revolution begins	Political liberty (common people vis-à-vis aristocracy)
1822	Mexican independence	Political liberty (colony vis-à-vis mother country)
1819–1831	Independence of South American countries	Political liberty (colony vis-à-vis mother country)
1832	British electoral reform law	Political liberty

1833	Britain promulgates prohibition on slavery in its colonies	Economic liberty
1848	Second French Revolution	Political liberty
1848	Vienna Uprising	Political liberty
1848	Hungary establishes a new government; Hungary–Austria war the following year	National liberty
1848	Italian Revolution starts	National liberty
1848	German states' attempt to unify fails	National liberty
1848	Italy, Switzerland, Denmark and the Netherlands proclaim constitutions	Political liberty
1861	Russia frees the serfs	Economic liberty
1863	Greece achieves independence from the Ottoman Empire	National liberty
1863	Polish uprisings against Russia begin	National liberty
1863	American Civil War over prohibition on slavery	National liberty
1867	North German states federation established	National and political liberty
1870	Third French Revolution	Political liberty
1871	Italy is unified	National and political liberty
1875–1878	Ottoman colonies of Montenegro, Serbia and Herzegovina begin agitation for independence	National and religious liberty
1881	Alexander II of Russia is to promulgate a constitution and is soon assassinated by Nihilists	Political liberty
1882	General strike begins in America; thereafter, general strikes occur repeatedly around the world	Economic liberty

1889	Brazilian independence, establishes republican government	Political liberty (colony vis-à-vis mother country)
1893	Britain promulgates Irish self-government	National liberty
1899	Philippine–American War	National liberty
1899	Boer–British War	National liberty
1901	Australian self-governing federation established	Political liberty

Looking at this chart of the major world events of the last few centuries, which of them has not been driven by the motive force of liberty? The liberties that people were seeking often differed by time period, by country and by the type of liberty they needed; and so the causes giving rise to liberty generally differed from one another. But liberty was the same insofar as it was to be used in practical action and not empty talk, and to fight public enemies and not for personal gain.

Let me assess conditions in China in terms of the six achievements discussed above. As for the first – the equality of the four classes – this does not apply to China, because China abolished its hereditary nobility in the Warring States period and thus the abuses of a class system were eliminated early. As for the third – colonists' self-government – this does not apply to China either, because China possessed no colonies outside its borders. As for the fourth – religious freedom – this does not apply to China at all, because China had no state religion and has had no religious wars for thousands of years. As for the sixth – workers' associations – this has not yet emerged, though it may in the future, because the Chinese economy is stagnant without much competition. However, it is the second outcome – political participation – that is most urgently needed in China today, along with the fifth outcome, the nation-state. These two outcomes share the same cause. If we successfully build a nation-state, then political participation will naturally develop. If we institute political participation, then even if we fail to build a nation-state, no harm will be done. Here we can see what we mean by liberty and how we can attain it.

By definition, liberty means that people enjoy liberty as long as they do not violate the liberty of others. Since people are not permitted to violate the liberty of others, their liberty is quite limited. Then why is this termed the ultimate principle of liberty? The concept of 'liberty' refers to the liberty of the group, not the liberty of the individual. In the barbarian era, individual liberty prevailed over group liberty, but in the civilized era, group liberty has overtaken individual liberty. Each era has a certain, unmistakable ratio of individual to group liberty.

If only individual liberty counts as liberty, then no one enjoys more liberty than the Chinese today. Village elites do what they want and run roughshod over people, while their victims have no redress. Merchants abscond owing money, while the victims they cheat have no way to make them pay. And since everyone can become their own village elite and everyone can become their own merchant, everyone's liberty is virtually unlimited. Not only that, but in the capital, men and women use the boulevards like their personal toilet. What liberty! In the cities, young and old consume opium like their daily meal. What liberty! If such abuses happened in a civilized country, minor cases would result in fines, while more serious cases would result in exile and forced labor. The total sum of such abuses, if we tried to count them all, would be incalculable. In this regard, who truly enjoys liberty? The Chinese or foreigners? This is why the wise see that free countries exist in the West, not China. Why is this the case? Barbarian liberty is the enemy of civilized liberty, while civilized liberty is liberty under the law, its every movement as mechanical as a piston and crankshaft, and as swift as a military maneuver. From the barbarians' perspective, they think there is no greater deprivation of liberty than this. Why is there no alternative to civilized liberty? It is because no country can compete with foreign countries without maintaining domestic order. Since foreign competition never ceases, the people must constantly be equipped with the tools required for this competition. If people abuse their liberty to violate others' liberty or the group's liberty, then they certainly cannot be independent and will be enslaved by others. Then what liberty can they claim?

Therefore, true liberty necessarily lies in obedience. Obedience to what? To the law. The law is what we establish to protect our liberty and yet also to restrict our liberty. For example, the British – of the nations of the world, none are more naturally obedient than the British while none enjoy greater liberty than the British. So we know that obedience is the mother of liberty. Alas! Today's youth are all full of excited talk about liberty, which they think demonstrates their civilized thought. What they fail to understand is that the six achievements of Western liberty discussed above were entirely aimed at the group's common interest, with no room for the self-indulgence or tyranny of private individuals. Today, if we fail to advance to constitutionalism on the basis of liberty, and if we fail to resist the foreigners by expanding state powers on the basis of liberty – but instead merely adopt one or two ill-digested theories – then we would be pursuing self-interest and destroying public morality and end up reverting to the darkest barbarism. Even when they are admonished, today's youth still dare to brazenly retort, 'This is my liberty! My liberty!' I am deeply worried that 'liberty' will not only become an alibi for autocrats, but actually become the public enemy of progress in China.

'Love' – altruism – is a good universal doctrine. But can those who indulge in loving themselves claim to be following the doctrine of love? 'Benefitting' – utilitarianism – is also a good universal doctrine. But can those who seek to benefit themselves claim to be following the doctrine of benefitting? 'Happiness' – hedonism – is also a good universal doctrine. But can those who pursue personal happiness for themselves claim to be following the doctrine of happiness? Therefore, whether ancient sages or modern philosophers, if they promoted an overarching doctrine to change the world, they never did so in support of the individual's private interests. Comparatively speaking, groups are large while the individual is small. The basic principle of governance is to promote the group over the individual. It has indeed often happened that people have chosen to love the group, benefit the group and work for the happiness of the group over loving themselves, benefitting themselves and thinking only of personal happiness when the interests of the individual and the group have been in conflict. A Buddha said, 'If I do not enter the hells, who will go there to save souls?'[3] Is this not the Buddha's expression of his desire to rescue all sentient beings from the hells? To do this, he has to personally enter the hells. Similarly, it is clear that persons of resolution can push past their physical and mental limits and sacrifice their own liberty to bestow liberty on the group and the country they love.

Those advocating liberty today are not trying to smooth the way of group and country toward liberty, but are simply promoting their personal liberty to pursue their own trifling interests. How is this any different from skinflints who haggle over chicken-feed while saying they understand the philosophy of utilitarianism? Or from wastrels who drink and gamble while saying they follow the ethics of hedonism? Like the half-educated boy in the *Strategies of the Warring States*, 'a little knowledge is a dangerous thing'.[4] I reckon this is the problem of all those people who do not understand the true meaning of liberty. Yet how can liberty not refer to individual liberty? I answer, huh! What kind of question is this? The liberty of the group is made up of the sum of the liberty of individuals, while no one can survive outside the group. If the group does not protect its liberty, then outside groups will attack, suppress and destroy its liberty. In that case, what sort of liberty is left for the individual? For instance, if an individual grants their mouth the liberty to eat whatever it wants without restriction, then eventually they will become gravely ill, and their mouth's inherent liberty will be lost. If an individual grants their hands the liberty to take a stick and kill someone, then eventually they will face great punishment, and their hands' inherent liberty will be lost. Therefore, if one can master a temperate approach to one's diet and one's actions, one may rectify all the parts of the body and preserve their liberty forever. This is exactly how we should deal with others.

Individual liberty is the liberty that belongs to the self. However, people all have two selves. First is the self in relation to all sentient beings, which is the physical body that exists in the world. Second is the self in relation to the body, which is the glittering spirit that exists in the mind. (Mencius said, 'The faculties of hearing and sight do not themselves think and can be misled by external things.

When the outside world is encountered by the faculties of hearing and sight, it is merely transmitted.'⁵ The self is relative to these things – all sentient beings and the physical body – that is, the faculties of hearing and sight. In sum, these things are all the non-self. What is the self? It is simply the 'faculty of the mind'. Now, 'If one first establishes what is of greater importance, then what is of lesser importance cannot displace it.' It is only the self that is of greater importance, while both these 'things' – all sentient beings and the physical body – are of lesser importance. As long as that which is of lesser importance does not displace the greater, this is the highest standard of liberty.) Therefore, I need not fear being enslaved by others, for this is no worse than enslaving myself to others. And I need not fear enslaving myself to others, for this is no worse than enslaving myself to myself. Zhuangzi said, 'Of all causes for sorrow there is none so great as the death of the mind, while the death of one's body is secondary.'⁶ I would add: of all causes of shame none is greater than the mind's enslavement, while the body's enslavement is a trifle. If I am forced into slavery, I will not be happy, but I can always rise up and break out of my fetters. We see this in the revolts around the world throughout the nineteenth century. When people's bodies are enslaved, others may rescue them from this torment out of compassion or impelled by justice. We see this in the American emancipation of the black slaves. It is only when people's minds are enslaved that this is not the result of outside forces, and so their liberation cannot rely on outside forces. Like silkworms that are gradually wrapping themselves in their cocoons, or like fat that is gradually rendered into oil – to seek true liberty, people must start by eliminating their own mind's enslavement. Please allow me to further address the types of slavery and discuss ways to eliminate them.

First, do not enslave yourself to the ancients. The ancient sages and heroes all made enormous contributions to the group, and it is right to love and respect them. However, the ancients lived then while we live now. Was it not because the ancients were able to develop their selfhood that they could become sages and heroes? Otherwise, there would have been former sages but no later sages, there would have been past heroes but no new heroes. For example, Confucius followed Yao and Shun while we follow

Confucius; furthermore, I reckon Confucius became Confucius by carving his own path. If Confucius had enslaved himself to Yao and Shun, then after a hundred generations there would have been no more Confucians. Do my words shock you? Have you not noticed that the times are continually progressing and human intelligence is continually advancing? Even when there are great philosophers, their theories still rectify only their own times and benefit their own society, but cannot help people thousands of years in the future. Was the West, during the Christian era of the Middle Ages, not a center of civilization? However, in its decadent stages, it became more restrictive and its problems grew out of control. But for sages like Luther, Bacon, Descartes, Kant, Darwin, Mill and Huxley emerging to rescue the West, it would not have become the West it is today.

China is different. Not only do people never dare to challenge the words and actions of the ancients, they do not even dare to entertain a shadow of doubt. Now, we all are the masters of our own minds and whenever we encounter some new ideas, we say, 'I'll consider it; I'll accept this one and reject that one.' Does this lead to punishment? I cannot say that no one in the world dares to challenge the ancients. But in the case of the Boxers, their masters went around with their hair wild, carrying swords, and pacing and muttering magic spells, and if the Chinese could have thought for themselves, they would have detected something suspicious.[7] Surprisingly, their believers spread across several provinces; they must have feared something about the Boxers which they did not dare to speculate about. Or else the Boxers used tricks to deceive and awe the people. In sum, this exemplifies the people's enslavement to the Boxers. Of course, I am not comparing the ancients to the Boxers. Yet, essentially, not all of the moral principles found in the Confucian Classics can be mechanically applied to the present day. Even if you put a knife to my throat, I would still speak out fearlessly. I do not see any difference between those who enslave themselves to the ancients and those who enslaved themselves to the Boxers. With my own eyes and ears and with my own mind, I will investigate things and plumb Principle from the top to the bottom.[8] As for the ancients, I sometimes take them as my teachers, sometimes as my friends and sometimes as my enemies, without bias, based on my own judgment of universal principles. This is liberty.

Second, do not enslave yourself to popular fashion. How very weak is human nature. *City fashion favors high-coiled tresses, everywhere hairstyles rise by a foot / City fashion favors wide-open sleeves, everywhere clothes require a whole bolt of cloth.*[9] The ancients created this lampoon, and if we can say that country bumpkins are just ignorant, in fact so-called fine scholars are no better. During the late Ming, the whole country was engaged in the Learning of the Heart-and-Mind, and all of China's scholars shot off in their own direction.[10] In the eighteenth century, the whole country was engaged in evidential learning and all of China's scholars became bookworms.[11] We can say that fashions always change with the times. Turning to recent years, during the reform movement of 1897–1898 the whole country worshipped Western Learning, then during the Boxer Uprising of 1899–1900 the whole country rejected Western Learning, and now rejection has turned back into worship. That the same set of scholars could change their views of Western Learning so drastically in just a few years was because they were in thrall to intellectual fashion and lacked liberty. I have seen performing monkeys. When one jumps, they all jump; when one throws objects, they all throw objects; when one dances, they all dance; when one laughs, they all laugh; when one makes a commotion, they all make a commotion; and when one is upset, they all run around cursing. According to the proverb, when one dog barks at a shadow, all the dogs join in. How pathetic! Humans are formed out of the vital elements of Heaven-and-Earth – so don't they differ from animals? How can we defile ourselves by behaving like monkeys and dogs? Ideally, we should establish a new society. But if we cannot do this, at least we cannot let ourselves be swallowed by the old society and just drift along with it. A true man stands tall even amid surging waves and keeps a clear head even in a land of drunken dreams. This is liberty.

Third, do not enslave yourself to fatalism. We live in a world of competition and must struggle unceasingly with the circumstances that surround us. Those who enter the fray and emerge victorious will survive. Those who fail to enter the fray will be crushed and perish. Such people can be said to be the slaves of the movement of heavenly bodies. The baleful influence of heavenly bodies can impact a group and can also impact an individual. But if people who want to struggle for their country simply accept their fate, then America would never have fought for independence or Hungary for self-government, while Germany and Italy would have remained divided vassals of the Austrian Empire. If people who want to make something of themselves simply accept their fate, how could Disraeli, a man from a despised race, ever dare to imagine he would win glory by defeating Russia? (Disraeli is a former prime minister of Britain who was Gladstone's equal, though he was originally Jewish, which the British considered to be the lowest of races.) How could Lincoln, born to a fishing family, ever dare to undertake the great task of freeing the slaves? (Lincoln is a former president of the United States who was the son of a fisherman and was very poor in his youth.) If Saigō Takamori simply accepted his fate, he would have changed his principles when he encountered adversity. If Mazzini simply accepted his fate, he would have despaired over his frequent exiles.[12]

I see today that the supposedly best people who have adapted to the times invariably say, 'Heaven is destroying China. Its doom of war and devastation has arrived, and there is nothing to be done.' On a personal level, if they are not debased by poverty, they will be corrupted by wealth, while even the best of them will bend before force. As soon as they encounter frustration, their willful confidence in their own stratagems and righteousness utterly collapses. How can we let trifling concerns cast our minds adrift? Mozi put it well when he refuted theories of fate, saying, 'Those who hold onto "there is fate" overthrow righteousness in the world and mislead the people.'[13] No one believes in fate more than the Chinese, and its people are withering away waiting to die. They do nothing but follow fate. Thus we humans, supposedly subject to the movements of the heavenly bodies and nothing but automatons, entirely lacked the autonomy necessary to fulfill our own purposes. So what was the purpose of life? Wherein lay its happiness? The British scholar Thomas Huxley said, 'Today, those who wish to create good order must struggle for victory over Nature ... Certainly we must keep a cool head and remain steadfast to make ourselves stronger, manifesting a resolute spirit and never turning back, struggling and never surrendering. When we meet with the good, we must treasure and cherish it, and when we meet with evil, we must remain unfazed.'[14] Lu Xiangshan said, 'Gain, loss, slander, praise, honor, ridicule, suffering, and joy – these are called the Eight Winds. Unmoved by the Eight Winds, one can attain meditative concentration.'[15] Some lines in a poem by Shao Yong read,

> In or out of office, ever responsible for the rise and fall
>   of the state;
> Roaming deep in the mountains and streams, wandering
>   freely.[16]

How trifling a matter is fate, which can barely harm even one toe of a hero. How could it trap a true hero? This is liberty.

Fourth, do not enslave yourself to desire. How can anyone truly lose their autonomy because of others? Mencius said, 'What I formerly would not accept even when it was a matter of life and death, I now accept as a matter of elegant palaces, a matter of wives and concubines, and a matter of needy friends. Can such desires not be stopped?'[17] Indeed they can be stopped, but only with the greatest of difficulty. How very deeply desires poison us! The ancients said that the mind is slave to the body. An enslaved body can still be freed, but what can be done for an enslaved mind? A mind enslaved to other things can still be freed, but what can be done for a mind enslaved to the body? The mind cannot be independent of the body for even one moment. As long as one's life is a captive of the six senses and six sensory fields, the sprouts of liberty will be all cut off.[18]

I often see noble and outstanding youths with the highest aspirations and talent who could launch a new age, but they become dejected after a few years. And after more years have passed, they become even more dejected. The precise reason for this is that people of extraordinary talent necessarily have extraordinary desires. But in the case of people of extraordinary talent and desires who do not possess extraordinary morality to restrain themselves, their talent will become the very slave of their desires.

And before long they utterly collapse. Therefore, it is primarily religious thinkers in the last few centuries in the West whose great accomplishments have shaken the world. Of course, it is not a good thing to make oneself a slave through excessive belief in religious doctrines. However, it certainly cannot be denied that people can restrain their desires with the help of religion, which allows people to free their minds from their attachment to their bodies and attain personal freedom. The Japanese who promoted and carried out the Meiji Restoration did so either through the Learning of the Heart-and-Mind or through the Zen sect. In China's modern period, no one is as well known for his achievements as Zeng Guofan.[19] When you read Zeng's complete works, you see how he pressed through all obstacles to practice what he learned and tempered his will to behave with self-restraint. No one can overcome hardship and become a man of great accomplishments without such cultivation. Without cultivation, people spend all their days recklessly crying out, 'Liberty! Liberty!' Such people are simply driven by the five thieves (which Buddhist scriptures refer to as the five organs – eyes, ears, nose, mouth and skin), strenuously running around in the name of liberty only to satisfy their five thieves. I do not know where there is any liberty here. Confucius said, 'Restraining the self and returning to ritual is humaneness.'[20] The self is defined as the 'self' in relation to all sentient beings, while it is defined as an 'object' in relation to the original mind. It is the self that is restrained, and it is the self that is doing the restraining. Restraining oneself by oneself means that one conquers oneself. When one conquers oneself, one develops one's strength. Conquering oneself and developing one's strength – this is liberty.

Ah! Ancient and modern philosophers in the West have devoted endless writings to analyzing the meaning of liberty and have still not finished the job. How can I, a person of shallow learning, elucidate liberty in just a few words? Although contemporary scholars have already touched on the essential principles of liberty, I have selected those simple and straightforward ideas of group liberty and individual liberty to share with my intellectual circle. If there is anyone who really loves liberty, they must be careful not to poison the world by poisoning liberty.

13

Self-Government[1]
(*The New Citizen*, chapter 10)

Liang's title of this essay, Zizhi *in Chinese, normally refers to self-government in the political sense, that is, closely related to democracy. But it also refers more generally to all types of self-governance, including individual autonomy. First published in* Xinmin congbao, *June 1902.*

What is governance? Governance means we are not living in chaos. What is chaos? Chaos means we are not living under good governance. This is an exegesis that everyone can understand; nonetheless, I have investigated the meaning of these two terms and given them careful thought.

When I walk into someone's courtyard and the garden is a mess, and when I go inside and see the house is in a shambles – in such cases, even if I do not see the family quarreling, I know it certainly lacks good governance. Lacking good governance, this is a family in chaos. When I travel across the countryside seeing people fighting in the villages, with no way to pacify them, and when I arrive in cities seeing people defecating in the streets, with no way to stop them – in such cases, even if I do not see battles or plagues, I know this state certainly lacks good governance. Lacking good governance, this is a state in chaos. A person who fails to maintain regularity in their daily activities, proper posture and facial expressions, and good manners in speech and gestures – in such cases, even if I do not see their immoral behavior, I know this person certainly lacks good governance. Lacking good governance, this is a person in chaos.

Nothing in the world can remain in a state of chaos for long.

When people cannot govern themselves, outside forces will come in to govern them. It is inevitable that people incapable of self-government will be governed by others. Animals are governed by humans, children are governed by adults, and barbarians are governed by civilized peoples – this is all due to their inability to govern themselves. If people cannot govern themselves, they are not human but animals pretending to be human; they are not adults but children pretending to be adults; they are not civilized adults but barbarian adults.

There is no other race in the world today as great and powerful as the Anglo-Saxons. They have boasted that if we British and some other country each sent a hundred people to the same place at the same time, within ten years we British would have gloriously founded an independent country, while those foreigners, like a sheet of loose sand, would have completely fallen under the rule of the British. They also claim that even if the natives in some half-civilized (that is, between civilization and barbarism) barbarian lands numbered in the millions, it would only take one or two British people a few decades to colonize them. I have examined the facts, and I believe that their boasts are not lies. Look at how the North American continent and the South Sea islands were originally opened up by the Spanish and the Dutch, while today it is the Anglo-Saxon race that receives all their benefits. Look at how fewer than ten thousand British people live in India today, while they have tamed 200 million Indians to be as obedient as a flock of sheep. And look at how British officials, merchants and missionaries across China's eighteen provinces number fewer than four thousand, according to arrival statistics, while they occupy all our strategic points as if it is enemy territory. How are they able to do this? It is because the Anglo-Saxons possess the greatest capacity for self-government of any race in the world.

The Book of Documents says, 'Regulate their nature, and they will advance daily.' Xunzi said, 'Human nature is bad. Any goodness is the result of deliberate effort.' What does 'regulate' mean? It refers to restraint. What does 'deliberate effort' mean? It refers to human action (Yang Liang's commentary on the *Xunzi* says it refers to going against human nature, which means anything that is not compliant with human nature but a result of deliberate action[2]).Therefore, human nature comes in all kinds of different flavors; it is heterogeneous and does not follow a single pattern. Let human nature run its course and the result will be unbounded chaos, and we will dissolve into fights with no way to group together. At that point, we must take deliberate action to establish laws and restrain human nature. However, these laws do not stem from outside forces, nor from a single leader, but rather are established to regulate group life. Given that innate knowledge of the good that germinates in the human mind is the same for all, it can be taken for granted that such laws are suited for humanity; they protect individual liberty while prohibiting violation of the liberty of others. Thus, neither encouragement nor compulsion is necessary for people to voluntarily work within the rules. This is what is meant by self-governance.

The ideal of self-governance is for individuals to act like machines. When it comes to a career, they decide how to prepare for it, how to set about it and how to carry it out. When it comes to daily activities, they decide when to start their day, when to work, when to receive guests, when to eat, when to rest and when to amuse themselves. If an individual feels that any inborn traits or learned desires threaten their career or morality, they can suppress and eliminate them on their own. No matter how they act or speak, no matter whether they are happy or sad, it is as if they are always bound by an iron law of self-governance. When first one person and then everyone behaves accordingly, it leads to the formation of the group's self-government. The ideal of self-government is for the group to act like an army, advancing as one and halting as one. I have never heard that an individual or a group fails to claim their independence once they abide by the common laws of the group, the common interests of the group and the common duties of the group. I have never heard that anyone can achieve independence otherwise.

Some might ask: given that machines are lifeless objects and that armies are the embodiment of autocracy, how can you think it is good for people to behave like such things? In addition, Chinese culture may not surpass others in some respects, but precisely in their addiction to following rules and orders, the Chinese people surpass all others. For thousands of years, autocrats policed them and scholars suppressed them, which has left the people weak and lifeless. And you still want to promote this poison to poison the future!? Isn't this absurd?

My reply is: no, a machine is a dead thing, but it requires an operator. As ancient philosophers said, when the mind is composed, it can command the body. If a person can turn their daily life into a well-oiled machine, their mind is in an ideal state of freedom and vigor. In form, an army is autocratic, but it has a certain *esprit de corps*. An army is a kind of group wherein the generals represent the law, which was created out of the moral judgment of all its members. Armies are thus command institutions – but cannot be called autocracies. Since their laws originate from all the people, not just one leader, every single soldier in the army is literally a general in command. Therefore, 'self-government' here is certainly different from those autocrats policing the people and scholars suppressing the people. Why is this? Because the latter is governing people, while the former is self-government. Moreover, what rules and norms do you think the Chinese people are following? Everyone speaks of respect for the law, but although there are laws in China, officials do not obey them, let alone the ordinary people. Everyone speaks of reverence for Confucianism, but although there are the sages' teachings, even the scholars do not respect them, let alone the lower classes. The 'Canon of Yao' says, 'Heaven prescribed our social relations and social classes with different duties and rituals established for each one.'[3] The social order is the foundation of how a group is governed collectively. Let's look at the officials and people of China today – what social order do they ever uphold? Looking at the government, we see a place filled with demons and monsters, dark and wicked, devoid of humanity. Looking at society, we see a lair of thieves and a den of greed and fraud, just as in the barbarian era before the establishment of government. Why is this? It is due to the incapacity for self-government. The reason that people are incapable of self-government and are governed by others lies in their inability to practice true governance.

However, we know what we need to do.

The first step we need to take is to develop individual self-governance. Since ancient times, all those who achieved great deeds had developed the strength to conquer themselves. Disregarding examples from the West and ancient times, allow me to discuss more recent cases. As a youth, Zeng Guofan developed the bad habits of smoking a water-pipe and sleeping late, but later resolved to reform. At first, such habits were hard to break, and Zeng lacked self-control, but he treated them as a formidable enemy that must be totally wiped out. Later, he was able to annihilate the traitorous Taiping rebels, who had occupied Nanjing for over ten years, with exactly the same spirit that he had displayed when he wiped out the evil habits that had troubled him for over ten years. When Hu Linyi was leading his armies, he insisted on reading ten pages of *The Comprehensive Mirror in Aid of Governance* every day, while when Zeng Guofan was leading his armies, he insisted on writing several entries in his diary, reading some pages of his books and playing a game of Go every day.[4] When Li Hongzhang was leading his armies, every day, upon rising, he insisted on copying out a hundred characters of the *Lantingji xu*, a habit he maintained throughout his life.[5] In the view of ordinary people, these are trivial concerns irrelevant to the general well-being. What they do not know is that the first step in cultivating one's character lies in the persistent and conscientious practice of self-restraint. This is what people who know how to judge character look for. Someone commented on Chen Fan, 'While wanting to clean up the whole world, Chen Fan could not even clean his own rooms. So I know that goal was beyond his abilities.'[6] (NB: I have forgotten who said this. If my readers can remember, I hope they will instruct me.) Although this comment seems too harsh, it is exactly on target.

Common practice in the West is that every Sunday is a day of rest, while on other days people go to work at 8 a.m., take a break at noon, return to work at 1 p.m., and end their workday at 4 or 5 p.m. This applies to everyone in the whole country from the ruler and officials at the top of society down to peddlers and butchers. When it's time to work, the whole country is working. When it's time to rest, the whole country is resting. Is this not to operate like an army or a machine? In the Chinese language 'order' is defined as being logical and systematic, while 'chaos' is defined as being arbitrary and contradictory. If we compare the daily lives of people in China and the West, we can truly see the difference between the chaos of the one and the order of the other. Do not say these are trivial matters. You should know that they are precisely the reason why the West today has been able to administer a perfect constitutional system in an orderly way. Montesquieu said, 'We cannot live without the law even for a moment. The distinction between the civilized and the barbarian lies in the former's possession of law and the latter's lack. This is true in the case of countries and individuals alike.' All 400 million Chinese today are lawless people. I have never heard that a country can be founded by grouping together 400 million lawless people. And do we need to wait until we actually confront the West amid the clamor of war to know which side would win?

The second step we need to take is to develop group self-government. It is through the constitution of the state that the citizenry possesses self-government. It is through assemblies of provinces, counties, townships and cities that localities possess self-government. All good political structures develop out of self-government. Although the scale of self-government differs – individuals govern themselves, a handful of people govern their families, some hundreds or thousands of people govern their towns and cities, and up to hundreds of millions of people govern their countries – they all reflect the same spirit. What is this spirit? It is simply the law. Guanzi said, 'The regions contest with the royal court for authority', and, 'If the royal court cannot unify the different regions, then they should govern themselves.'[7] Western political thinkers emphasize that nothing is more important than that a state include smaller units of governance. These units – provinces, prefectures, departments, counties, townships, cities, companies and schools – all assume the form of a state. Provinces, prefectures, departments, counties, townships, cities, companies and schools are simply scaled-down versions of the state, while the state is simply an enlarged version of these smaller units of governance. Therefore, as long as these smaller units can practice self-government, then the state can do so as well.

Otherwise, people will be ruled by others. If a people are ruled by others, then they just have to accept whatever is done to them, for good or ill. If tyrants of the same race conquer and dominate a people, they just have to accept it. And if oppressors of a foreign race seize and subjugate a people, they just have to accept that as well. Thus the reason people let themselves be ruled is because they have been completely crushed.

Why were Westerners able to achieve self-government? Because they imbued punishment, order and law with the spirit of self-government. If a country has true self-government, others cannot intervene in its affairs even if they want to. If a country lacks self-government, others cannot but intervene even if they do not want to. There are thus no alternatives to self-government. The Chinese people have been subjugated for thousands of years, assuming it to be the natural order of things and never daring to think otherwise. How could the Chinese have turned the job of providing for their interests and happiness over to others? And how can they let idlers take on the job of dealing with today's problems?

Today, more and more scholars are affirming democracy, liberty, equality, constitutions, assemblies and the separation of powers, but whether in the future the people can enjoy the happiness of democracy, liberty and equality, and whether they can carry out a constitution, assemblies and the separation of powers all depends on the extent, strength and stability of self-government. O! My compatriots! Do not take self-government as a trivial matter! Do not take self-government as a worn-out cliché! Do not just rely on groups to realize self-government but begin with the individual! We should first try to realize the self-governance of the individual, then try to realize self-government of a small group of individuals, and then of a larger grouping of small groups, then of an even larger grouping of large groups. Thus will a country of complete and perfect liberty, equality, independence and autonomy be created. Without self-government, chaos will follow. Self-government and chaos are irreconcilable, and ultimately only one or the other will prevail. The task facing the Chinese now is to engage in honest reflection. The task before the Chinese now is to make their choice.[8]

14

The Relationship between Buddhism and the Social Order[1]

Liang Qichao is not known as a Buddhist thinker, but he had been a serious student of Buddhism at least since the early 1890s. Here, he had the models of Britain's Church of England and Japan's State Shinto in mind as well. 'Social order' (qunzhi – literally 'the group's rule') might also be translated as 'community', 'society' or even 'democracy'. First published in Xinmin congbao, *December 1902.*

The future of our ancestral land is facing a big question. Can the Chinese social order make progress without a faith, or should it adopt a faith to make progress? Indeed, it needs a faith, and faith is certainly rooted in religion. Religion is not the ultimate expression of civilization. However, since today's world is far from attaining true civilization, we cannot do without religion. Some people say that education can replace religion, but I am not sure of this. Even if this were the case, it would only work in countries with universal education where everyone is getting so accustomed to learning that it has become second nature. As their virtue and wisdom develop equally, even if the people lack faith, no harm results. But that time has not yet arrived in China, and thus we must discuss the question of faith.

Following this first question, a second question emerges. Since China needs a religion, which religion should it choose? Indeed, when I raise this question, you may have your doubts. 'Since China already has its own Confucianism, what more is there to discuss?' But I believe that Confucianism is an educational teaching, not a religious teaching. As a teaching, it is about practice, not faith. Therefore, in a civilized age, the impact of Confucianism may be more profound, but in a barbarian age, its impact may be less. There are people who are infatuated with the West and think that Europe and America became powerful because of their Christian faith; they want to abandon Confucianism and adopt Christianity in its stead. Such people simply do not grasp the heart of the matter. Given that Christianity has long been incompatible with our national sentiment, it is undermining China's development; at the same time, given that there are desperate people turning to it, the Western powers use it as bait. Even a slight mistake could plunge us into unfathomable disaster. Furthermore, Christianity lacks profound doctrines that can encompass all existence and mold all sentient beings. I believe that if a country has had no religion but now wants to adopt a new faith, it should simply seek the highest form of religion rather than follow fashionable trends. Most of my teachers and friends study Buddhism. Please allow me to discuss Buddhism.

1. The Buddhist Faith Rests on Wisdom, Not Superstition

Confucius said, 'When you know a thing, acknowledge that you know it; and when you do not know a thing, acknowledge that you do not know it: this is knowledge.' He also said, 'Do I really have knowledge? I do not have knowledge.' And, 'Ultimately, there is that which even the sage does not know.' And finally, 'If you do not know about life, how can you know about death?'[2] Thus, fundamentally, Confucianism is based on the principle that questions remain open to repeated discussion, which is indeed the only way to practice Confucianism. The principle of other religions, however, is that belief comes first. Yet while one may base belief on knowledge, to force oneself to believe without knowledge is sheer self-deception. Superstitious folk have accosted me with the most abstruse and mystical reasoning, saying that that which God knows is not given to us to know. How is this any different from the laws of the autocrat, which the people have no voice in?

Buddhism is otherwise. The greatest precept of Buddhism is the 'combined practice of compassion and wisdom'. From the first arousal of the determination to seek enlightenment to becoming a Buddha, one must constantly aim to turn delusion into enlightenment. 'Enlightenment' refers to more than knowledge of the Buddha and blind belief. Therefore, according to a tenet of Buddhism, the sin of proclaiming that one believes in the Buddha without knowledge of him is greater than the sin of denigrating him. Why is this? People denigrate the Buddha because they have doubts, but once their doubt turns into belief, that is true belief. The World-honored-one preached the dharma for forty-nine years, and 80 to 90 percent of his teachings were philosophical in nature.[3] They were disputed back and forth until all was clear so that people could attain true wisdom and true belief. Shallow-minded people may think that such profound discourses are not useful for social order. I would ask, have the philosophies of ancient Greece and modern Europe benefitted world civilization or not? The ideas of their philosophers are not even one-tenth as comprehensive as those of Buddhism. How can we reject Buddhist ideas while Western scholars have begun to eagerly adopt them in their own work? In sum, when other religions speak of faith, ultimately they compel their followers to believe, because they assume that their followers will never grasp the wisdom of their founder. But when Buddhism speaks of belief, its dharma-teaching lies in awakening faith, because it assumes that their followers will be able to grasp the wisdom of their founder. This is precisely why Buddhist faith is not superstition. In his discussions of philosophy, the modern scholar Herbert Spencer distinguished between the knowable and the unknowable in an attempt to rectify the Christian error of compulsion and seek a reconciliation between religion and philosophy – which is like Confucius's teaching that questions remain open to discussion. As for Buddhism, ultimately it seeks to extract the knowable from the unknowable. Spencer's discussion represents a transitional learning, while Buddhist teachings represent complete learning.

2. The Buddhist Faith Promotes Universal Virtue, Not Personal Virtue

Those who found religions do so to change the world, and it follows that they all want to achieve universal virtue. No other religion places the emphasis on universal virtue that Buddhism does. Buddhist teachings say, 'As long as a single sentient being has not attained Buddhahood, I vow not to become a Buddha.'[4] This is still a personal vow made to oneself. For teaching others, Buddhist teachings say that only those who follow the path of the bodhisattva can attain Buddhahood, while those who pursue solitary enlightenment will never attain Buddhahood.[5] Who are those who pursue solitary enlightenment? They are persons satisfied with cultivating just themselves to achieve self-enlightenment. There are two approaches to studying Buddhism. One is for ordinary unenlightened people to strictly embark on the path of the bodhisattva to attain Buddhahood. The other is for ordinary unenlightened people to become Arhats, Non-returners, Once-returners and Self-enlightened ones.[6] Self-enlightened ones have attained the fruit of self-enlightenment and are also called Hinayana disciples and the Two Vehicles.[7] The Self-enlightened ones are just steps away from reaching Buddhahood, while the Hinayana disciples at this level have entered nirvana by themselves. Therefore, the Buddha vowed not to preach the dharma to them. Why are the fruits of Arhatship so bad that even Buddha despises them? Because even ordinary unenlightened people and those who denigrate the Buddha may still one day become buddhas, while the practitioners of Hinayana cut themselves off from their buddha-nature.

What is it – the path of the bodhisattva? According to Buddhist teachings, it is the Buddha-deed of entering the state of nirvana but returning to liberate others, and it is the resolution to attain enlightenment by liberating others before liberating oneself. Therefore, although the attainments of a first-stage bodhisattva are perhaps inferior to those of Arhats and Non-returners, nonetheless, because of their resolution to liberate others, they are laying the ground for attaining true

Buddhahood. Such bodhisattvas have not yet attained Buddha-hood (I cannot say if some bodhisattvas are actually avatars of Buddhas.) Why is this? Because, as long as a single sentient being has not attained Buddhahood, they vow not to become a Buddha themselves. The ultimate hope of all of Buddhists is to achieve Buddhahood, but if bodhisattvas can give up this great hope in order to liberate all sentient beings, there is nothing they can't give up. Therefore, it is only Buddhism that can take up the great task of saving others at one's own expense. It is not that these bodhisattvas are trying to prove themselves, but rather that they understand that the nature of sentient beings and the buddha-nature share the same root. Thus they will not seek enlightenment while others are mired in delusion, or seek bliss while others are suffering. In the case of the nation, once I am born in a certain country, there is no way that I alone can be wise among an ignorant populace, nor that I alone can be safe among a popu-lace in danger, nor that I alone can flourish among a shattered populace. Those who understand this truth will never refuse to sacrifice their own interests for the sake of their country.

3. The Buddhist Faith Engages with the World and Does Not Forsake It

Now that the difference between the path of the bodhisattva and the pursuit of solitary enlightenment is clear, we can see that Buddhism is not a religion that forsakes the world. The Song Confucians who denigrated Buddhism generally understood it as being solely the search for nirvana, which is precisely the oppos-ite of the goal of Mahayana Buddhism.[8] Christianity extends Hinayana Buddhist ideas, and constantly preaches about a King-dom of Heaven totally separate from the human world, to appeal to the populace. Isn't this a strategy to fool people? Yet, from a Buddhist perspective, Christianity is as degraded as Hinayana. Buddhism does speak of heavens, but it directs us to formless heavens, not physical heavens, not heavens of other realms but heavens of one's original mind. Thus it speaks of 'no hatred of the cycle of birth-and-death, no love of nirvana'.[9] And, 'Hells

and heavens are both the Pure Land.' Why is this? It is due to the
bodhisattvas' resolution to liberate others before attaining their
own enlightenment; therefore, since sentient beings have not all
become buddhas, how can bodhisattvas enter the enlightened
realm of ultimate bliss? Since most people are deluded and ignorant, waiting for others to rescue them, they have no hope of
creating a new world. As for the enlightened and wise, if they
long for higher realms and despise their people, then who will
take responsibility to better the world?

When the Buddha's disciples asked him who should go into
hell, Buddha replied: 'Buddhas should go into hell, and not
only go into hell but also stay in hell, and not only stay in hell
but also take joy in staying in hell, and not only take joy in
staying in hell but also adorn hell with their compassion.' From
their first steps on the path of enlightenment to adorning hell
with their compassion, the greatness of their vows and the
extent of their divine powers are beyond measure. If they do
not stay in hell and take joy in it, how can they extend their
compassion to hell itself? A few hundred years ago, Europe and
America were virtually lands of hell, but now they have leapt
ahead to become what they are today. This is all because of a
few hundred public-spirited persons who stayed in hell, took
joy in it and adorned it with their compassion. At the very
least, those who understand this truth may save their country;
and, ultimately, they may save the world.

4. The Buddhist Faith is Infinite, Not Limited

Religion differs from philosophy because it deals with the soul.
When people know of the soul's existence, their hopes expand;
otherwise, lack of hope may lead them to depravity. However,
the teachings about the soul in other religions are not as complete as in Buddhism. Christianity preaches about eternal life in
Heaven and the Final Judgment. The Christian idea of eternal
life makes some sense insofar as it is souls that go to Heaven, not
bodies. But as for the Final Judgment, when all the dead rise out
of their graves to be judged by the All-Knowing and Almighty,

what is being judged is actually their bodies, not their souls. In this regard, if the soul is sustained with the body and perishes with the body, what is special about the soul?

Confucianism attends to the body, claiming that good and evil in this life will be repaid to one's descendants, while Buddhism attends to the soul, claiming that good and evil will be repaid across endless kalpas.[10] Although their approaches differ, each is complete in itself, while Christianity falls in between. Therefore, I believe the Christian doctrine of Judgment Day has not yet broken away from the superstitions of the barbarous religion of the ancient Egyptians. (The Egyptians developed skills of mummification to preserve corpses for the sake of their future rebirth in the land of the immortals. Furthermore, Christianity often mixes the body into their doctrines on the soul. One example is their claim that Adam committed a sin and his descendants were all depraved. If the teaching of Jesus is that although our bodies all came from Adam while our souls come from God, then how could the punishment for Adam's personal sin be passed on to his descendants for millions of years? This is just like our common saying that your good deeds will incur good fortune for your descendants, and your bad deeds will incur disaster for your descendants. Thus Christianity remains a doctrine of the body, not the soul. Jesus's doctrine should not be completely rejected, given that his teachings on salvation have their good points, even though his doctrine of the Final Judgment is severe and terrifying. The only problem is that his doctrines of the soul are not as complete as those of Buddhism.)

Now, human life is limited, but knowledge is unlimited. Therefore, whoever pursues religious faith, if they do not think beyond their limited physical existence, then their beliefs will be obstructed. In his *Exposition on Benevolence*, Tan Sitong said, 'Those who love life and hate death may be said to labor under a great delusion. For they are ignorant of the fact that there is ultimately neither arising nor ceasing. Their ignorance gives rise to delusion; hence even though they know what is righteous, they are overwhelmed by the fear of death, and they refrain from doing it. But when their lives are not endangered, they take to the pursuit of evil. And when they feel alone and oppressed on all sides, they take to the pursuit of pleasure. This being the case, how can the world still be ordered? But now that the concept of soul is understood, even the most benighted know that there are great consequences to our actions and infinite suffering and happiness to experience after death; they therefore will not weary of the world only because of the temporary suffering or happiness of their present life. As long as they know of the existence of heaven and hell, they will certainly not dare to deceive and behave wantonly, but each day will move toward goodness out of fear for their future. As long as they know that the self is an immortal thing, which, even when slain, will not die, they will be prepared to die for righteous causes because they have no fear. Besides, since what is left unaccomplished in this life may certainly be made up for in a future life, how can any fear make them irresolute?'[11]

Ah! This amounts to 'applied Buddhism' (Westerners always divide the academic disciplines into their pure and applied forms, such as pure philosophy and applied philosophy, or pure economics and applied economics, and so forth. In this sense, Tan Sitong's *Exposition on Benevolence* can be called applied Buddhism). Tan Sitong's whole life benefitted from his Buddhism, which is why we revered him and followed him. Without Buddhism, Tan would not have achieved his insights.

5. The Buddhist Faith Rests on Equality, Not Distinctions

In other religions, all the members are in thrall to a single venerated figure. Buddhism is otherwise. Therefore, it proclaims, 'All sentient beings possess buddha-nature.' And, 'All sentient beings are originally buddhas, and transmigration and nirvana are both but last night's dreams.' The objective of Buddhism is simply to make everyone equal to the Buddha. Now, by definition, autocratic political systems demand obedience, and constitutional political systems also demand obedience. Yet they are opposites, in that one demands our submission to others, making us obey without understanding, while the other demands our submission to ourselves, giving us the responsibility for our fate. Therefore, although other religions are good, and while in the end they can cultivate people of the Age of Chaos or the Age of Lesser Peace, only Buddhism can cultivate people through all three ages up to the Great Peace.[12] Other religions may have some errors, but Buddhism is faultless.

6. The Buddhist Faith Rests on Oneself, Not Outside Forces

All religions speak about good and bad fortune, which stem from outside forces, and claim that the best way to cultivate merit is through practices like praying and worshipping. Buddhism does discuss outside forces, but only in the context of Hinayana, not Mahayana. The core principle that weaves through all three of the Buddhist vehicles and their canons is the law of cause and effect, which truly permeates every Buddhist teaching, large or small, fine or coarse.[13] The Buddha said that the present is the effect of past actions, while the future will be the effect of actions in the present. If you create an evil cause now, you cannot hope to avoid evil effects in the future. Conversely, if you create a good cause now, you don't need to worry about any lack of good effects. The law of cause and effect is like sending a telegram. If someone on the eastern shore sends telegrams, no matter how long or how many, the recipient on the western shore, even if they are thousands of miles away, will receive exactly what was sent. So, actions creating karma stem from the individual's ālayavijñāna consciousness and in turn form that consciousness. (Ālayavijñāna is the eighth of our eight consciousnesses. There is no way to translate this term, and therefore it was merely transliterated. Whoever wants to know more about it should read the *Laṅkāvatāra Sutra* and the *Discourse on the Perfection of Consciousness-Only*.[14])

Therefore, those who seek enlightenment are very careful about creating karma-causes. No one can extinguish the karma that we ourselves create. No one can create our karma for us. Not only are we ourselves formed out of karma, but also the

Buddha said that this polluted world is permeated with the collective karma of all sentient beings. One part of this evil karma created by sentient beings is common to all, while the other part is specific to each individual. The karma that is shared in common continually accumulates to form this 'container world' (the Buddha said that there is the 'container world' and there is the 'animate world', which refer to the cosmos and to all sentient beings, respectively). The karma that is specific to each individual means that in consequence of their actions, each individual soul stews in its own juice (originally we were all one soul, but delusion gave rise to the differentiation of self from others). These two kinds of karma have always permeated one another and will continue to do so forever. Therefore, those who seek enlightenment must first urgently create true, good karma-cause in order to save themselves from depravity, and second must urgently create profoundly good karma-cause in order to save the container world in which they live from depravity. Why is this? Because if the container world is still in a polluted state, then we ourselves have no common ground for reaching the Pure Land. The saying that 'as long as a single sentient being has not attained Buddhahood, I cannot become a Buddha' is true, not empty talk.

Those who understand this truth will know how to govern a country. A country does not become corrupt and weak overnight. Rather, we are now reaping the evil harvest of what previous generations sowed. However, we cannot simply place all blame on the previous generations in order to avoid our responsibilities. We must urgently create good karma-cause today so as to see their good karma-effect in two or three years, or perhaps in ten years or several hundred years. If we persistently create good karma-cause, the country will advance forever. The same logic applies if we create evil karma-cause. The seeds of previous evil karma-cause have sprouted, and if we water and propagate them further, then there will never be an end to their evil consequences.

As well, this applies not only to the group, but also to the individual. We are contaminated by all the evil karma of this society, and once we absorb it, we in turn contaminate society. But if we

have not purified ourselves to make a new start and yet still will-
fully claim, 'I am perfecting my group, I am saving my group',
then we are either great idiots or are deluding ourselves. Thus the
Buddha's teaching about the law of cause and effect is the world's
most elevated, wide-ranging, profound and flawless doctrine.
None of the laws and principles proposed by modern advocates
of evolution like Darwin and Spencer fall outside the law of cause
and effect. Indeed, they complement the Buddhist law of
cause and effect by illustrating its workings, which shows how
Buddhism is a pragmatic teaching relevant to human affairs. The
only shortcoming of ordinary religions is their failure to guide
people to rely on their inborn spiritual capacity. Although they
make up for this shortcoming with the saying 'God helps those
who help themselves', people have lost much of their sense of
freedom and independence because they cannot help believing
that God will help them in the end. But according to Buddhism,
even our parents cannot help us, and even our enemies cannot
harm us. There should be nothing we are attached to or repulsed
by; there should be nothing deluding or terrorizing us. All sentient beings are alone on their paths and make their own choices.
The ancient Chinese philosophers said, 'Calamities sent by
Heaven may be avoided; but from those brought on by oneself
there is no escape.'[15] And, 'One is better off relying on oneself: my
fate is in my hands.'[16] In terms of the law of cause and effect, such
statements are not as profound or enlightening as Buddhist doctrine. Buddhism is truly the most noble of all the teachings.

*

The six statements above describe what I believe Buddhism
rests on. Alas! Given the vastness, profundity and subtlety of
Buddhist learning, how can an insignificant scholar such as
myself grasp more than a tiny portion of it? If the Buddha hears
my words, I am not sure whether he will think I am praising
Buddhism or slandering it. But even if my remarks happen to
slander Buddhism, I hope they can still serve as a gateway to
the study of Buddhism. I wish to create such a karma-cause,
and indeed a karma-cause that will benefit all the sentient

beings in this world. The powers of the buddhas are boundless, and my wishes are also boundless.

My critics might say: you speciously claim that Buddhism can promote social order, but if so, how has India, the fount of Buddhism, come to its present parlous state? My reply: oh! How can you be so ignorant of history? The fall of India was not because of Buddhism but precisely due to the failure to practice Buddhism. Ten centuries after the Buddha entered nirvana, Buddhism had totally disappeared from India and the remaining Brahmins completely replaced it. The Buddhist concepts of equality and engagement with the world were totally lost, while the old customs of castes and ascetic practices endured in India the whole time. Later, India became even more chaotic when Islam entered, resulting in its downfall. In what way was Buddha to blame for the downfall of India? Given what you say, let me ask: where is Israel, the land that gave rise to Christianity, today? Do you really think that the fall of Israel was attributable to Christianity's greater fitness in the struggle for survival? Neither of the two great world religions, Buddhism and Christianity, are practiced in their ancestral lands, and their ancestral lands no longer exist today. Indeed, this can be called a strange phenomenon.

PART THREE
CULTURAL REFORM:
EXILE 2, 1904–1911

After his return to Japan from America in 1903, Liang spent less time exploring new political theories and more time communicating with reformist elites in China, including high-ranking Manchus. There was still a price on his head, but Liang was beginning to think about the role he could play in a future China (the Qing announced its commitment to constitutional reform in 1905). He studied technical subjects such as economics, taxation and law to prepare himself for power. Meanwhile, he still engaged in political debate, though now his main targets were young revolutionaries rather than old conservatives. Repeatedly, he insisted that revolution risked chaos, and that chaos amounted to an invitation to the foreign powers to carve up China. He criticized the idea of 'destruction', trusting that that which should be destroyed could be destroyed through gradual and peaceful means. And finally, he criticized the revolutionaries' socialism, though their socialist commitments were shifting and vague. For Liang, neither nationalization of land nor nationalization of capital made sense in China, even if they might make sense in industrialized countries. China needed to encourage its own capitalists to increase production and not worry, for the time being, about questions of distribution. The global class divide was between rich and poor countries, not rich and poor classes. Liang also worried that state ownership of the means of production was a recipe for inefficiency and corruption. This did not mean that he was committed to laissez-faire principles, and he labeled himself a social reformer favoring progressive income taxation and inheritance taxes, public ownership of utilities, factory laws, social insurance and anti-trust regulations.

The two essays translated in this part illustrate a shift in Liang's thinking from his more radical earlier period – or at least illustrate that his tone became more conservative. But how substantive his 'conservative turn' was depends on how we read the earlier essays. The two essays here reflect Liang's disillusionment with the moral character of the Chinese people and his sense that character ultimately determined political conditions. The foundation of a strong nation had to be a strong sense of morality.

As a nationalist, Liang now turned more wholeheartedly, at least briefly, to statist solutions, which had previously existed in tension with his libertarian and democratic beliefs. He even promoted autocracy in a 1905 essay on 'Enlightened Despotism'. Here he was influenced by the writings of the German legal scholar Johann Kaspar Bluntschli and Bluntschli's Japanese translator, Katō Hiroyuki. They taught that the 'state' had a will and a personality of its own; that it stood above the nation but also represented the nation. Yet soon Liang abandoned this version of statism, even if he did not explicitly reject it, as he responded to the constitutionalist movement in China by calling for greater speed in the writing of a constitution and the establishment of assemblies. Supporting constitutional monarchy, as ever, Liang followed Japanese scholars in distinguishing between state structures or the body politic (*guoti*; Japanese *kokutai*) on the one hand, and forms of government (*zhengti*; Japanese *seitai*) on the other. For Liang, whether the state structure (*guoti*) was a monarchy or a republic was less important than whether its government (*zhengti*) was constitutional or despotic; the question was how power would actually be distributed. (Immanuel Kant, on whom Liang had written a lengthy essay in 1902, distinguished 'form of sovereignty' from 'form of government' in his well-known essay 'An Answer to the Question: What is Enlightenment?') In other words, Liang believed that a truly constitutional monarchy was essentially democratic; in spite of the German and Japanese statist influence on his thought, Britain remained his model of a strong people living in a strong state.

15

Personal Morality[1]
(*The New Citizen*, chapter 18)

Written after Liang's return to Japan from America, this essay directly responds to Liang's own 'Public Morality' (translated above), taking his earlier arguments in a sharply different (and more extended) direction. The title could also be translated as 'private morality'. This essay has been generally read as an attack on the revolutionaries who were promoting anti-Manchuism in the name of Han Chinese nationalism and who wished to establish a republic. However, it also speaks to broader questions; above all, what kinds of private virtue are suitable for a complex society? To answer questions that touched on the private sphere and individual subjectivity, Liang turned to the resources of Chinese philosophy; he was at least partially inspired by nineteenth-century Japanese interest in Wang Yangming. Readers should note that by 'destroy' (pohuai), Liang meant revolution and revolutionaries, but chose to use the term 'destroy', which elsewhere he also applied to his own earlier views. This essay has a greater density of acknowledged and unacknowledged citations and historical references than most of the other essays translated in this volume, and in this regard is typical of much of Liang's writing. First published across three issues of Xinmin congbao, *October 1903 – February 1904.*

When I began writing *The New Citizen* last year, I had it in mind to write on several dozen topics and to begin with a chapter on public morality. By focusing my discussion of morality on public morality, I did not mean to dismiss the importance of personal morality. But since people have long appreciated and practiced personal morality, and also since the former sages and worthies had already discussed the matter thoroughly, there seemed to be no need for an ignoramus like me to pontificate further. However, in recent years the whole country has been caught up in clamorous arguments without producing any plans to benefit our nation or our society. Furthermore, the worsening situation today gives the reactionaries an excuse to say that new ideals are harming the people and poisoning the empire. Ah! Unable to stay silent, I decided to write on personal morality.

1. The Relationship between Personal Morality and Public Morality

Personal morality and public morality are not opposites but relative to each another. Herbert Spencer said, 'All groups are made up of individuals, and the morality of grouping is determined by the morality of its individual members. The group is called the "aggregate" while the individual is called the "unit". The character and properties of the aggregate are made up by its units, while what is not found in the units cannot be found in the aggregate. And what is found among the units cannot suddenly disappear when they combine into an aggregate.'[2] How true! (The above passage is based on Yan Fu's translation of Spencer's *The Study of Sociology*. The term 'aggregate' corresponds to 'group' in Chinese, while 'unit' corresponds to 'individual'.) In terms of its substance, 'public morality' refers to the moral nature held in common by people in a given group. In terms of its formation, it refers to the way the individual's morality contributes to the group's collective understanding. We cannot produce a Li Lou by assembling blind people together.[3] We cannot produce a Shi Kuang by assembling deaf people together.[4] We cannot produce a Wu Huo by assembling cowards together.[5] Therefore, when individuals lack their own personal morality, even if we assemble millions of such individuals together, we will still have no way to produce public morality. This is obvious. A blind person will not suddenly be able to see by joining a group of seeing people. A deaf person will not suddenly be able to hear by joining a group of hearing people. A cowardly person will not suddenly become brave by joining a group of warriors. If I am not inherently trustworthy, how can I expect others to trust me? And if people cannot be loyal to other individuals, how can they be loyal to their group? This is obvious as well. Accordingly, young scholars today are constantly speaking of public morality, but the results of any such public morality are nowhere to be seen. In other words, it is simply that the personal morality of our citizens has great defects. Therefore, if we want to mold citizens, we must cultivate the individual's personal morality, but when we engage in molding our citizens, we must start by cultivating our own personal morality.

How could there ever be a boundary that clearly distinguishes public morality from personal morality? Morality originated in the interactions among people (if a single individual is living on a deserted island, as in *The Life of Robinson Crusoe*, then there is no 'morality' and no 'immorality'). The framework of moral behavior differs, but the essence of morality is the same regardless of whether the interactions are among large groups or small groups, or private occasions or public occasions. Therefore, in both the Orient and the Occident, 'morality' simply means to increase public order and public good, while 'immorality' simply means to harm public order and public good. 'Public' and 'personal' are merely terms to provide a gateway for people to conform to morality. In its general meaning, morality is simply a single entity, without separate public and personal spheres, but when it is broken into those spheres, we only emphasize the pure and beautiful of personal morality and neglect public morality. Yet, if personal morality declines, it is impossible for public morality to replace it. Mencius said, 'The ancients came to greatly surpass others simply because they well understood how to extend the influence of their conduct to them.'[6] Public morality is the extension of personal morality. Those who understand personal morality but not public morality simply lack this extension. But to disdain personal morality for the sake of public morality is to destroy personal morality and the public morality that is its extension. Therefore, once we have cultivated personal morality, the battle for moral education is half over.

2. The Causes of the Deterioration
of Personal Morality

Personal morality has deteriorated to an extreme degree in China today. The causes for this are too complex to list, but five are worth noting.

(A). Personal morality has been
shaped by despotic government

Montesquieu said, 'Occasionally despotic countries might have wise and able rulers, while virtuous subjects are exceedingly rare. As we see in history, in monarchical countries the so-called great ministers or ministers close to the king were for the most part all third-rate, servile, bitter and treacherous men, as has been true regardless of time or place. Not only that, but if the rulers commit injustices while the ruled abide by the law, and if aristocrats swindle and deceive while commoners uphold a sense of shame, then the people will be even more exploited and oppressed by their rulers. Therefore, in despotic countries, everyone tries to cheat and swindle everyone else regardless of their rank or status. No one can choose to act otherwise. It is thus very clear that the principle of virtue is not at all necessary for a despotic government.'[7]

According to the law of natural selection, only the fittest can survive. The Chinese people have lived under despotism for several thousand years. If anyone tried to advance their careers, they had to lie and cheat; if they wanted to stay safe, they had to bow and scrape. Those who excelled at these skills came out on top in Chinese society, while those who lacked these skills were defeated and eliminated, no longer able to sire descendants. This thus became a deeply embedded legacy that took hold of the whole society, and these skills have become second nature, further permeating society every day. This is why, although heroes emerged from time to time, the Chinese were still unable to free themselves from this legacy. Furthermore, putting aside those who were terrorized by a despotic government and contented themselves with keeping safe and hoping to curry favor, a few farsighted and dedicated scholars were willing to roll up their sleeves and fight for the people. But sometimes they had to adopt illicit and radical approaches. As long as they upheld their principles, they could resist this temptation and hold true to their purpose, but by the time they became accustomed to illicit and radical approaches, their moral sense had already greatly declined. How many weak characters could stand against this depraved trend and defy it? Now, are so-called farsighted and dedicated scholars who are willing to fight for the people not the great men that any country longs for? If they were born in a free country, these people would become great statesmen, educators and philanthropists who use their pure moral characters and moderate methods to benefit their group. But now in China they are forced to adopt illicit and radical approaches, and so 80 or 90 percent of them have become degenerates. Ah! They are not fully at fault for what happened to them.

(B). Personal morality has been destroyed by modern despots

Such is the legacy of despotism handed down in China for thousands of years! During these thousands of years, the rise and decline of imperial governments was entirely in the hands of the emperors – as a Western philosopher said, in despotic countries the ruler is omnipotent. These are not empty words. In Gu Yanwu's discussion of public morals, he said the Eastern Han dynasty was best, followed by the Song, giving credit to Emperor Guang Wu and Emperors Xiao Ming and Xiao Zhang of the Eastern Han, and Emperor Taizu and Emperors Zhenzong and Renzong of the Song dynasty.[8] (In chapter 13 of his *Record of Daily Knowledge*, Gu Yanwu wrote, 'In Han times, subsequent to Emperor Xiao Wu's proclamation commending the Six Classics, although the study of Confucianism flourished, its central meaning remained obscure. Therefore, when Wang Mang assumed the regency, those who praised his virtue and offered auspicious omens came forward throughout the empire.[9] Emperor Guang Wu took these as his examples. Therefore, he honored and revered purity and righteousness, and regarded name and entity as important, so that those he employed in official positions were invariably men who understood the Classics and were cultivated in their conduct. As a result, customs changed for the better. In the last years of the Eastern Han, the court and administration were disordered and corrupt, the nation's affairs declined by the day, and yet those of the proscribed party and those given to independent action, who followed the path of benevolence and righteousness, continued to risk their lives. "Wind and rain, all is dark / Yet the cock crows without ceasing."[10] Since the Three Dynasties, the customs of no other dynasties attained the excellence of those of the Eastern Han.'[11] Gu Yanwu also said, 'It is written in *The History of the Song Dynasty*, "The spirit of the loyalty and righteousness of the literati was nearly exhausted in the period of the Five Dynasties.[12] Emperor Song Taizu first honored Han Tong and then commended Wei Rong in order to give the people moral exemplars.[13] During the time of Emperors Zhenzong and Renzong, such worthy men as Tian Xi, Wang Yucheng, Fan Zhongyan and Ouyang Xiu frankly and candidly stated their opinions at court.[14] Thus high officials and nobles of the court and the regions came to esteem reputation and integrity and to uphold both their sense of honor and their sense of shame, completely eliminating the evil practices of the Five Dynasties. Therefore, when the Jingkang Incident occurred, the army instantly rose up to rescue the emperor, indomitable in the face of all dangers and without doubts. Although the Song dynasty fell, the spirit of loyalty and integrity continued to flourish." '[15]) Gu Yanwu later added, 'When we observe the shift from the reigns of Emperor Ai and Emperor Ping of the Western Han to the Eastern Han, and from the Five Dynasties to the Song dynasty, we realize that the realm has no moral customs that cannot be changed.'[16]

Although these passages may not have explained all the main causes behind the rise and decline of popular morality, they certainly point to an important factor. I have systematically studied the changes in customs over the last three thousand years. Although the period before the Three Dynasties is too remote from us to research in depth, some of the descendants of the former kings survived into the Spring and Autumn period.[17] Virtuous customs declined from the Warring States era through the Qin dynasty and down to the Western Han on account of the tendency toward centralized despotism.[18] All the rulers of the time had their own strategies to degrade their peoples. Although the Warring States period was chaotic, the righteous act of helping the weak had not yet disappeared. But then the early Han crushed local strongmen such as Zhu Jia and Guo Jie, who gradually became popular objects of ridicule.[19] Therefore, when Wang Mang founded the Xin dynasty, people came forward from throughout the empire to offer auspicious omens and to fawn on him, as had been encouraged by the Han emperors Gaozu, Hui, Wen and Jing.

A change for the better came with the rise of the Eastern Han, as Gu Yanwu clearly demonstrated. But after Cao Cao took Jizhou, he rewarded his dissolute followers and swindling and treachery grew unchecked.[20] (In the eighth month of 217, Cao Cao issued an order to seek men capable of administering the state and commanding troops, regardless of their evil reputations and eccentricities, or their cruelty and lack of filiality.) The beneficence of Emperor Guang Wu and Emperors Xiao Ming and Xiao Zhang was completely lost, and public morals declined until they reached their nadir in the Five Dynasties. It was also emperors' debaucheries that led to the decadent trends in popular customs seen over the last thousand years.

Another change for the better came with the rise of the Song dynasty. Song Taizu ruled as a prudent emperor, using his autocratic powers to suppress the populace in order to consolidate his power. (The institution of rulers and ministers discussing good governance together was abolished in the Song. When Fan Zhi and the future Song Taizu served the Later Zhou together, Fan held the higher rank, but once the Song was established and he became prime minister, he found his authority drastically circumscribed.) Emperors Zhenzong and Renzong followed the institutions of the Former Kings, understood the general interest and promoted good morale. The credit for the excellence of Song customs is not mostly due to the emperors, but they did make a contribution. When the barbarian Yuan dynasty took the throne, civilized ethics and manners were struck down as these nomads ran roughshod over our people. Ninety years of darkness followed.

After this, a further change for the better came with the rise of the Ming dynasty. This was not, however, because of the emperors. A harsh and brutal man, Ming Taizu ravaged popular morale and executed disgraced officials, and he established a law that made it a capital offense to refuse service under the emperor.[21] Reputation and integrity could no longer guarantee the safety of officials or commoners. Given the oppression caused by this kind of despotic power, it is no wonder that its evil consequences surpassed even those of the Western Han. The Donglin Academy and Fushe Society activists who were critical of the late Ming government remained constant even unto death.[22]

After the Ming fell to the Qing dynasty, the standards for determining who counted as loyal and righteous changed. During the early Qing, Imperial Examinations for Eminent Scholars were held to bind Ming loyalists to the new dynasty, while later the Qing compiled the *Biographies of Twice-Serving Ministers* to insult them.[23] The resolute spirit of the late Ming was gradually extinguished. By the time of Emperors Yongzheng and Qianlong of the Qing dynasty, these sovereigns were employing their outstanding skills in terror and treachery to carry out masterful strategies of manipulation and pacification.[24] These sovereigns searched out anything remotely suspicious in people's writings as the basis for false prosecutions, and they insulted the great and the good among court officials to destroy their sense of honor. (In the sixty years of Qianlong's reign, none of his grand secretaries, ministers and other high officials escaped disgrace and dismissal.) In addition, the emperors sponsored massive compendia like the *Annotated Catalog of the Complete Library of the Four Treasuries* and the *Combined Overview of Comprehensive Mirrors to Aid in Government*, which excluded the learning of the Way and suppressed integrity and righteousness.[25]

Ever since Cao Cao, no one has dared to so brazenly confuse right and wrong as the Qing. Indeed, the Qing seems to have adopted the School of Legalism's paranoid vision of threats to the state, turning everyone into a suspect.[26] This was a strategy to degrade the people by abusing Confucian ideas, deluding the age. Alas! How can it be that tempered steel becomes soft enough to wrap around one's finger?[27] The seeds of disaster planted over a hundred years ago have now flourished and ripened, and the people are reaping the consequences. Our corruption is the most depraved of all times and all places. This is not happenstance!

(C). *Personal morality has been set back by repeated military defeats*

The chaos of war is deeply connected to the moral character of a nation, and if the nature of wartime chaos changes, then its consequences change. This chart illustrates the basic categories of wartime chaos:

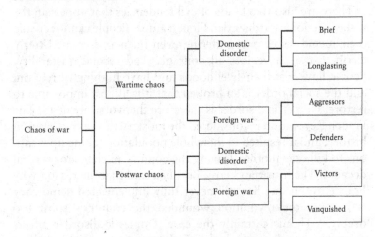

Domestic disorder is the worst of curses. Countries in constant disorder can never nurture a pure and cultivated people. During domestic disorders, six evil tendencies arise among the populace. First, opportunism. Smart people do not seek to benefit the group but only to develop treacherous schemes to grab a chance for their own advantage. Second, cruelty.

Once killing people has become like scything grass, people become used to it and harden their hearts. Third, power struggles. People engage in in-group strife, everyone is out for themselves, banquets turn to murder and fates are determined in an instant. These are the three evil tendencies of wicked people. Fourth, duplicity and hypocrisy. To escape from threats, people maintain numerous bolt-holes to protect themselves. Fifth, apathy. If a person cannot even safeguard himself, how can he care for his wife? If people cannot extend their love to those who are dear to them, how can they love other people? Thus is the quality of humaneness gradually extinguished. And sixth, aimlessness. It is better not to have been born than to be like this. Life hangs by a thread, so *carpe diem*. Since no one feels safe, no one makes plans. In the end, such people are the same as barbarians who have no concept of the future. These are the three evil tendencies of weak people.

There are also two kinds of evil tendencies that appear in the wake of a domestic disorder. First, trauma. People cannot escape their memories of past suffering even in their dreams. Utterly terrified, they have lost all courage. And second, instability. People have lost their livelihoods and have nothing to rely on, and the social order is so broken that it is almost impossible to restore. Domestic disorder is therefore the worst of curses. The French Revolution is considered the most earth-shaking event in history, and it resulted in the whole population taking up weapons to kill one another, leaving the country in chaos for several decades. The historian Leroy-Beaulieu said that the reason why France to this day has still never fully implemented democracy is because the revolution wounded the country's spirit too deeply.[28] This is certainly the case. Domestic disorder affects everyone regardless of which side they are on, since they belong to the same nation. After peace is restored, the level of the populace's morality depends solely on how well the government encourages the people to return, resettles them, supports them and cultivates them, regardless of whether this is the old government or a new one. When domestic disorders are brief and sporadic, their impact is shallow and easily overcome, but when they are long and frequent, their impact is great and difficult to overcome. This is a general comparison.

Wars with foreign countries are totally different. The attacking country focuses on the deployment of its armies, while its people continue to live in peace. It thus promotes the people's martial spirit and encourages their sense of pride, which should be heartening, not distressing. For as a Western philosopher has said, war is a basis for the education of the people. A country that is defending itself is different from a country suffering from domestic disorder – it can transform opportunism into ambition for glory, cruelty into common cause against the enemy, power struggles into national awakening; and, as well, duplicity and hypocrisy into confronting the enemy, apathy into daring and aimlessness into a sense of self-worth. Why is this? Because in a country that is in disorder there is nowhere to escape to, and one's only hope is the restoration of peace after the war, while in resisting foreign invasion one's very survival hangs by a thread and one fears that there can be no recovery after the war. Therefore, some people welcome foreign invasion to promote the national good, though this is hardly an ideal method. In foreign wars of aggression, the more battles a country fights, the higher its popular morality soars.

Here are two cases. After Germany defeated Austria, patriotism increased, and after it defeated France, it increased even more. It was the same after the Japanese defeated Korea and then China. However, when a country is defeated and conquered, its people's inherent character may suddenly collapse and be utterly lost. The martial spirit of Sparta shines forth in the books of history, but why, once it surrendered to Persia and became a permanent vassal state of a foreign race, was its acclaimed militant legacy lost? Before the eighteenth century, Poland nearly came to dominate all Europe, but why, once it was divided by the powers, was it unable to restore the intrinsic character of its people? In ancient China, it was said that the kingdoms of Yan and Zhao were renowned for their many passionate patriots, but when we pass through their cities today, the flags of surrender are fluttering in the wind.[29] Let me ask about the savage peoples of the past. Why are they so quiet now?

Because after six or seven conquests in the course of several hundred years, they have completely lost their savage instincts – for example, the Wu Hu, Northern Wei, An Lushan and Shi Siming, Khitans, Jurchens, Mongols and Manchus.[30]

Under a despotic political system, the sole way to stay safe and advance one's career is through bowing and scraping and through lying and cheating. Not to mention when the despotic regime is a foreign race. Therefore, domestic disorder and foreign subjugation have this in common – namely, that the moral character of the people steadily declines. Chinese history is a history stained with blood, accumulated from thousands of years of unceasing domestic disorder. It has constantly been under attack, but never attacked others, and it has often been conquered, but never been able to conquer others. The evil legacy of this constant degradation has permeated our society. Today, in the wake of the ten-plus years of earth-shattering disorder caused by the Taiping Rebellion, and since the European powers have made their way to China, the Manchu–Qing conquerors have themselves been conquered.[31] First one gang of thieves arrived at our doorstep, then they became five or six gangs, all tigers eyeing their prey. No wonder the people have lost their moral character.

(D). Personal morality has been undermined by lack of the basic necessities of life

Guanzi said, 'When the granaries are full, the people can follow propriety; when food and clothing are sufficient, the people can behave with honor.'[32] Mencius said, 'The people will not have constant hearts if they lack a constant livelihood. Without constant hearts, they will fall into excesses and depravities. When they can only try to save themselves from death, afraid it will not be enough, how can they have time for the rites and righteousness?'[33] Alas! How could it be otherwise?

The peoples that have the best moral characters in the world today are, first, the British and the Americans, and second, the Germans. These three nations are the best in the world at securing the basic necessities of life for their citizens. A few hundred years ago, Spain and Portugal possessed a strong spirit of militancy, vigor, resolve and discipline, but today each of these qualities has turned into its opposite, precisely because their people's livelihood steadily declined. The worst off are the Koreans and Annamese of the Far East, who are in utter distress from their lack of the basic necessities of life. The Russian government is as fierce as a lion waiting to pounce, and terrifies the five continents. But its people feel they live in a world of utter darkness and condemn their government as evil, which is, again, because the livelihood of the Russian people is so desperate. (A Japanese book, *The Collapse of Russia*, has worked this out in detail.[34]) The Nihilists are also stymied by this dire poverty of the Russian people – they tried to rouse the people for years, but, unable to muster much popular support, they have had to gamble on acts of terrorism. Japan's governance is almost the equal of the West's, but its social morality is much worse. And again, this is because its economic growth has not kept up with its political progress.

In every age and in every country, there are always a small number of extraordinary eremites who can neither be restrained by despotic power nor weighed down by poverty. However, not everyone can follow this course. Most people, after taking care of their parents and their families, will certainly, if they have sufficient financial resources, conduct themselves with dignity and cherish their reputations, and love others and practice charity. If they have sufficient mental capacity, they will engage in learning to nourish their high ideals. If they have sufficient time, they will think beyond themselves to develop their group spirit. But there are also people who do not know where their next meal is coming from or what they will wear when winter comes. Even if they possess benevolent natures, how can they condemn themselves to cold and hunger for the sake of others? Even if they are farsighted, how can they sacrifice the present to plan for the future?

According to Western sociologists, the distinction between civilized people and barbarians lies in whether they are cognizant of the community and how much they understand the concept of the future. And what determines this distinction is, above all, the extent to which they have been able to secure the necessities of life. Greed, narrow-mindedness, apathy, hypocrisy, sycophancy,

dispiritedness and resignation – over half these traits are created
by lack of the necessities of life. Popular morality is thus strongly
tied to people's livelihoods. For thousands of years, the Chinese
have suffered from forced labor, from natural disasters and
plagues, and from the calamity of war. We have not seen a time
that everyone was able to live and work in peace for generations.
These evil traits of hypocrisy, narrow-mindedness, greed, apathy,
sycophancy, dispiritedness and resignation have been cultivated
by thousands of years of clan society. The nation's wealth never
increases, while expenditures on construction projects for the
imperial court, and official malfeasance, exceed the government's
revenues by several factors. Statistics show that the national
wealth of China on a per capita basis comes to just a little over
7.1 jiao.[35] (This is equivalent to a bit over 7 yen, according to the
studies of the Japanese statistician Yokoyama Masao.[36]) Our foreign debt has nearly reached a billion Haikwan taels (not
including interest), and thus any wealth we produce is permanently lost to the nation.[37] How can the people earn a living under
these circumstances? Moreover, China is facing storms of economic competition that are sweeping across the entire globe. And
we are just now doing something? Popular morality is becoming
more and more corrupt and decadent. Alas! I do not know where
this will end.

(E). Personal morality has not been rectified by learning

The four causes of the deterioration of personal morality
addressed above explain most of the evil traits found in the
people. However, although movements for social change since
ancient times were aimed at the majority of people, they were
always led by a small group. If learning can rectify personal
morality, then it can make up for the above four causes of the
deterioration of personal morality, and even though China
would still have problems, they would not be unsolvable.
Although 30 percent of the credit for the triumph of integrity
and righteousness in the Eastern Han belongs to Emperor
Guang Wu and Emperors Xiao Ming and Xiao Zhang, 70

percent actually belongs to Confucianism. Compared with the
Song dynasty, the despotism of the Tang was about the same,
and the virtue of its emperors was also similar, but the practices
of their scholars were as different as Heaven and Earth. Tang
scholars amused themselves with literary stylings, while Song
scholars took Confucianism and integrity as their standard of
virtue. Although the causes of the corruption of the Wei, Jin
and Six Dynasties period were quite complex, the Pure Discussion school of Daoism holds half the responsibility.[38] Ming
Taizu was cruel and unfeeling, and he completely suppressed
integrity and righteousness, but due to the merit of Wang Yangming Learning, which was comparable to the achievements of
Yu the Great, the resolute spirit of the late Ming surpassed that
of the ancients.[39]

However, it is clear that popular morality has declined over
the last two hundred years, for the prestigious men recruited for
Emperor Kangxi's Imperial Examinations for Eminent Scholars
simply disgraced themselves, even though they were esteemed as
venerable across the empire.[40] After the Manchu–Qing invasion,
the Learning of Wang Yangming – Wang Learning – which had
dominated popular sentiment for a century, was completely
wiped out. When great scholars like Wang Fuzhi, Huang Zongxi,
Sun Qifeng and Li Yong retired from public life, the tradition of
Wang Learning was cut off.[41] Li Guangdi and Tang Bin were
both renowned for their learning of the Cheng-Zhu school.[42] Li,
who left his family and friends behind and made his way through
flattery, and Tang, who fawned on his superiors and was a two-
faced hypocrite, were both honored as great Confucians for
helping to build the Qing state and were enshrined in the Shrine
to the Able and Virtuous.[43] There is no doubt this was the result
of a society in moral decline. (Li Guangdi falsely blamed Koxinga for the fall of the Ming dynasty, but until Quan Zuwang,
no one had criticized his fraudulent claim. Although Tang Bin
held high office, he never treated himself to grilled chicken and
he used nothing but the thinnest burlap to screen himself from
the sun. He once said to the emperor, 'I have never lied in my
whole life.' Later the emperor realized that Tang was as two-
faced as Gongsun Hong.[44])

After this, men like Lu Longqi, Lu Shiyi, Zhang Lüxiang, Fang Bao and Xu Qianxue disguised their treachery with abstruse scholarship that conformed to the desires of the Qing court.[45] Their moral character was even worse than the moral character of Xu Heng and Wu Deng of the Mongol-Yuan dynasty.[46] The same is true of nearly all of the biographical subjects in *A Genealogy of Song Learning in Our Imperial Dynasty*.[47] But by the eighteenth century, men like Yan Ruoqu, Wang Niansun, Duan Yucai and Dai Zhen proclaimed themselves to be so-called Han Learning scholars, and celebrated each other's work while doing everything possible to rebut the learning of the Song and Ming.[48] Song–Ming Learning certainly has its flaws, but I myself cannot permit these reckless and muddled Han Learning scholars to dismiss it. In what sense is Han Learning actually 'learning'? During Qianlong's reign, the Inner Court enjoyed opera.[49] Since most operas were depraved and licentious, however, opera troupes did not dare to perform them for Court lest they be denounced for violating a taboo. Instead, they performed operas about gods and spirits and about ghosts and demons to entertain the court without offending it. As far as I can see, all the learning of the scholars over the past two hundred years of this dynasty is nothing but ghosts and demons, and the purposes of the Han Learning scholars are precisely the same as Song–Ming Learning.

The righteous spirit and militant enthusiasm associated with Wang Learning were what emperors of the day truly detested, and so they endorsed Cheng-Zhu Learning instead. But since Cheng-Zhu Learning exemplified righteousness and faithfulness, it was still not what emperors of the day really liked and they changed again to endorse Han Learning. As for the Han Learning scholars, they lived entirely in their own world, burying themselves with two-thousand-year-old fossils. They wrote hundreds of volumes, but not one word spoke to the times. Their arguments were copious, but they never spoke their minds. There was no better way to stay safe. When brilliant scholars used Han Learning as a secret key to wheedle their way to fame, integrity and self-reflection were completely lost. Although Song Learning is flawed, its followers at least pretend to be righteous,

while the advocates of Han Learning do not even pretend. Why
is this? They saw that the most prestigious scholars of the previous generation brazenly got away with what people who cared
for their reputation never did, and they coolly enjoyed the worship of society and the scholarly community. And so they figured,
why should we torture ourselves by trying to put up a façade of
sageliness? Wang Mingsheng once said that a reputation for corruption lasts only fifty years, but the fame of one's writings lasts
for five hundred. (Wang, who compiled *Final Notes on the
'Book of Documents'* and *A Discussion of the Seventeen Histories*, was a great scholar of the Han Learning school.)[50] This
remark perfectly represents the psychology of all the Han Learning scholars. Zhuangzi said, 'There is nothing sadder than a
withered heart.' Indeed, Han Learning scholars turned the whole
empire into a lifeless world. As poisonous as the eight-legged
essay, their ridiculous notions became entrenched at the heart of
scholarship for over two hundred years.[51] Not until after the
Sino-Japanese War did their ascendency begin to show cracks.[52]
We are now reaping the consequences of their creation of this
world without sensation or feeling. Alas!

In the last five years, following the invasions by the great
powers, new ideas from abroad entered China. At first one or two
people advocated them, but soon thousands of people began to
parrot these new ideas. It is not that they completely despised
traditional learning, but that they were trying to compensate for
the inability of traditional learning to deal with the complex
needs of the day. Furthermore, they were laying out all kinds of
ideas, which encouraged freedom of thought, so that young
scholars could choose what to think for themselves. However,
they did not fully realize that a society rotten for so long could
not be instantly transformed by civilized ideas. Thus, when the
idea of freedom arrived in China, it led people to disrupt the
social order instead of promoting happiness. When the idea of
equality arrived, it led people to despise the law instead of taking
responsibility. When the idea of competition arrived, it led
people to divide their own group instead of uniting to resist outside forces. When the idea of rights arrived, it led people to
conceal their private interests instead of pursuing the public

good. When doctrines of destruction arrived, they led people to destroy the national essence instead of saving the people.[53]

Herbert Spencer once said, 'In a period of decline, even if there are government reforms, abuses eliminated in one place will simply arise in another, and calamities eliminated in one place will simply re-emerge in another. If we examine the whole society, we will see that these abuses and calamities often remain unsolved. Thus, without popular solidarity, disaster may strike in new places but there is no stopping it.'[54] Alas! As I witness the influence of new ideas on our youth over the last few years, I cannot but admire Spencer's empirical observations, and I feel worse and worse for my people. Hardly one out of ten can understand how the benefits of the new ideas can fix the flaws of the present system. *The Book of Rites* says, 'What is sweet may be moderated, and what is white may be colored. Those who are upright and sincere are readily taught the rites.' And, 'The orange trees of the south produce sweet oranges, but in the north their yield is sour.'[55] Who could have anticipated that the purest and noblest of the new ideas to benefit the group and improve customs, once they landed in China, would be swallowed up by China's immense capacity to assimilate the foreign? In a word, the Pure Discussion of the Wei–Jin period and the Han Learning of the eighteenth century – and the ideas of freedom, equality, rights and destruction that are on the lips of young scholars today – all show the same capacity to monopolize the discourse. And today, the most obsessed of the young scholars promote the newest and most powerful of these ideas in accord with their own evil natures and habits, whether longstanding or recent. Popular morality was transformed during the two hundred years of the Qing dynasty. In the period dominated by the Cheng-Zhu school, its followers pretended to be righteous, but still knew that evil conduct was shameful. In the period dominated by the Han Learning school, its followers did not even pretend to be righteous and so failed to regard evil conduct as shameful. If we do not salvage the situation today, I am afraid that after the period dominated by Western Learning, evil conduct will be regarded as glorious. Indeed, we already see this beginning to happen with a portion of our youth. Can words like 'floods' and

The Causes of the Changing Levels of Popular Morality across Chinese History

	State structure	Kingship	War	Scholarship; thought	Economy	Popular morality
Spring and Autumn (770–476 BCE)	Various states; aristocracies	Weak power; little influence	Numerous but not very intense	Numerous schools sprout; not yet developed; mostly following the former kings	Transportation embryonic; competition limited	Simple and honest; pure and kind
Warring States (472–221 BCE)	Various states; gradual concentration of autocratic power	Kings reward subordinates for military and diplomatic skills	Extremely violent	Freedom of thought develops; contestation among Confucian, Mohist, Daoist, Legalist and Diplomacy schools; Legalist and Diplomacy schools dominate	Commercial activity gradually rises; much business consolidation; high taxes and war impose great hardships on the people	The good: righteous acts of helping the weak; the bad: indecency and deception, destroying the social order

	State structure	Kingship	War	Scholarship; thought	Economy	Popular morality
Qin (221–206 BCE)	Centralized power; despotism	Aims to suppress popular intelligence and morale	Extreme violence continues	Eliminates the various schools; favors Legalists	Widespread destitution	Servile and unsettled
Western Han (202 BCE– 9 CE)	Centralized power; despotism	Founding emperor Gaozu maintains Qin institutions; crushes righteous acts of helping the weak; cruel and unfeeling	Few wars	Both Confucianism and Daoism practiced	During the reigns of Emperors Wen and Jing, the populace is provided for; after the reigns of Wu and Zhao, the populace is poorer	Even more servile than the Qin
Eastern Han (25–220)	Centralized power; despotism	Emperor Guang Wu and Emperors Xiao Ming and Xiao Zhang reward reputation and integrity	Few wars	Confucianism prevails and benefits the realm	Recovery	Esteem for moral integrity; upholding a sense of honor and shame; its customs were known as the finest

Three Kingdoms (220–280)	Disunity of the Han Chinese	Cao Cao of Wei promotes evil practices; the kingdoms of Wu and Shu reward political machinations	Violent	Scanty	Difficult	Base
Six Dynasties (222–589)	Foreign invasions	Frivolous and extravagant practices rewarded	Numerous; Han Chinese always defeated	Both Buddhism and Daoism practiced; literature and Pure Discussion flourish	Straitened conditions	Turbid and dispirited
Tang (618–907)	Han Chinese recovery of central power; then division again	Arrogant and extravagant	First half: peaceful; second half: great rebellion	Scholars focus only on literature; Buddhism develops	First half: considerable recovery; second half: grave difficulties	First half: dispirited and servile; second half: turbid

	State structure	Kingship	War	Scholarship; thought	Economy	Popular morality
Five Dynasties (907–979)	No true state	No true ruler	Military defeats by foreign races	None	Populace unable to meet its needs	Lowest imaginable
Song (960–1279)	Weak sovereignty; frequent foreign attacks	Emperors Zhenzong and Renzong love the people and uphold the rites	Military defeats by foreign races	Neo-Confucianism flourishes; central figures Zhu Xi and Lu Xiangshan	Some recovery	Esteem for integrity and righteousness; refined and weak
Yuan (1271–1368)	Foreign sovereignty; despotism	Nomads trample on the Han Chinese	Complete defeat of the Han Chinese; the people not affected by war	Adopts the last dregs of Cheng-Zhu Learning, without its essence	Difficult	Servile; little sense of honor and shame
Ming (1368–1644)	Restoration of Han Chinese rule; despotism	Ming Taizu is cruel; suppresses popular morale	Lasting peace after victory of the Han	Wang Learning flourishes; intellectual level raised	Some recovery	Esteem for reputation and integrity; almost on level with Eastern Han

Qing (1644–)	The Manchu–Qing race assimilated; despotism	Emperors Yongzheng and Qianlong command their officials through cruelty and treachery	Lasting peace after defeat of the Han	Scholars retreat to Han Learning and literature, abandon true learning; crafty use of corrupt and hypocritical Cheng-Zhu Learning to disguise their treachery	Prosperity	Weak, timid, base and sly
Present-day	Civilized races invade; sovereignty is lost	For forty years, rulers oppress and neglect the people; conditions worsen	Domestic disturbances, foreign aggression; after defeats, populace in ferment	Old Learning destroyed, New Learning not yet mature; fallacies set in	Wealth flows out as global economic competition arrives; nationwide straitened conditions	Turbidity at zenith; evils prevail

'wild beasts' even begin to describe the horror of regarding evil conduct as glorious? When any persons of integrity think about this, they tremble in fear.

The Changing Level of Popular Morality across Chinese History

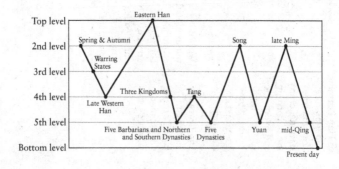

3. The Necessity of Personal Morality

Just as people need food, no one can live without personal morality, even for a moment. However, if I were to talk about my ideas with the majority of people, who are illiterate, there is no way they could understand me. Even if I talk to the minority of people who have received a traditional education, there is no way they will listen to me. My sincere advice can only reach the tiniest minority of the minority of the Chinese people, but I believe that in the future the influence of this tiny minority will be so tremendous that ultimately they will influence the great majority of the people. I cannot express how joyful and yet how fearful this makes me.

Today, what most dazzles and enchants our promising, out-spoken and resolute idealists? Is it not the doctrine of destruction? Whether the doctrine of destruction can be carried out in today's China is a separate issue that I will not pursue for now. But today's radicals all seem to think that while morality is needed for construction, it is not needed for destruction. I beg to differ.

Across all history, the great projects of national construction always involved some destructive characteristics. In addition, the great leaders of destructive movements always exhibited the spirit of construction. Indeed, destruction and construction have always been interdependent and inseparable, and the abilities that are needed to carry them out are precisely the same. Without such abilities, neither construction nor destruction is possible. Today's advocates of destruction frequently cite the principle of the division of labor in economics to argue thus: we humble persons cannot shoulder all the world's responsibilities; our job is to meet the current situation by focusing on destruction; we will leave it to others of outstanding merit to take on the job of construction, which is not our concern. What grand and noble intentions they profess! But, for my part, I believe not only in construction after destruction but also in construction before destruction. Otherwise, even if we are daily preaching destruction, its goals will never be met. Why is this? Because, as the principles of sociology tell us, the group must be consolidated before it can compete with others. When a society competes with other societies or when a nation competes with other nations, if their institutions or defenses are not consolidated, they will certainly be defeated by their first opponent, unless indeed they self-destruct first.

The core idea of the doctrine of destruction is to mobilize a newly emerged but still-weak minority of a society or nation to recklessly challenge a deeply rooted and powerful majority. But what we really need to worry about is our nation being too weak, not our enemies being too strong. Then how do we vanquish our enemies? Simply by consolidating strong and stable institutions. In the case of a society or nation whose inherited ways of life were built over generations, it is quite easy to establish institutions that are based on their natural development. However, in the case of a political party with no precedents or resources to rely on, it is extremely difficult to establish institutions that would have to be completely man-made. What I mean by the construction that precedes destruction is simply this kind of construction. And can we achieve this without morality?

Today's advocates of destruction often talk about destroying everything, which is not credible. For the rest of us, what do we mean by destruction? Simply, to eliminate the causes of social problems. For to speak of destroying everything would mean to destroy society as well. Take the physical body, for example: of course people suffering from chronic diseases should get treatment, but if they were treated with acupuncture and moxibustion and given harsh medicines regardless of which parts of the body were diseased, this would virtually amount to suicide. I am also well aware that the goal of the 'resolute idealists' who advocate destruction is not actually to destroy society, but they do not realize that once people are accustomed to talk of 'destroying everything', and this notion is seared into their brains, moral sanctions will be useless and society itself will be destroyed. And I am also well aware that these 'resolute idealists' who advocate destruction clearly see that virtually all of today's society is so diseased that they become enraged to the point they must fix the problem at its roots. This makes sense, but no matter what kind of strong medicine patients are given, they must have a 'vital essence of life' that gives them the strength to drive away their illness. Otherwise, before their first disease has been cured, the patient is afflicted with another disease, and this second disease will be even harder to cure than the first.

Therefore, all this talk of destroying everything has led in the end to thousands of abuses without a single good result. Why is this? Because only if we know both what should be destroyed and what should not, can we reap the benefits of destroying what should be destroyed. If we destroy everything, not only will we be unable to create what should be created, but also in the end what should be immediately destroyed is still not destroyed. I can say with certainty that this is what will happen.

I previously believed that China's traditional morality was no longer fully able to guide the people, and I hoped to develop a new morality to supplement the moral tradition (see my essay 'Public Morality' above). Reflecting on this idea today, it was all idealistic talk which was impossible to put into practice given current conditions. Whoever speaks of the social order must promote morality, intelligence and strength. But while it is easy to cultivate intelligence and strength, morality is extremely difficult to nourish. If we wish to transform the people with new morality, we cannot merely rely on a few tidbits of Western ideas. Having read all of the works of Socrates, Plato, Kant and Hegel, we might claim that they expressed new moral theories, but not a new morality as such. Why is this? Because morality is conduct, not words.

When we speak of morality, we note that it is rooted in liberty of conscience; because morality is universal, existing everywhere and at all times, there is no such thing as new morality or old morality. But when we practice morality, we adjust it to accord with the nature of our particular society; thus its legacy of the sublime words of the ancient philosophers and the virtuous deeds of the ancestors is passed down. This is how a society is continually sustained. To suddenly switch to that which sustains another society in order to sustain our own society is easier said than done. I examined the origins of Western morality and discovered that it is partly derived from religious sanctions, partly from legal sanctions and partly from reputational sanctions. But will today's China be able to use these three sanctions? Now that I know this is impossible, I cannot continue to say that I hope to transform the people with a new morality. This would be like trying to grind a brick to make a mirror or to boil sand to make rice. I am well aware that, when it comes to moral education, in the end we will be forced to add some Western morality. However, this cannot be achieved overnight but certainly must wait until education has become universal. As in a time of dearth before the harvest, listening to people talk about food can never feed you, so in a time of transition with no basis on which to establish universal education, empty talk will never bring it about.

This is why, even if we brought in the new morality, it is hopeless. Then, what is the one hope we have to sustain our society today? It is nothing but the traditional morality that has been handed down from our ancestors. (Morality is different from ethics in that morality includes ethics, while ethics cannot encompass all of morality. The interpretation of ethics might change as circumstances change, while morality is the same around the world and remains true after a hundred generations. The traditional view that close kin serving together in the imperial court is a transgression and that polygamy is not immoral are examples of ethical norms that are not suitable for the present age. Yet the morality of loyalty and the morality of love are constant regardless of time or place. Examples like this are too numerous to list. We may therefore say that Chinese ethics is flawed, but we cannot say that Chinese morality is flawed.) With the rise of the call to 'Destroy everything!' they will eventually come for traditional morality and destroy it as well. Alas! What may seem trivial at first can become immense as the end approaches. Long ago, when Xin You saw someone with unbound hair offering sacrifices by the Yichuan River, he was able to foresee that ritual propriety was collapsing and that within a hundred years the territory would be taken over by a barbarian Rong tribe.[56] Do not tell me that all your talk of 'destroying everything' is just a result of getting carried away. If your talk is inconsequential, why bother saying it? And if it is influential, you will be poisoning the world. I hope that you will take responsibility for your words and think it over carefully.

Do your readers not ask: why do you keep blathering on about your theories when our nation is in imminent peril? Do you not acknowledge your personal responsibility for saving the nation? Since the 400 million Chinese have already been corrupted for so long, it should make no difference if your small number turned out to be corrupt. Yet the fate of China lies on your shoulders; therefore, the very survival of our nation depends on whether you value morality or scorn it. As we are discussing the great enterprise of destruction today, do you also know what kind of person was the hero of the English Revolution two hundred years ago? Cromwell was truly the purest of the Puritans. Or what kind of people were the heroes of the American Revolution a hundred years ago? The men Washington led were all the most conscientious and upstanding citizens. Or what kind of people were the heroes of Japan's revolution thirty years ago? Yoshida Shōin and Saigō Takamori and their comrades were all masters of Zhu Xi Learning and Wang Learning. Therefore, unless you possess a compassionate mind, you should not advocate destruction. Unless you possess a pure and noble nature, you should not advocate destruction. Yet to develop a compassionate mind and a noble and pure nature is easier said than done. Now, we understand this is a difficult task which requires constant dedication, but we might accomplish it if we conscientiously restrain ourselves, diligently encourage ourselves, treat each other with sincerity and trust, and admonish our friends to do good. But if you are going to destroy the very virtues that enable you to pursue the course of destruction, I really cannot congratulate you.

When I look at public comments today, they have become so enthralled with revolution that some people idolize Hong Xiuquan and Zhang Xianzhong.[57] I am aware of the purpose behind these comments, but should you yourselves be creating any more of such evil karma? It may be thrilling to create such karma, but the consequences are incalculable suffering. Zhang Xianzhong is not worth mentioning, but in the case of Hong Xiuquan, some people praise him for being a kind of fighter for the nationalist cause. But was Hong Xiuquan really motivated by nationalism? Even the people who believe this do not dare to swear to it. When we judge a person, we must look into their true character. Even if Wang Mang praised Yi Yin and the Duke of Zhou, and even if Cao Pi followed the examples of Shun and Yu, we still need to evaluate their characters.[58] You cannot call a despicable person a virtuous person just because their goals happen to be in accord with your own. For example, we all praise Han Tuozhou for advocating attacks on the Jin.[59] However, while we can praise his advocacy, we cannot praise his character. And you cannot call a virtuous person a despicable person just because their goals happen to be opposed to your own. We all despise Wang Meng for serving Emperor Fu Jian of the Former Qin. However, while we can despise his actions, we cannot erase his whole character.[60]

Who can stop ideologues if they do not take their moral character seriously? If their words are valued by society, I fear that they will influence the character of the whole society. Now, don't the revolutionaries want to save the nation? But who doesn't want to save the nation? The nation will never be saved by a revolution led by the 'Trouble-Makers' Party'. And not only will the nation not be saved, but also its doom will be sped up. We must consider this prospect calmly and collectedly.

According to the thinking of these ideologues, they would certainly counter, 'If our "Trouble-Makers' Party" did not plant the
first seeds, the "Consolidation Party" would not be able to harvest the fruits of our efforts.' Whether this theory is true is
another question, which I will not pursue here. Let me ask this:
do you ideologues want to join the Trouble-Makers' Party
yourselves and also want to convince my readers to join it as
well? I am afraid, however, that even if you want to debase
yourself in this way, your social position would never allow it;
and even if it did, people across the nation are already flocking
to join the Trouble-Makers' Party now. They have already engaged
in many actions and will be taking more in the future. Why
would they let you join when you could serve no purpose? And
why would they listen to what you have to say from the side-
lines? Furthermore, you are only talking to people who, like
yourself, are outside rebel circles, and nothing you say can possibly influence the rebels.

Today, we should be devoting ourselves to the task of true
national salvation and cultivating people of ability to carry this
out. If we could do this, then I could stop issuing this kind of
frank criticism. Cao Cao once issued an edict seeking officials
who knew how to order the state and command the military
regardless of whether they were benevolent or filial. I suppose
Cao Cao would say he was taking temporary measures to shore
up the nation, but no one knew that once these kinds of norms
came to prevail, by the time of the Jin dynasty, virtues of honor
and shame would be lost, the Wu Hu would repeatedly invade
and the Northern Wei would seize power.[61] This is when the
descendants of the Yellow Emperor started to weaken.[62] Thus
the interplay of cause and effect works remorselessly without
the smallest deviation. Alas! Is it not terrifying? So if the father
steals, the son will kill. If city fashion favors high-coiled tresses,
then hairstyles will rise by a foot everywhere. Today, a tiny
minority of 'people with foresight', who proclaim themselves to
be pioneers of a new era, are regarded as brothers by a younger
generation of activists. Yet if they are being misled by these
people's doctrines, I am afraid that nothing they accomplish will
ever compensate for their crimes. Did an ancient philosopher

not say, 'When two armies go into battle, the side that deplores the situation will win'?[63]

How should scholars of some understanding and resolution prepare themselves and gather their strength in the face of the great threats coming from the government, as well as another great threat coming from the foreign powers? Where will this strength come from? It will, I believe, come solely from following the guidance of morality; developing knowledge and preparing for action are secondary. If two people associate without a conception of morality, they cannot form a group, much less make plans. If someone builds a house and burns it down, or if they grow plants and trample them, then they can certainly be considered capable of destruction – except that what they destroy is theirs rather than their enemy's.

Zeng Guofan is the target of the harshest condemnation by the anti-Manchu camp, but the more I have gained experience of the world, the more I admire him.[64] I believe that if Zeng had been born in our times and was still in his prime, then he would certainly be the one to save China. Destruction was permissible for Zeng because of his extremely frank and honest temperament. Malleability was permissible for Zeng because of his extremely strict practices of self-cultivation. In his words, 'Set forth for the battle, fight to the death.' And, 'More clear thinking, less big talk.' And, 'If you do not become a sage or worthy, then you will become a beast. Do not ask about the harvest but ask about the plowing and weeding.' It was Zeng's self-discipline that enabled him to carry out his great enterprise. It was Zeng's ability to inspire trust among people and guide them well that enabled him to lead worthy men to plan their great enterprise together. If you do not wish to restore peace to the empire, I have nothing more to say, but if you do have this goal, then I say you must read the works of Zeng Guofan thrice daily. The heroes of England, America and Japan, like those mentioned above, as well as the heroes of our own fatherland, show how we can form an army to take on the task of national salvation.

You may be unhappy that I have said that what the advocates of destruction generally end up destroying is theirs rather than their enemy's. The advocates of destruction never deliberately intend to destroy themselves, but this is the probable outcome of their actions – which is true not only of other factions but their own faction as well. Why is this? As I have said, learning together and working together are often at odds, which is why those who wish to form a group must be extremely careful. When people are learning together, their circumstances are the same, their aspirations are the same, their thoughts are the same and their words are the same; they are all still naive, and they promise to transform the world hand in hand. But when they enter the real world to work together, each has their own character, each has their own position, and when it comes to actually dealing with each other, their opinions and their methods are never in complete accord. It is often the case that initially they encourage each other, then they compete with each other, then they resent each other and finally they end up hating each other. Such cases are common in both Chinese and Western history, and even heroes are not exempt. There is a proverb, 'To meet with each other is delightful, to live together is difficult.' This is the case even with familial relations, such as those between parents and children, siblings and couples, to say nothing of friends trying to live together. When people live together, only those with a profound sense of morality can admonish one another to do good without ruining their relationship. When we observe how Zeng Guofan dealt with Wang Pushan and Li Ciqing, we can see the problem.[65]

Dear reader, do you still doubt my words? Please remember this until you actually start working with others – then the truth of my words will dawn on you. It is clear that the resolute idealists of today cannot save the nation from imminent peril if they are distant from each other. To be of any use, they must cooperate to form an organization with specialized departments and solid unity. I have thought endlessly about this. Can such an organization possibly be established without a sense of morality?

Furthermore, morality deteriorates greatly when people are working with others, and even more so when they are engaged in destruction. How can we say that the paths to the Taihang and Mengmen mountains are dangerous when compared to a whole world where people are so corrupt that they have become constantly opportunistic and manipulative? In a letter to his younger brother, Zeng Guofan said, 'I believe myself to be an honest and sincere man. Yet if only because I have experienced so many events over the course of my life, I came to learn some political tricks and have demeaned myself.' If even such an admirable man as Zeng Guofan could not avoid moral degradation, what can we say about other people? In sum, it is easy to uphold morality as students, but extremely difficult in the real world. Since the advocates of destruction are constantly facing great enemies, they need to think strategically about their every move. What I mean by thinking strategically is not like actual combat between two countries, but rather how a country will covertly seek a secret agreement when an enemy with massive forces at its disposal is approaching – that is, unless they execute brilliant tactics in reaching an accommodation, they will inevitably join the ranks of the defeated. Therefore, the position and the nature of advocates of destruction were incompatible with morality. They may have started out as the most sincere and principled of people, but they were gradually and imperceptibly transformed due to their position and their nature. There are people who will become cruel and deceitful in just a couple of years. The school of destruction is truly the most horrible of laboratories, but when we look into it, we see that whoever embarks on the path of cruelty and deceit will certainly never be able to accomplish anything.

I am not engaged in empty talk of theories selectively cited from the *Scholarly Annals of the Song and Yuan Periods*; rather, I can deduce how things will turn out based on what I have personally seen and experienced.[66] It is difficult to cultivate morality when you are working with others, but this is precisely when the need for morality is most urgent. In such a situation, who would not fear to lose their sense of morality? Who would not do their best to restore it? *The Book of Odes* says, 'Do not teach monkeys to climb trees, as it is like mixing more muck into muck,' or, do not encourage the wicked.[67] Even if you constantly practiced self-restraint, you would still fear that nothing could save you. But if you relax a little or if you cover up your errors, you will suffer moral collapse.

You may ask: the moral rot running through China's decrepit society is greater than we can imagine, but your argument puts all the blame on the youth who are pursuing the new learning. While these youths may commit some moral lapses, do you still think they are worse than the old society? My answer: no, but I think the old society is hopeless and there is nothing we can ask of it; anyway, it is beyond what I can deal with. China has already been destroyed at the hands of the old society. Our only hope is that the youth with new learning will revive this dying China. But if they are even slightly careless, they will become just like the old society, and then China will be beyond salvation. This is why I have to go on at such length.

The Book of Rites says, 'Only after the superior man possesses goodness himself will he demand it of others; only after he is himself free of evil will he condemn it in others.'[68] In view of this principle, for a humble person like myself – whose grasp of morality is narrow and whose commitment to morality is shallow and who particularly regrets his growing jealousy and greed – how dare I brazenly preach morality to the scholars of the empire when I myself am at fault? However, as the religion from the West also says, 'To first save yourself and then devote your merits to the salvation of others: these are the deeds of a Buddha. To first save others before you can save yourself: this is the resolve of a bodhisattva.' Since my capacity for self-examination is weak, is there anyone more eager than me to cure myself with the help of good friends and good advice? On the one hand, I follow the principle of learning from others to rectify my faults and strengthen my virtue, and on the other hand I reflect on exhortations written on my waist sash to improve myself. Although my words are inadequate, how can I stop?

I have observed that there are still a few followers of the new learning movement who are raising the issue of moral education. However, their efforts come to nothing. This is entirely because their so-called moral education is nothing more or less than the education of the intellect. They stuff their arguments with citations from the Confucians of the Song, Yuan and Ming dynasties, and they pack them full of their shallow understanding of the history of ethics in England, France and Germany.

Such erudition! But what does any of this have to do with morality? What is the relevance of Pattern and Substance? Of the Supreme Polarity and No Polarity? Of Already-Manifest and Not-Yet-Manifest? Of Intuitionism? Of Epicureanism? Of Evolutionism? Of Utilitarianism? Of Liberalism? To make their arguments, they go from scraping the surface to diving into the depths, but what does any of this have to do with morality?

It is not that these kinds of theories are not worth studying, but when I study them I simply treat them as scientific disciplines – like chemistry and physics, engineering, law and economics – as ways to increase my knowledge. Any claim to find moral education here is just so much empty talk that leads nowhere. If they follow these kinds of theories, I am afraid that not only today, but even after decades or centuries, their efforts will still come to nothing. Alas! The intelligence and the morality of the people of the West progress in direct ratio to one another, but the intelligence and morality of the people of the East progress in inverse ratio. Based on what is happening in China today, we can see which way the wind is blowing, and if this is so, then our education of the intellect will undermine our moral education. Education of the intellect that is disguised as moral education will be another obstacle to moral education. If we use education of the intellect to undermine moral education, the world will blame education of the intellect; if we use 'intellectualized moral education' to undermine moral education, the world will blame moral education. Can we take this lightly? Those whose ambition is to save the world must ponder deeply on the true scope of moral education.

'To pursue learning, learn more day by day; to pursue the Way, unlearn it day by day.'[69] These words hit the mark! Today, we may be diligent in pursuing gain day by day, while we lose sight of what we lose day by day. Alas! Thus does the true Way diminish daily. I think that if young scholars do not wish to seek the Way, then that is the end of it. But if they do wish to seek the Way, they do not need to look for any grand philosophies; rather, they should just select a few short maxims of the ancients which they can follow for the rest of their lives to correct their faults and help them improve. This is the key to building a good and meaningful life. Huang Zongxi said, 'Learning is true only when individuals make use of it themselves.' And, 'Every teaching usually has its basic objective. This is where the thinker in question applies his most effective effort. It is also the student's starting point. The moral principles of the world are inexhaustible. Unless one is able to define them in a few words, how can they be summarized and become one's own?'[70] This truly expresses the only path for students to seek the truth. Since, as Huang Zongxi said, it is up to individuals to make use of learning themselves, it is also up to individuals to decide what to learn for themselves. But then, should I be intervening with my advice? Since I want to take responsibility for my ideas to help our people, I hope my comrades and I can discuss the questions I am anxious to learn more about. OK?

(A). Rectification from the root

I have read Master Wang Yangming's 'Pulling Out the Root and Stopping Up the Source', which says, 'The teachings of the Sage became more and more distant and obscured, while the current of success and profit ran deeper and deeper. Some people were deceived by Buddhism and Daoism, but in the end there was nothing in these teachings that could overcome their desire for success and profit. The scholars modified the teachings of the Sage to suit their own discourses, which still had nothing that could destroy the view of success and profit. For up to the present time, it has been several thousand years since the poison of the doctrine of success and profit has seeped into the innermost recesses of people's minds and has become second nature to them. Their extensive memorization and recitation merely served to increase their pride; their tremendous sum of knowledge merely served to help them do evil; their abundant experiences merely served to help them indulge in argumentation; their talent in literary composition merely served to conceal their artificiality. Under false pretenses, they might say, "I want to work together with others to help complete the work of the empire." In reality, their purpose lies in their belief that unless they do so they cannot satisfy their selfishness and fulfill their desires. On top of such long-held hypocrisy and such deeply rooted motives, they still preach such doctrines! No wonder that when they hear the teachings of our Sage, they look upon them as useless and self-contradictory ...'[71] How awe-inspiring are Wang Yangming's every word and every sentence! It is as if he were speaking directly to us today.

'Utilitarianism', or the doctrine of success and profit, has even developed into an ideology promoted by the major nations today. Young scholars not only feel no shame in discussing it, but even think it can make their reputations. Wang Learning was already considered useless and self-contradictory in its own time, and today it is still despised and rejected. However, if we were to establish a certain goal today, our actions to achieve that goal would look the same regardless of whether we took action for its own sake or for selfish reasons, yet the true nature of our actions and their outcomes would be very different. Take, for example, patriotism. Patriotism is absolute and pure. If someone masquerades as patriotic under false pretenses in order to satisfy their selfish desires, truly they are even worse than the people who know nothing of patriotism or the people who never talk about it. This is the distinction Wang Yangming drew between those who strive for success and profit and those who do not. If we were to reflect on ourselves through a long, quiet night, would we be exempt from the reproaches of Master Wang? This is not something other people can judge.

When we resolve to take action, most of us are reacting to the events of the day and are influenced by the opinions of wise persons. Our first thought is of patriotism, which is absolute and pure – this is true for everyone. But gradually patriotism may be corrupted, or gradually other ideas may come to the fore, in which case patriotism dissolves and people can no longer lay a claim to it. Yet since people still crave a reputation for being a patriot to impress other people, they continue their masquerade, but as this goes on they themselves forget that it is nothing but a masquerade. In the beginning they are surely sincere, but later they are just putting on a show. This is not because they are evil by nature, but because their learning is incomplete and because they did not put in the hard work to carry out Wang Yangming's teaching to 'pull out the root and stop up the source' of corruption. Wang said, 'As the art of killing a person lies in targeting their throat, so the discipline of learning lies in the effort to cultivate the innermost recesses of one's mind.'[72] If we are content to give up and remain backward, then that is the end of it. But if not, we must resolve to cultivate our mind's innermost recesses by means of our own self-discipline, from which there is no turning back.

I recently came across a certain journal that criticized me for preaching morality. It said: 'What we need today is selfless patriotic heroes, not pedants devoted to self-restraint and avoiding errors. As they are heroes, we should overlook any small flaws they may have and only admire their passion.' And, 'You want to turn every resolute youth who possesses a daring, vigorous and martial spirit into a prim and proper rule-bound scholar who can barely keep breath in their body. We cannot imagine how such rotten and useless pedants can save the nation from imminent destruction.'

I believe my critics' self-exculpatory remarks are actually worse than those people who simply try to cover up their flaws. I agree that there may be true heroes with small flaws, but I fear that only one out of a hundred is a hero, while ninety-nine are just flawed. Are you a true hero, or one of those ninety-nine? Only you yourself can know. If you think heroes do not need to 'pull out the root and stop up the source' of corruption as Wang Yangming demanded, I believe such heroes will achieve nothing, for without sincerity there is nothing. If you think that your inherent nature is already so pure that you do not need to put in the work to 'pull out the root and stop up the source', then even though you are pure, you lack what is needed for us who are sunk in corruption and stupidity to turn to. Are you not frightened by this? Moreover, what I mean by 'traditional morality' is not limited to self-restraint and following rules. Indeed, to uphold self-restraint and rule-following as the ultimate morality – this would be similar to what Master Wang called sailing around a lake to get to the sea. Without the resolution to cultivate the innermost recesses of our minds, the pretense to self-restraint and avoiding errors is as bad as the pretense to selfless patriotism, and the pretense to rule-following is as bad as the pretense to daring and martial spirit. Why is this? It is because they have completely diverged from our inherent nature. If this is what happens to patriotism, it applies to other virtues as well.

(B). Vigilance in solitude

To 'pull out the root and stop up the source' is the first step in the study of the Way. Without the will to do so, without the courage to do so, people would be throwing their lives away, and would not be able to accomplish anything else. The corrupt influences from society over thousands of years and the old habits we have acquired from a time before we determined to follow the Way are still floating around in our consciousness, ready to erupt at any time. Even if we establish our will and summon our courage, there is no guarantee we can hold onto them unless we find a simple method to control and correct old influences and habits. This method is precisely 'vigilance in solitude'. For my generation, from our teenage years we were all more than familiar with the meaning of 'vigilance in solitude' from *The Great Learning* and *The Doctrine of the Mean*.[73] But there was hardly anyone who actually benefitted from practicing it. This was because they did not establish their will, and also because they did not completely carry out what the practice of vigilance in solitude requires. Furthermore, I heard that Master Wang Yangming said, 'Vigilance in solitude is practiced to attain innate-knowing' (in a letter to Huang Mianzhi).[74] Indeed, Wang Yangming's teaching of innate-knowing can only be reached through vigilance in solitude.

A disciple once said to Master Wang, 'In my recent efforts, although I seem to know the basics to a degree, I have found it difficult to find any sense of security.'[75]

The Master replied, 'It is nothing but the extension of knowledge.'

The disciple asked, 'How does one extend knowledge?'

The Master said, 'Your innate-knowing is your own standard. When you direct your thought, your innate-knowing knows that it is right if it is right and wrong if it is wrong. You cannot keep anything from it. Just don't try to deceive it, but sincerely and truly follow it in whatever you do. Then the good will be preserved and evil will be removed. What security there is in this!'

This really hits the nail on the head! (Indeed, the maxim of *The Great Learning* – 'making the thoughts sincere means allowing no self-deception' – already went straight to the point and said everything that needed saying.) The disciple Qian Xushan added, 'When we have realized that innate-knowing is the basis, then our task is to direct our attention to discerning right or wrong for every fleeting thought, whether we are amid millions of people or alone.'[76] In other words, innate-knowing is the true mind itself, while vigilance in solitude is the means of attaining it. Wang Yangming in the East and Immanuel Kant in the West both came up with this same notion, echoing each other as it were, even though their lives were separated by a hundred years. These sages of the East and the West shared the same mind and the same rationality, and they conveyed their concepts of the Way simply but in profound and thorough compositions from which we can continue to learn endlessly. Yet although we generally want to follow this principle, we still fail to do so. Why is this?

Wang Yangming also said, 'We can always infer the essence of the Way, which permeates the universe in every direction in constant changes and transformations, but ordinary scholars have a partial view and embellish it. Used to such practices, they become self-confident and are content with their arguments and citations. Thus they deceive both themselves and others to the point they can never climb out of the pit they have made or awaken. Unless they have a sincere determination to become sages, they will not be able to diagnose the root of their disease and unveil this underlying demonic evil.'[77] And, 'Unworthy as I am, I too was stuck in those kinds of bad practices of ordinary scholars for many years, until I happened to come to an understanding of innate-knowing. Then I regretted my actions of the past, which were nothing but harboring evil intentions and behaving falsely, all my schemes ending in nothing. After more than ten years, although I committed myself to correcting my faults and remaining vigilant, the roots of my disease were very deep and new sprouts constantly re-emerged.' The learning of Master Wang is pure and noble and has ascended to the precincts of sagehood, but in his own account of his achievement, he still spoke of 'harboring evil intentions' and 'behaving falsely'; and he still said, 'the roots of my disease were very deep and new sprouts constantly re-emerged'. Is there any limit to the underlying demonic evil of our scholars who have never inquired about the Way, never set their will on the Way and never learned the Way? Thus our absolute priority is to 'pull out the root and stop up the source'.

After Master Wang died, the essence of his profound thought was gradually lost. The Zhezhong school of Wang Learning over-emphasized the concept of 'true mind'.[78] By the late Ming, Wang Learning had greatly decayed, but then Liu Zongzhou restored the principle of 'vigilance in solitude' and thus revived Wang Learning.[79] He truly did nothing more than correct false Wang Learning with true Wang Learning by strictly adhering to this principle alone. Today, the poisons affecting the scholarly circles are different from those of the late Ming – they are ten times worse. In the late Ming, the 'streets were full of sages', and wine, sex, wealth and arrogance did not block the road to enlightenment. And today the streets are full of 'resolute idealists', and in addition to wine, sex, wealth and arrogance, they are capricious, treacherous, cunning and apathetic – and it is taken for granted that this is how heroes behave. The scholars of the late Ming were reckless as they misused the straightforward and simple teachings of Wang Learning to justify themselves. The people of today are reckless as they misuse all the popular platitudes of 'patriotic sacrifice' and 'liberty and equality' to justify their behavior. They are ashamed to be a virtuous person, but not ashamed to be a despicable person, and consequently they brazenly behave as despicable people. Yet in the whole empire no one criticizes them, and indeed they worship one another and take it for granted that this is their naturally endowed right. Don't these rabble-rousers know that they are actually sacrificing their lives for an underlying demonic evil? Alas! If we want to be an upright person in this world, who can help us? Who can advise us? Besides constant vigilance in solitude, what can we rely on? What else is there to rely on?

I have often said that Christianity was the source of moral education in the West, but how did it work? It worked through prayer. Prayer is not for wishing for one's own good fortune. All prayers – prayers upon rising in the morning, prayers at meals, prayers before bed and prayers at Sunday assembly – are recited with total concentration to calm one's heart in order to thank and praise God, as well as to reflect on the day's every action and every thought. At normal times not in prayer, people may hide their evil deeds and celebrate their good deeds, but when they are praying they know that no one can deceive an omniscient and omnipotent God. Therefore, sincere and pure thoughts will come naturally to them, which is extremely helpful in undertaking self-cultivation, self-reflection and self-control. This is a common way to practice vigilance in solitude. If individuals practiced it every day, their morality would gradually improve. If everyone practiced it, the morality of society would gradually improve. This is the essence of Western civilization. *The Book of Odes* says, 'The Lord-on-high is near you / Let there be not treachery in your hearts.' And, 'You are seen in your house / You do not escape even in the curtained alcove.'[80] Are there any differences between the teachings of the East and the West?

In a word, the thousand sages and ten thousand wise ones enlighten their disciples depending on their capacity and according to the path of awakening that is suitable for them – sudden or gradual – but the basic principle that runs through these different practices is nothing but vigilance in solitude. Do you insist that the path to heroism is different from the path to pedantry? According to the proverb, 'Even a hero can deceive', but while there may be heroes who deceive people, I have never heard of heroes who deceive themselves. As Wang Yangming said, 'It is easy to rid the mountains of thieves, but difficult to rid one's mind of its thieves.' Since those who proclaim themselves to be resolute idealists are imbued with demonic evil beyond their control, it is no wonder that the demonic evil that forever imbues the nation is beyond all control.

(C). Attention to small matters

'So long as a person does not transgress the boundary line in the great virtues, he may sometimes transgress it in the small virtues.'[81] This is of course a teaching passed down from the former sages. However, since our natural capacities are weak and our self-discipline is generally not strong enough for us to protect ourselves, our learned habits leave us morally adrift. As our transgressions of the boundary line of small virtues increase, our transgressions of the great virtues follow. This is what is meant by 'Trickles of water that are not stopped will become a great river. Thread that is woven continuously will become the reins of government.'[82] Qian Xushan said, 'If our studies are not straightforward and direct, it is only because we are haunted by misgivings. How is it not clear whether something is in accord with our innate-knowing or contravenes it? But if we cannot decide right away, we may spend every day steeped in such misgivings as: (1) Will I be harming Principle?[83] (2) Will I be in accord with social custom? (3) Will I be deceiving people without their knowledge? (4) Will I seek to reform myself later? It is such misgivings that haunt us and give rise to regrets.' And, 'People often take it for granted that the mere impulse to temporize on small matters will not harm the Way. But now we know that even a speck of dust can blind you and even one finger can block the sky – this is truly terrifying!'

Yes! Every single word and every single sentence here is nothing less than a call to awakening. When I reflect on my whole life, my failure to improve morally is all as a result of being blocked by those four misgivings. When the mind of the Way and the mind of humanity are at war, the mind of humanity is often able to hire various pettifoggers to make an unlimited number of clever excuses for them. There was a poem:

> My learning of the Way was not too late, but I did not
> establish my will.
> My irresolution gives rise to wickedness, and my flattery
> appeases my enemies.

Saying these are but small flaws, why should I attend to
  them so promptly?
Saying they are to be corrected, for the time being I put
  off reform.

This is the proof of the weakness of my character, which I dare
not conceal. Of course, there are plenty of us who share this
problem, and thus we must offer one another encouragement.
We have read in Zeng Guofan's own account how he quit
smoking, started to rise early and kept a daily diary, and while
we may have initially doubted that these tasks were so difficult,
once we have some experience of our own, we will know that
such trivial matters are not easy at all. In this regard, we can
predict that none of us will ever match Zeng Guofan's achievements. This is not to say that trivial matters alone can be the
wellspring of great achievements, but rather that they show
how Zeng Guofan's self-discipline far exceeds our own self-
discipline. Thus a trivial matter can illuminate a great one.

Liu Zongzhou said, 'Since our habits have become ingrained,
nothing we do is a minor mistake but rather an evil deed. Therefore, what students face now is the need to eliminate their evil
conduct, not their mere mistakes.' And, 'We commit evil deeds
but exonerate ourselves with the excuse they are harmless – but
little do we realize that even if the cosmos has the capacity to
accommodate all creation, it will have no room for those who do
evil.' And, 'When occasionally our mistakes are exposed, other
people think nothing of it. What they do not realize is that when
you investigate the mistake, you will see that it stemmed from
dozens of previous mistakes and has already led to dozens of
subsequent mistakes. Therefore, our constant mistakes inevitably turn into evil deeds; in other words, once you have started
down this road, there is no turning back.' Liu's remarks are
equivalent to the saying 'Every lashing leaves a trace, every slap
leaves a red mark', which is intended to enlighten us.[84] Anyone
of even a little intelligence who reads Liu Zongzhou's words
should reflect deeply on themselves. If our minor mistakes were
isolated events with no cause and no effect, then indeed such trifling mistakes might not give rise to any harm, nor be enmeshed

in a chain of causation with dozens of previous causes and dozens of subsequent effects. Even if this were the case, how could you say that a small matter is unimportant? Take the case of governing a country. A remote district suffering from famine and banditry is a very small matter, but a look into the causes of the problem will reveal the failures of government administration and the unevenness of social progress. As abuses worsen, famine and banditry will spread from one district after another, and this disaster will eventually spread across the whole nation. Or take the case of preserving one's health. A couple of days of a cold or scabies is a very small matter, but a look into the causes of the problem will reveal a deficiency of *qi* and blood and a mismanagement of hygiene. As the disease worsens, it becomes chronic over time and may eventually become fatal.

What is the true thinking behind our self-exoneration of our minor mistakes? Our repeated failure to examine our minor mistakes is certainly due to our deeply ingrained habits and our weak self-discipline. Our impulse of self-exoneration is the same as admitting, 'I cannot dwell in humaneness or follow righteousness.'[85] It also means abandoning Kant's 'liberty of conscience'. It is for all of these reasons that we have come to accept self-exoneration of small mistakes, so how can we say they are minor? Furthermore, as we continue to engage in self-exoneration, we are changing along with it and our originally pure moral nature cannot withstand its daily assaults. Mencius said, 'If our minds are filled with aversion for "transgressing boundaries of morality", then our righteousness will be boundless.'[86] Conversely, we know that when people's minds are filled with apathy, they can kill their fathers; and when their minds are filled with treachery, they can betray their countries. What we truly fear is not the symptoms that have already appeared, but the source of those symptoms. As for our self-proclaimed flawed heroes, they should reflect on this.

*

The three practices above describe how I wish to encourage myself to do better. The moral principles of the world are inexhaustible, but to follow Huang Zongxi's teaching to define them in a few words, I only raise these three practices. Given my limited learning, my understanding of those ideas of the wise that I discussed at length above is not as profound as theirs. The specific theories of Master Wang Yangming and his followers that I discussed were what I wanted to learn, but although their theories are brilliant, I am not quite able to grasp them. In ancient times scholars certainly had a thorough understanding of their teachings, and they faithfully practiced what they taught. Even without saying a word, and through their practice alone, they could exemplify how to transform the empire, while speech was superfluous for them. Yet for a person ignorant of the Way, like myself, it is preferable to speak out, for as I like to say, I will save others before saving myself – echoing, as it were, the resolve of bodhisattvas. If you ask me whether I have mastered these three practices, I will not have the confidence to reply. But I hope my readers will not say that because these three practices are impossible, they will reject them. Even if someone's thinking is different from mine, as long as they have one or two worthwhile ideas, we should not reject them. It is thus my modest hope that my words will be of some use to society.

As for a certain journal that said I was admonishing people non-stop, I cannot deny it. As Mencius said, 'To admonish our friends to do good is the principle of friendship.'[87] Following this principle, the purpose of my discourse is to befriend all the scholars of the empire. Is this not proper? Readers, too: do not hesitate to admonish me and always help and encourage me, so that I will feel ashamed of my faults and inspired to do better in the hope of one or two achievements in the future. Thus would I gain countless benefactors!

16

Defects of the Chinese People[1]

Liang wrote this essay – actually, a chapter from a small book he published under the title New World Travel Notes *– after his return to Japan from America in 1903. Whether the Chinese were 'ready' for democracy was a point of controversy between elite reformers like Liang and the growing revolutionary movement. Perhaps Liang's criticisms could only have been made by a fellow Chinese, though they echo some Westerners' derogatory comments on the Chinese character. First published as a supplement to* Xinmin congbao, *February 1904.[2]*

The defects of the Chinese people can be summarized as follows:

First, the Chinese people possess clan identity but not citizen identity. The organization of Chinese society is based on clans, not individuals, which embodies the ancient concept: 'After the family is governed, then the state can be ruled.'[3] Although the clan system of the Zhou dynasty has been abolished in form, it survives in spirit.[4] I have already discussed the self-governing capacities of the Aryan race. They were certainly the first to develop this capacity, but the local self-government of the Chinese was probably just as developed. So how is it that they were able to form nations while we were not? It is because what they developed was the self-governance of cities, while we developed the self-governance of clans.

If we visit the Chinese countryside, the scale of self-government is certainly undeniable. Even in my own home village, which only has two or three thousand people, the legislative and executive organs do not interfere with each other. Other peoples admire this. This being the case, local self-government can become the foundation of state-building. But if we visit Chinese cities, we see that they are in a state of unbelievable turmoil. This can be best explained on the grounds that clan members cannot become urban citizens, which I believe even more after visiting America. Although the Chinese people who emigrate to America leave behind their village clans and travel to the world's freest cities as individuals, nonetheless what they have inherited and what they build is just the same clan system. In addition, what they use to maintain social order partly relies on this very clan system. We can thus see that the legacy of thousands of years is deeply rooted and still dominates the Chinese people. I cannot repeat this too often.

Second, the Chinese people possess local consciousness but lack national consciousness. I heard of Roosevelt's speech advocating that Americans today must abandon their local consciousness, meaning their loyalties to their own provinces and towns. However, from the perspective of historical development, the reason that America was able to perfect republican governance was completely due to local consciousness. If it is excessive, however, it becomes a major obstacle to state-building, though it should never be dismissed. This is a fine line that cannot be determined without precise judgment, but China is surely a case of excessive local consciousness. It is not only the Chinese in San Francisco who display such excessive local consciousness, but such is the case throughout China. Even the wisest are no exception. While serving Chu, Lian Po could not help recalling his soldiers of Zhao, and while serving the Han dynasty, Zifang could not help recalling his natal Hán kingdom.[5] Yet without breaking down these boundaries of localism, it would have been very difficult to consolidate the empire.

Third, the Chinese people are only fit for autocracy and cannot enjoy freedom. Such words are truly offensive, but such is the simple reality – how can we pretend otherwise? In the whole world, I have seen no one as disorderly as the Chinese of San Francisco. What is the reason for this? Freedom. The character of the Chinese in China is not necessarily better than that of the Chinese in San Francisco, but in China they are still under the rule of local officials and the control of the heads of their families. Although the Chinese in Southeast Asia are different from those in China, the British, Dutch and French treat them very strictly. Any assembly of more than ten people is ordered to disband. All freedom is abolished. The restrictions are harsher than in China, and thus people are more obedient. The Chinese people who have the same freedoms as Westerners according to the law are those who live in America and Australia. In cities with few Chinese, they have little influence and so there is less trouble, but in the free cities with the greatest numbers of Chinese, most notably San Francisco, the situation is as described above. A fellow townsman told me that the Chinese of San Francisco were most tranquil back when Zuo Geng served as consul-general.[6] He asked the San Francisco police to arrest and punish Chinese criminals. Then no one dared to carry out vendettas, no one dared to riot and no one dared to be idle; all the secret societies died out, the nights were safe and everyone diligently carried out their professions. After he left, conditions reverted to their original state. This clearly proves that autocracy provides stability while freedom is dangerous, which points to the advantages of autocracy and the harms of freedom.

When I read the bylaws of various Chinese associations, they generally follow those of Western societies, which are civilized and comprehensive, but when I look at how their members actually behave, not one fails to violate their bylaws. The Chinese Consolidated Benevolent Association operates like a city government, but whenever it meets, fewer than one out of ten of all the chairmen and directors of its various member associations attend, and nothing gets done. These associations find trivial reasons to refuse to pay their dues, and there is nothing the Consolidated Association can do about it. Even more ridiculous are its meetings. I have witnessed dozens of association meetings abroad, and there are only two types. First, those with a few powerful elites. When they speak, no one dares to object, and everyone just yesses them. Not a meeting, but just pronouncements and orders. Meetings like this I call the oligarchy form of autocracy. Second, those with supposed elites who have no real power and are afraid to make decisions. When they finally make a new proposal, all the young hooligans who are surrounding them shout them down, so that nothing is done in the end. Meetings like this I call the mobocracy form of autocracy. Such meetings frequently end in quarrels and fights.

This is true not only of associations abroad. Are the so-called public bureaus and public offices in China any different? And are the groups formed in recent years by people who claim to be resolute reformers, such as 'mutual assistance associations' and 'study societies', any different either? This shows that a group cannot rely solely on one or two individuals – and the same applies to countries. This is exactly what Gustave Le Bon meant by saying that a people's national psychology is always obvious.[7] So, is it possible for our people to ever practice parliamentary government? Indeed, when looking into their elections, there is much that is shocking. Each association elects a chairman to be its representative. Yet the actual process sets district against district (most associations comprise several districts); and within each district, clan against clan; within each clan, village against village; and within each village, household against household. Every election sees copious bloodshed. Given the abuses that arise from struggles within a single association over who gets annual control of just a thousand dollars in a couple of districts, the consequences of bigger elections are unimaginable. I am afraid it would not merely result in a revolution every four years like those in South America. In fact, is it ever possible for such a people to practice parliamentary government?

My critics will say that these problems only occur in San Francisco and ask if I expect China will be governed by these crude Cantonese customs.[8] However, according to my objective observation, I do not believe that the character of the Chinese people in China is any better than the character of those in San Francisco; on the contrary, their level of civilization is far lower. May I ask, in all China is there a city of twenty or thirty thousand people that has six newspapers? No, there is not. May I ask, in all China are there any groups that have drafted bylaws as perfect as those of the eight associations of San Francisco? No, there are none. The conditions in San Francisco simply throw a spotlight on the situation in China. And even if the Chinese people in China were superior to those in San Francisco, it would just be the pot calling the kettle black – for they are the same in their lack of capacity for freedom.

Now, are there not one or two outstanding Chinese people who are in no way inferior to Western elites in terms of their idealism and morality? But can we rely on just one or two outstanding people out of a population of millions to establish the country? It is possible for just one or two outstanding people to strengthen the country through authoritarianism, but we cannot say that the general populace can have freedom just because there are one or two outstanding people. Now, freedom, constitutionalism and republicanism are general terms for majoritarian government. No matter how big a majority can be mobilized in China, if today we chose majoritarian government, it would amount to national suicide. Freedom, constitutionalism and republicanism in China would be like wearing summer clothes in the winter, or fur coats in the summer – it is not appropriate, no matter how good they look. Today, we should not indulge in dazzling illusions or beautiful dreams. In a word, today's Chinese people can only live under an autocracy, not in freedom. I pray, I hope – I can only pray and hope – that China can find men like Guanzi, Shang Yang, Lycurgus and Cromwell who will emerge today determined to mold and forge the Chinese people with iron and fire for twenty years, thirty years or even fifty years, and only then teach them Rousseau, and only then talk to them about Washington.[9]

(The above three points all show that the Chinese people lack political abilities because of their extreme conservativism. There is no need to speak of republicanism again.)

Fourth, the Chinese people lack noble goals. This is the fundamental defect of the Chinese. The world consists of national citizens, but why are some nations great and strong while others are small and weak? All persons occupy space, but they should have a higher purpose than just food, clothing and shelter. And all persons live in time, but they should have a higher purpose than just prosperity and glory. Only through these higher purposes can people consistently evolve and progress; otherwise, they will merely stagnate and degenerate. Since the individual unit must have a higher purpose, when individuals assemble to form a nation, this totality must have a higher purpose as well. The noble goals of the Westerners are not all the same, but in my view the most important of them are, first, love of beauty. (When the Greeks spoke of virtue, they essentially meant the true, the good and the beautiful, but the Chinese emphasize goodness while neglecting beauty. Confucius proclaimed Shao music to be both perfectly good and perfectly beautiful, while according to Mencius that which commands our liking is goodness and that which fulfills goodness is beauty.[10] Confucius and Mencius spoke of goodness and beauty together, but few others have done so. Relatively speaking, we can say the Chinese are a people who do not appreciate beauty.) The second important goal of Westerners is to earn the respect of society. The third important goal lies in their religiously inspired concept of the future. The development of the West's spiritual civilization is based on these three goals, while China lacks all three. The reason why the Chinese people are stagnant and degenerate is truly because they focus only on their own needs and only on the present. It is not just the Chinese living abroad who are like this, but the whole country is this way. After traveling abroad, I was inspired to reflect on this. Thus I raise the issue here, though there is more to say than I can finish today.

In many other respects as well, the character of Chinese people is inferior to the character of Westerners. I wrote down some examples when they crossed my mind, but some I have forgotten. Listed below are some of these examples, though not in any particular order:

· Westerners only work eight hours a day and rest on Sundays. Chinese open their shops every day at 7 o'clock and work for the next eleven or twelve hours, sitting upright in their shops the whole day and never resting on Sundays, but they are still no richer than Westerners and their job opportunities are fewer. Why is this? When it comes to work, the worst problem is exhaustion, but when people work all day, all year round, they get fed up with work, and so they become tired of work and their performance declines. Proper rest is truly a requirement of life. That Chinese people cannot have noble goals can also be blamed on lack of rest.

- American schools are only open an average of 140 days a year, and only hold classes for an average of five or six hours a day, yet Western students are better than Chinese for this very reason.

- For a very small shop, Chinese may employ up to ten or more people, while an average Western shop only employs one or two people, each of whom accomplishes about three times the work of a Chinese employee. It is not that Chinese are lazy, but that they are sluggish.

- Sunday rest is excellent. After every six days, people revitalize themselves and their energies are thus truly restored. The sluggishness of the Chinese runs deep, and even if we do not adopt the Western week, we must institute a day of rest on every tenth day.

- Any time more than a hundred Chinese people are assembled in a meeting hall – even if they are very solemn and quiet – they will produce four sounds: most will be coughing, some will be yawning, some will be sneezing and some will be blowing their noses. During talks, I have listened quietly to the audience and heard these four sounds in unceasing quick-fire succession. I also have listened quietly to audiences at Western meeting halls and theaters and not heard a sound from even thousands of people.

- In the Orient, the trains and streetcars all provide spittoons which are constantly filled with filthy gobs of spit, while American trains rarely have spittoons and even when they do, they are rarely used. In the Orient, on train trips of two or three hours or more, over half the passengers are dozing, while in America no one falls asleep even on trips that take a whole day. The racial differences in strength and vitality between Orientals and Westerners are evident.

- The Westerners in San Francisco often propose to move Chinatown somewhere else. This is because it occupies the city's most expensive real estate which they covet for themselves, though they offer the excuse that the Chinese are dirty. A Chinese diplomat once told me that I should urge the Chinese to move of their own accord. Because Chinatown's businesses attract only Chinese customers, they cannot compete for Westerner customers – while if they moved, they would still attract their Chinese customers.

· If we moved Chinatown to a new location and spruced it up to give it a better atmosphere, then wouldn't our American neighbors cease regarding it as an eyesore? But if we fail to move voluntarily, the Westerners will still force us to move eventually and then the Chinese community would collapse. This is another thing that people say. However, one may ask whether this is achievable, or if it is just empty talk.

· Both sides of the streets in San Francisco have sidewalks (with the middle reserved for vehicular traffic); it is not permitted to spit or to litter. Violators are fined five dollars. New York's streetcars do not allow spitting and violators are fined five hundred dollars. This is how much they value cleanliness, stringently restricting freedom to such a degree. Yet the Chinese are a people so dirty and disorderly that it is no wonder the Americans despise them.

· When Westerners walk, they always walk upright with their heads raised, whereas the Chinese are bent over and looking down. We Chinese can't help feeling ashamed of our inferiority.

· When Westerners walk, they walk swiftly, a sight that reveals a city full of people busy at their work. When the Chinese walk, they walk mincingly, with mannered grace, their jade pendants clinking, which shows how contemptible they are. One can instantly spot a Chinese person walking toward one on the street a mile off, just from their small builds and sallow faces.

· When Westerners walk together, they are like a skein of flying geese, whereas the Chinese are like a flock of straying ducks.

· When Westerners speak, if they are talking to one person, they make themselves heard by that person alone; if they are talking to two people, they make themselves heard by those two people only; if they are talking to ten people, they make themselves heard by those ten people only; and if they are talking to a hundred, a thousand or several thousand people, they make themselves heard by a hundred or a thousand or several thousand people. Their voices are properly regulated. But when Chinese people get together to chat in a room, the noise is like a thunderstorm; when several thousand people are in a meeting hall, they buzz like swarms of mosquitoes. When Westerners are discussing matters, they do not interrupt one another. But when Chinese assemble in a hall, the hall is filled with their clamor and certain famous scholars from the capital try to dominate the meeting – all this shows a complete breakdown of order.

Confucius said, if you do not learn the *Odes*, you will not be fit to converse with, and if you do not learn ritual behavior, your character cannot be established. My friend Xu Qin has also said that the Chinese people have never learned how to walk or how to speak.[11] He was not exaggerating. And although these are small matters, they illuminate larger problems.

PART FOUR
SYNCRETISM AND
PROGRESS: TEACHER,
1912–1929

Liang Qichao could claim some of the credit for the defeat of Yuan Shikai's attempt to restore the monarchy in 1916, but the last years of his life were more concerned with scholarship than politics. His thought became more explicitly syncretic than it had been just a few years before, as seen in his 1920 essay on 'The Self-Awakening of the Chinese People' below. That essay, though it essentially stands alone, was originally written as a section of Liang's much longer record of his 'impressions' from a trip to Europe in 1919 – a shattered and distressed Europe. Liang had to ask what had gone wrong in the lands he had long admired from afar. In his answers, he rejected both calls for 'total Westernization' and calls for a return to traditional ways.

To the May Fourth generation that had taken to the streets in 1919, Liang seemed conservative and, perhaps worse, not even interesting. It is as if time moved especially fast in China in the early twentieth century, and what was radical in 1902 was passé by 1912 and downright reactionary by 1922. Liang dismissed calls for 'science and democracy' in the 1910s and for 'class struggle' after about 1920 as crassly reductionist, but there was no denying their popularity. That said, many people continued to listen to Liang when he spoke out; now, however, his voice was but one among many. Amid his scholarship and teaching, he did continue to contribute to the political discussions of the day. He condemned the Versailles Treaty in 1919, and in the tumultuous year of 1925 – a hightide of anti-imperialist actions – he spoke out against the imperialist powers and in effect warned them to back off. Liang had long seen class conflict as central to European modernity, but only a minor current in China. He thought a different kind of conflict afflicted China, as his essay below on 'The Proletariat Class and the Idler Class' suggests. Liang also argued that, since most capitalists in China were actually foreigners, class struggle and the national struggle were coming together.

17

The Self-Awakening of the Chinese People[1]

Liang's trip to Europe in 1919 was his first extended trip abroad in almost a decade. He was excited to be traveling to what in some respects had been, we might almost say, his spiritual motherland, the lands of Rousseau and Montesquieu, of Herbert Spencer and John Stuart Mill. He tried to study French and English on the trip out and claimed to have acquired a certain reading ability in English, though he depended on his younger colleagues fluent in English, French and German – leaders of the new generation of Chinese intellectuals – to translate for him. Liang was happy to meet with foreign scholars and politicians, and to see the parliaments and universities he had written about years earlier. He was fascinated by the new intellectual currents ranging from Spenglerian exhaustion to neo-Kropotkinist enthusiasm. He was also, understandably, distressed by the war's destruction. Whether the trip changed Liang's mind in any fundamental way is debatable. In the last few weeks of his European sojourn, he holed up in a house outside Paris to write up his extensive notes. He knew he would have little time to do so once he returned to China. Liang had left China in December 1918 and returned to a quite different China in March 1920, a China still in the grip of student protests and commercial boycotts in opposition to the Versailles Treaty. Liang was distressed and angered by the treaty, but not so sympathetic to the students. Written in the newly popular vernacular style, 'The Self-Awakening of the Chinese People' was a kind of sidebar to Liang's Impressions from My European Travels. *First published in* Shishi xinbao *(Shanghai) and* Chenbao *(Beijing), March–August 1920.*

1. A Universal State

We need to understand that it is still too early to build a global utopia. States at this time absolutely cannot be eliminated. At the same time, each state must replenish the national strength that was weakened in the war with resources from other countries. Looking around the world, China is the only easy target left. Naturally, countries from near and far are all greedily eyeing us. If we think we can rely on the protection of the League of Nations without standing up for ourselves, we are living in a fool's paradise. Even so, we cannot dismiss the idea of the League as completely worthless and must still endeavor with all our might to help it develop. Generally speaking, the League is initiating a synthesis of universalism and statism, which will bring the concept of the mutuality of states into the popular consciousness. People will thus understand that the will of the state is not absolute but is fettered by many outside restraints. To put it plainly, this adds a new factor in the relationship between states. Under these conditions, we want to construct a kind of 'universal state'. What is a 'universal state'? We must be patriotic, but we cannot consider mulish and narrow-minded old ways of thinking to be patriotism, because states in today's world cannot develop in that way. On the one hand, our patriotism cannot recognize only the state and not the individual, while on the other hand it cannot recognize only the state and not the world. Under the protection of their state, every individual must develop their natural abilities to the utmost and make great contributions to human civilization. This is the future of every country, and this is exactly why we are promoting universalism.

2. China Will Not Perish

We absolutely cannot be pessimistic and think that China is doomed. In terms of fiscal and economic difficulties, other countries are actually a hundred times worse off than China. If we are frustrated by some slight difficulties, then the Europeans should be throwing themselves into the Atlantic. If you want to give up simply because of warlord domination and government corruption, please go and study European history from the first half of the nineteenth century and see what it was like then. Aren't Britain and France generally acknowledged to be models of democracy today? But didn't they previously suffer from the same oligarchical domination and corruption as us? How did Britain and France reach the point where they are today? We should not focus on the distant past, but on how the capitalist class today has achieved domination. Simply speaking, they were incorrigibly wise and resourceful, not remotely comparable to China's warlords, who are merely paper tigers, or its bureaucrats, who are merely the products of favoritism. If the Chinese want to give up, the majority of Europeans can only wait to die. If today's widespread depravity and villainy leaves you feeling hopeless, then you are missing half the story.

Evils always come to light in chaotic transitional periods. This happens in every country, not just China. I certainly cannot agree that people are more depraved today than in the past. When has the past ever lacked for evils? Sometimes something was not considered evil as a result of a different perspective, and sometimes something was not considered evil because public opinion paid it no heed. For example, the political circles of the Republic of China are definitely corrupt, but can it be said that the political circles of the Qing dynasty were any purer? Nobody took any notice of these evils in the past, but simply accepted their oppression as a matter of course. Although we have not yet escaped from oppression, we have thoroughly exposed its evils. It thus seems more terrifying – as if it were worse than ever. This also applies to the other evils of the family and of society. In fact, the evils of the past and the present are the same evils – it is only that one is exposed and understood and the other is not. Since today's evil is the same as in the past, we cannot consider ourselves to be more depraved. On the contrary, exposure and understanding are themselves a kind of progress. Why is this? Because it is an expression of the people's self-awakening.

As the ancients said, the antidote lies in knowing the disease. In the past we were very diseased but knew nothing of it. Now we know it, and just from 'knowing it' a cure will naturally emerge. Today, Europeans are constantly wailing that the apocalypse is nigh and civilization is bankrupt. Whether their point is exaggerated or not, this very awareness of crisis is a guarantee of their revival. What people should fear most is contentment with the status quo, for that way they are bound to retreat, not progress, and they might as well be dead. But if we are dissatisfied with the status quo, naturally we will work hard, and this hard work is itself the way forward. Now that we know how evil we are, and that we live in an evil society, China can find a way forward. This is a good thing, not a bad thing. Whenever you learn that you are sick, get treatment immediately. Do not let the disease discourage you and undermine your survival instinct. The disease doesn't matter! There are no problems in the world that are impossible to solve, but if we do not try, then they become truly impossible. If we abolish the word 'impossible' from our vocabulary, then many solutions will emerge.

3. Factional Politics and Democratic Politics

Formerly there were two groups of patriots, both of which were on the wrong path.[2] The first group wanted to rely on the existing power structures to gradually reform China in a relatively orderly way. Who could know this idea would go completely wrong? It turned out this group was simply being manipulated, and it yielded no reforms. The second group wanted to completely abolish the existing power structures. What were they going to abolish them with? They ended up using the same kind of power structures as the existing ones, saying in effect, 'You are incompetent, it's my turn.' Who could know that this idea too would go completely wrong? They claimed to be eliminating warlords but turned out to be warlords themselves. They claimed to be eliminating bureaucrats but turned out to be bureaucrats themselves. They not only failed to remove a single one of these thieves, but actually helped to strengthen their powers. And, at the same time, they helped the rise of many more thieves. Can't you see that the recent rise to power of the warlords and bureaucrats is directly or indirectly thanks to the struggles of these two groups?

Given that both groups were patriotic at heart, how did they bring disaster on the country? As it happens, both groups shared an erroneous view – they were trapped in the thinking of the old society. This was expressed in Du Fu's poem: 'Two or three heroes emerged because of the times; they set Heaven and Earth aright, saving the nation.'[3] Neither group realized that a democratic country would have to wholly rely on the majority of its people and not on a few heroes. In the past, the constitutionalists pursued their constitution, which had nothing to do with the general populace, while the revolutionaries pursued their revolution, which also had nothing to do with the general populace – in a similar way, when you open a bottle of beer, the bubbles stream excitedly to the top, but exposed to the atmosphere for a while the bubbles dissipate and the beer returns to its still state. This is fundamentally contrary to the principles of a democratic movement. It is the reason for all the defeats of the last twenty years. If everyone admitted this mistake today, they could sincerely repent. The best path forward is for the constitutionalists to discard their despicable manipulation of warlords and bureaucrats and for the revolutionaries to discard their despicable mobilization of soldiers and bandits, and for each group to try to win over a majority of citizens to their beliefs. That is to say, the only true patriotism – the only national salvation – lies in trying to win over the whole people, not just a sector of the population of use to us. Only when the factional politics of the past is overturned will a truly democratic politics emerge.

4. Haste Makes Waste

We need to understand that nothing can be accomplished in haste. Only when you give up the quick-fix mindset will you achieve your goals. Some people say: given the dire situation, how can we not try quick fixes to keep China afloat? Once China perishes, then what can be done? I say: no matter what, China will certainly not perish, because even if other people want to destroy such a big country, it is not that easy. And even if China did perish, it's not such a big deal. Didn't Poland perish for several centuries? Yet here it is today. We must understand that it is the 'quick-fix mindset' that will truly destroy the country. If we do not want to perish, the only way is to fight long and hard to the death. This way simply cannot be pursued in haste.

Historically, the foundations of Chinese democracy have been very shallow; geographically, democracy has had even less opportunity to flourish. Thus Chinese democracy has developed more slowly than in the West. If we abruptly raise the banner of democracy today, we would inevitably make all kinds of fools of ourselves. But none of this is important because we are living creatures capable of learning. We only need to put in the time and effort and we will naturally transform ourselves to adapt to the situation. For this, we need to rely on the youth who have just emerged on the scene; we cannot look to the older generation. We are definitely not disparaging the older generation, because they were only able to do what was feasible in their own time. Old as they are, physically and psychologically their metabolic functions are all slowing down, so how can we expect them to be the same as us? Their positions in society will soon be passed on to today's youth, and their responsibilities will naturally become lighter. In turn, the responsibilities that today's youth are taking on are heavy beyond measure, but as long as they accept and fulfill these responsibilities, then there is nothing they cannot do. I have confidence that the majority of our dear youth do indeed hold this view and this aspiration. However, they have not yet finished tempering themselves, and the time for the older generation to pass on their responsibilities has not yet arrived. This is why we absolutely cannot move too hastily at this moment. Nothing can be accomplished in haste – if we insisted on acting hastily and something got accomplished, it would be insignificant; while if we failed, it would be catastrophic. If we understand this point, we will realize that we have to plan for the next two or three decades of the citizens' movement that we are now engaged in, even though our generation may not immediately see the results. Yet two or three decades only occupy a page or two in history textbooks, which is nothing. So don't hold back. Let's just roll up our sleeves and get started.

5. The Doctrine of Developing
One's Individual Nature

The principle of cultivating citizens lies in developing the individual's nature. There is a phrase in *The Doctrine of the Mean* that puts it best: 'Only those of perfect sincerity are able to develop their individual natures to the utmost.'[4] Here I borrow this idea as the basis for 'the doctrine of developing one's individual nature'. This doctrine means to develop the individual's innate abilities to the utmost. This is true for individuals lest they become social dregs; when everyone can be independent, they do not have to rely on others or live at their discretion. This is also true for society and the state, in that if everyone does what they excel at, they will naturally bring about progress and create a strong country and advanced society through mutual cooperation. The reason why Germany was defeated is because its statism was over-developed and warped to the point that the people's individuality was absorbed by the state. Thus when Germany encountered Britain, France and America, where individuality was most developed, it was simply unable to withstand them. Because Germany lost the advantage of 'people fighting on their own initiative', its soldiers were not allowed to lose. German statism cast everyone in the same mold, to be of use to the country based on the goals of the state. In the end, however, this proved to be very problematic.

As for China, it lacks so-called goals of state. But the individual's natural abilities are fettered and crippled from a young age by deformed social institutions and the authority of outmoded theories. Today, it is said that the Chinese people are ignorant or that they lack talent. This is true! However, we also need to understand that talent and intelligence cannot sprout in this old society that shackles the people. This is because the old society also casts people in the same mold. Anyone who deviates from that mold has no way to survive in Chinese society. No matter who you are, you must be willing to put on an act to fit in, and your innate abilities cannot be freely developed to their utmost. This is the reason that the talent and intelligence of the Chinese people lag behind that of Westerners. The most urgent task today is for everyone to hold to this doctrine of developing one's own individual nature. As Lu Xiangshan said, 'You must try to be a righteous person.'[5] We should make every effort to develop fully our inborn talent (to whatever degree, everyone has some talent) – do not be shy about it, and especially do not behave falsely. This, then, is the first principle of individual autonomy, and also the first principle of national survival.

6. The Liberation of Thought

To develop individuality, we must begin by liberating thought. What does the liberation of thought mean? It means that whenever someone tells me something, I will thoroughly investigate it and think it through in order to get to the truth. When we are thinking, we cannot fetter ourselves by any preconceived notions whatsoever, but must remain unclouded like a clear mirror reflecting an object. By thinking without preconceptions, we will follow what we think is correct, while we will resist what we think is wrong. 'After the Sage compiled the *Odes*, who dares to dissent?' is an extremely vapid remark made by Han Yu.[6] The Sage's approach to learning was not like that. Confucius taught people to select the good and follow it, but how can one know what is good without the process of selecting? The act of 'selection' is in itself the key to the liberation of thought. Contemporary European culture, whether in its material aspects or its spiritual aspects, was wholly produced through the 'freedom to criticize'. From their own perspectives, people may issue harsh criticisms of any theory that dominates their society – regardless of who invented it or whether it is new or old. Their criticisms may not necessarily be justified, but they must undergo a process of careful 'selection', which in turn opens the path to the liberation of their own thought. Their criticisms also stimulate other people to initiate a process of their own careful 'selection', which in turn opens the path to liberation of thought for the whole society. In turn, people inspire and correct each other so that the truth naturally becomes ever clearer and the world continuously improves. If the thought of one person is taken as an infallible law and sets limits on how people can think – regardless of whether this person is a modern or ancient figure, or a commoner or a sage, or whether their thought is good or bad – it will obliterate people's creativity and halt society's progress. If they didn't think it through themselves, how could they have created such an 'infallible law'? If we respect them and want to learn from them, the first task is to learn their methods of thinking. They had to break free from the fetters of both old thought and contemporary thought to conduct free and independent study for their own theory. Otherwise, the theory would not count as theirs. This being the case, why don't we follow their example instead of doing the opposite? This precisely accounts for the decline of learning and the lack of progress in China over the last thousand-plus years.

Some people say that they are afraid that the liberation of thought means everyone will abandon the Classics and rebel against the Way. But I say this is an absurd and unnecessary worry. First of all, if they are not the Classics and not the Way, then wouldn't abandoning and rebelling against them be the right thing to do? Yet if they really are the Classics and the Way, then the common saying nails it: 'True gold does not fear the flames.' When one person exercises their 'freedom to criticize' to attack a theory, naturally some other people will exercise their 'freedom to criticize' to defend it, and this cycle of 'cleaning and polishing' increasingly brings out its true value. If people are not allowed to criticize a certain theory, then it appears that the theory cannot withstand criticism.

Thus I urge China's erudite senior scholars not to feel anxious about this. No matter how our youth free up their thinking to cast doubt on any theories whatsoever – whether ancient or modern, Chinese or foreign – it doesn't matter, even if they go so far as to 'criticize Yao and Shun and slight Tang and Wu'.[7] If their words are of no value, then they can do no real harm and aren't worth our attention. But if you really think they amount to a threat to moral standards and popular sentiment, then you should denounce them. As long as both sides construct their arguments based on common principles of reasoning and engage each other's arguments with precisely targeted counter-arguments, then it will naturally become clear who is right and who is wrong. If you think that prohibiting criticism can pre-serve moral standards, then you are simply adopting the old trick of Qin Shihuang, who killed off anyone who dared to express themselves.[8] Can this succeed?

Let me be blunt. With the liberation of thought, moral stand-ards will certainly become unsettled, at which time society will experience many evils. This is inevitable, but it is not necessarily a real threat to our moral standards and popular sentiment. Moral standards are constructed according to the social condi-tions. (This is best illustrated by Confucius's notion of being in accord with the times.) As society changes, the old standards are naturally no longer suitable and naturally lose their disciplinary force, becoming just a lifeless ornament. The old standards have proven incompatible with the rise of new social institutions, but the new standards that we need have not yet been settled. How can we avoid the spread of moral uncertainty? Precisely because of this moral uncertainty, we advocate the liberation of thought; we will fight our way through thick and thin to new moral stand-ards that will give everyone the peace of mind to get on with their lives.

We don't need to debate the definition of 'morality' with those people who fear that the liberation of thought means moral col-lapse. Even if they can completely ban the liberation of thought, will people actually follow their so-called morality? Their old morality has long been a dead letter, while discussion of the new morality is prohibited. This is the true moral collapse. There are two reasons why social evils have emerged today. The first reason has nothing to do with the liberation of thought; rather, the old morality has already lost its authority and is unable to regulate society any longer, and thus evil people are running amok. Look at all the evils brought about by warlords, polit-icians, bandits and gangsters – how do they have anything to do with the new thought? The second reason involves the new thought, for the advocates of new thought naturally indulge in pushing boundaries. Sometimes they go too far, giving bad people the excuse to take new thought arguments out of context as protective amulets that let them openly do evil. However, this does not mean that liberation of thought is at fault, for these people were already essentially evil, though they had hidden it. Now that they have exposed their true natures and ended up denounced by everyone, doesn't this benefit society after all? The liberation of thought thus yields no harms but only benefits. I earnestly advise these great gentlemen who worry about moral standards and popular sentiment – there is no need to resist the coming liberation of thought.

7. Total Liberation of Thought

To promote the liberation of thought naturally depends on our dear youth, but I have some sincere advice: 'Liberation must be total liberation; otherwise, it's not liberation.' As for learning, we must always follow the principle that 'no preconceived notion can ever fetter us'. Therefore, we must not only reject the fetters of the old thought of China, but also the fetters of the new thought of the West. Whenever we come across a theory, we must study it with an open mind and boldly criticize it. Granted, this is easier to say than to do. Because the foundations of our learning are inherently shallow, whenever we come across a theory of any value, we become mesmerized and unwittingly fettered by it. We need to understand that it is certainly wrong to take the words of Confucius, Mencius, the Cheng brothers and Zhu Xi as infallible and treat them as sacred and inviolable.[9] So how can it be right to take the words of Marx and Ibsen as infallible and treat them as sacred and inviolable? We also need to understand that much of what we are calling 'new learning' has already become outdated in Europe and smashed to smithereens. And even if it were truly new, we cannot presume that 'new' is 'true'.

We also need to understand that intellectual circles in the West are still going through a chaotic transition. They are madly running around in the dark looking for the morning light, and many insightful intellectuals are proposing to import Chinese and Indian civilization for the sake of blending of East and West. But I am afraid that this is a great task that depends on us. Our youth will need to shoulder this great responsibility on behalf of all humanity, and their preparation must begin with the study of Western thought. First, since Western research methods are quite precise, we should adopt them; and second, since Western thought has long been liberated, producing a rich intellectual culture, we should study it in its various aspects. However, study is only study – we cannot follow it blindly. Regardless of whether any given theory is ancient or modern, Chinese or foreign, we need to act like an experienced old trial judge, treating these theories like confessions and testimony to help us reach a judgment. We cannot turn over the right of judgment to others. This is the first principle of the total liberation of thought.

As for our moral nature, to undo the fetters constraining us at this level requires even more strenuous effort. If our moral nature is not resolute, we cannot become upright individuals. Then how can we talk of liberation of thought? Yet our moral natures are also all fettered, and unless they are totally liberated, we will not be able to establish them properly. Both our ancestral legacy and social conditions exert enormous pressure, weighing us down to the point we are bound hand and foot. In addition, there is an even more ferocious enemy: our five senses and four limbs. This enemy never leaves us for a moment, constantly troubling and tempting us, wanting always to turn us into its slaves. We want to fully realize our individuality, but we are surrounded by this enemy on all sides. Therefore, we must struggle in our homes, and we must struggle when we go out to deal with personal matters, social functions and society. What we struggle against is no one but ourselves. And if we relax for a moment, we will suffer a crushing defeat; we will become captives and forever lose our freedom. Youth have the hardest time dealing with all kinds of critical moments, because their natural disposition is distorted by the impulsiveness that culminates at this stage of life. Indeed, sometimes the higher they climb, the harder they fall. If this happens to someone who is incapable of thought, it doesn't matter. But if this happens to someone who is capable of thought, then the vitality of the nation suffers irreparable harm. If we want to cure this disease, we must begin with the liberation of thought and engage in frequent introspection to realize our 'true self'.[10] Everything that fetters this 'true self' must be eliminated, layer by layer. This is the second principle of the total liberation of thought.

8. Organizational Abilities and the Spirit of Rule by Law[11]

The greatest flaws of the Chinese people are their lack of organizational ability and their lack of the spirit of rule by law. When we compare individual Chinese people with individual Westerners side by side – whether they are students, soldiers, merchants or artisans – our accomplishments are in no way inferior to the Westerners. Yet when Westerners bring ten people together, their strength increases tenfold and they can scale up their enterprises tenfold. When they bring together hundreds or thousands of people, their strength increases a hundredfold or a thousandfold, and they can scale up their enterprises a hundredfold or a thousandfold. The Chinese are different. When another person is added to a group, not only is it not strengthened, but it is actually weakened because its members struggle with one another, canceling out their abilities. The more people are brought together, the more their strength diminishes toward zero. Therefore, if someone opens a shop, they make money, but nine out of ten joint-stock companies run in the red. Soldiers are brave individually, but when they are brought together to form an army, they all become scoundrels. Our constitutional republic has been turned into a total farce. In a word, any undertaking that involves organization always becomes a complete mess in Chinese hands. And when an unorganized society comes up against an organized society, it will be shut down and will end up being eliminated. But where does the West's aptitude for organization come from? And why is it that we ourselves don't have it?

It occurs to me that in their competition the only difference between the West and China is that one has the 'spirit of rule by law' and the other lacks it. How is it that one bunch of people is able to unify? It is because they rely on a kind of 'rules for collective life'. The people all divide their labor and cooperate within the framework of these rules. But if no rules are established, or rules are established but not enforced, or people simply want to exploit the rules, each aiming for their own individual benefit, then however the group is established, it cannot pursue a collective life. In Western societies, at scales ranging from national politics to small group activities, people all accept a number of common rules that they should abide by, recognizing them as sacred and inviolable. These rules – whether called laws, bylaws, statutes or covenants; whether written or unwritten – are, in brief, not entered into lightly, but once they are affirmed, they can neither be violated nor exploited. With these rules, a group of people is now like a smoothly running machine with every gear slotting neatly together. The Chinese, however, have never fostered such rules for collective life.

Lately, as the term 'rule by law' has emerged around the world, the Chinese also want to join the parade. But as for the *spirit* of rule by law, we have not grasped it at all. We see our national assembly and provincial assemblies carrying on discussing laws and statutes day after day, but in fact the government does not take any of this seriously, and so neither do the people, nor even do the assemblymen themselves. There are companies and there are associations, and they all have dozens of elegant bylaws, but in reality these are nothing but a few lines of black ink on white paper. Every day lots of people are loudly proclaiming that we must unite and group together, but how can these people possibly unite when they ignore the spirit of rule by law? How can they group together? In fact, these people have made themselves the slaves of their ignorance. So, what more is there to say?

At first, I was thinking that it cannot be that Chinese people are innately flawed, but that if this did turn out to be the case, then eventually the laws of natural selection would lead to our extinction. This would be truly horrifying. Later, with careful consideration, I concluded this was not so. Rather, our past history has suppressed our innate abilities, which were left undeveloped for a long time. Because the Chinese previously lived simple lives, not a collective life, naturally they did not require any common rules. In the past, the state and the family were both built on a reciprocal relationship, giving orders and obeying orders. Those who gave orders held supreme power and did not allow common rules to fetter them. Those who obeyed orders were only waiting to do as they were told, and they also had no use for common rules. Therefore, in the old society, the term 'rule by law' was truly meaningless. Civilization tends toward collective life, which tells us that we cannot survive without organization. And if we do not once again arouse our innate ability for organization, then what can we depend on? What is this innate ability? It is simply the spirit of rule by law.

9. Two Key Constitutional Issues

Now we again turn to political questions. Given the devastation caused by the northern and southern warlords, it follows that there is simply no politics to speak of today. However, the warlords will collapse in the end. After this collapse, will politics improve? It will depend on the basic organization of the state. The most important organ of the state, of course, has to be the national assembly, but for the last several years its value has been completely trashed by the assemblymen, and the trust of the Chinese people in it has declined drastically. Unless their trust is restored, we will have no recourse at all. How can we restore it? May I ask, doesn't the national assembly have value because it represents the people? But now whom do the assemblymen represent? Actually, what we have now is nothing but a bunch of unemployed vagrants who live off politics. Just because they can flaunt the title 'assemblyman', they brazenly pretend to be the masters of the country. How can we expect the people to have any trust in them? Even if there were a new election, the same bunch of people would win, just putting old wine in new bottles with the exact same results. This is to say that if the organ of the people's will cannot be properly established and if our politics cannot be reformed, then in the end the country will be forfeit.

If we want to revive the national assembly – fundamentally calling for a national assembly that truly represents the people – then I think nothing would be better than establishing an election law that recognizes the professions. A bicameral legislature can have one body that still represents geographical constituencies, while a second body represents functional constituencies.[12] That is, the government grants the status of juridical person to various professional groups to manage elections. The qualifications of voters and candidates are determined by their professions. High-class vagrants like us who would lose our civic rights had better find professions quickly if we want to recover them. If we employed such a law, even if we failed to get rid of all the politicians who live off politics, at least we would get rid of 80 or 90 percent of them, which would let us wipe the political slate clean. If we employed such a law, then workers in the fields of agriculture, industry and commerce – just for the sake of their own interests – would naturally raise concrete political concerns. If we employed such a law, the 'bedrock of the nation' – scholars, farmers, artisans and merchants – would develop such a close relationship with the state that its democratic foundations would become unshakable. If we employed such a law, industry would take off, and then the capitalist and working classes would each have some representation in the highest organ of state, able to exchange their opinions and reconcile their interests at any time. The tragedy of social revolution may thus be avoidable.

I think every country in the world will adopt this kind of electoral system in the future, but since the power of their capitalists is quite great and they will put up every obstacle, it can't be put into practice without an ugly fight. China, however, is starting from scratch, and we have no class conflicts. Why don't we work together to carry out this kind of electoral system? China could not only lay a foundation for the state, but also gain recognition as an advanced country.

And another point. We should adopt the Swiss system of citizen voting.[13] Some have said this system only works in small countries. Nonsense! Isn't Germany now practicing it widely? And a few years before America revised its constitution, weren't some people urgently advocating this system? The people are the masters of the country, and national assemblymen are their representatives. This does not mean that we give away all rights to the representatives whom we send to parliament. Sometimes representatives cannot take on their master's business, and so the masters must personally take action themselves. For instance, the true popular will that underlies the North–South Peace Conference is visible to all.[14] What would be right is simply to resolve the disputes with citizen voting. Instead, we have the northern and southern warlords appointing their own representatives to surreptitiously divide up the political spoils. As people reach the end of their rope and begin to speak out, those grand old assemblymen glower at them and pronounce, 'This is the concern of we representatives of the people – who dares to interfere?' Isn't this outrageous! Thus, I say two key constitutional issues facing the Republic of China are functional constituencies and citizen voting, which must be instituted before our political foundations can be laid.

10. Self-Government

One more commonplace remark: that is, concerning local self-government.[15] Through personal investigation on this trip, I realized that the European countries have scaled up 'City Hall', as what was originally the right of the citizens to participate in local affairs gradually grew to encompass the democratic politics of the nation. The Europeans have a great creed: 'I live here, and so I concern myself with local affairs. Why? Because I have vital interests here.' This is the Europeans' view of the local, and it is also their view of the nation. Thus did their sense of political consciousness and responsibility naturally emerge. No one needed to teach them patriotism. As for China, we have called ourselves a republic for over eight years, but there is not a single municipal council in the national capital or any of our provincial capitals, nor is there a single district council in any of our twenty-two provinces. Only in our very highest administrative offices did politicians make a big deal about copying the idea of a national assembly and provincial assemblies, purely following the old bureaucratic thinking of the Qing dynasty in becoming assembly-men. How does this show even the slightest understanding of self-government? 'Officially sponsored self-government' is a joke, just like saying you have a Song edition of the *Kangxi Diction-ary*.[16] Those wise military governors and provincial heads simply assigned some of their redundant personnel the job of planning for self-government and counted the task as done. Some people say that all self-government amounts to is to have a fellow pro-vincial to serve as their military governor and for all provincial posts to be monopolized by fellow provincials and closed to out-siders. Other people do not bother about that, but only want to pacify these intractable political grandees by giving them their own fiefdoms to keep them quiet, which they call some 'feder-ation of self-government provinces'!

Alas! We call ourselves a republic, but no one even recog-nizes the term 'self-government'. So what can we possibly say about it? I can only say that if the Chinese people were able to establish a municipal council in Beijing and a town council in Fengtai, then we could finally build the Republic of China. Otherwise, extravagant political talk is all futile. To take polit-ical action, we must start with local self-government.

11. A Discussion of Socialism

In speaking of the people's livelihoods, socialism is of course the most valuable theory around today. Those advocating new thought in China have gradually begun to study it, which is a healthy phenomenon. However, in my opinion, in advocating socialism, its spirit and its practice should be discussed separ-ately. Its spirit is certainly worth adopting, and this spirit is not foreign but is indigenous to China. Confucius said, 'With equality, there is no poverty; with harmony, there is no loss of population.'[17] And Mencius said, 'If the people have reliable livelihoods, they will maintain their constant heart.'[18] It is no exaggeration to say that these remarks represent the core spirit of socialism.

As for the practice of socialism, it varies by country and era.

Under the general banner of socialism, Western scholars have developed a host of different schools. As for which we should adopt and to what degree, it must fit the immediate social conditions of our country. Why is there socialism in Europe? It was nurtured by the industrial revolution. Since industrial organization developed unjustly, the more it developed, the more harm it created. Socialists came up with various solutions to fix the situation – all good prescriptions for the disease. However, if we want to apply such prescriptions to a China that is not yet industrialized, regardless of whether it would be malpractice, the biggest problem is that they simply will not treat our disease. Let me give you a few examples.

If we want to form labor unions like those in the West to resist the capitalist class, then we must first ask whether China has a capitalist class. If not, then we are just shooting in the dark. Do China's warlords and bureaucrats, who are personally worth millions, count as a capitalist class? The capitalists of other countries play an important role in production, contributing to the overall livelihood of the people, but all of the money that China's warlords and bureaucrats grab by force and trickery is soon wasted on luxury and extravagance. Can we call them capitalists? There are legitimate Chinese businessmen trying hard to run their companies, being bruised and battered by foreign competition. How can we in good conscience insist on labeling them a capitalist class and make war on them?[19]

In the West, the Marxist theory of state ownership of the organs of production could bring about a needed cure, but if we want to adopt it in China, we must first ask what the organs of production actually are and whether they exist in China or not. If they do exist in China, I would be the first to oppose proposals to nationalize them. Haven't you seen what happened to the railways? Western socialists are especially insistent on nationalizing the railways, but hasn't China already done so? How did that turn out? Given China's current politics, to advocate Marxist collectivism would be shooting ourselves in the foot.

These cases above do not speak to whether socialist practice is good or bad but only to whether we should adopt it or not. Some people say that China now needs to focus on the issue of production, not distribution. I cannot completely agree with this. Rather, what I propose is that we use every means to promote production, while at the same time keeping an eye on the question of distribution. Since the war, every country has been striving to expand its exports and output competition among countries has become fiercer. Unless we try to resist this trend, how can we survive? Our industry is immature and still very fragile. To agitate workers to take action against the factory bosses would, I think, be a suicidal act. But when our industry has begun to mature, we should start to consider the consequences that a fully developed industry may lead to in the future.

Because Europeans failed to take any precautions during the industrial revolution, they now confront deeply embedded problems. Even though Europeans have expended herculean efforts to correct the situation, their efforts have accomplished little. Fortunately, we are a late-developing country. We can see clearly how the Europeans made mistakes on their road to industrialization. We can examine every one of the reform measures they took. We just need to avoid their mistakes and adopt their reform measures to ensure that industrial organization is built on a sound basis from the beginning. The future threat of social revolution may thus be avoided.

We need to understand that revolutions occur only when there are no alternatives. They are not a good sign and should be avoided if at all possible. Therefore, my suggestion for industry at the present moment is to develop a cooperative spirit between capitalists and workers. We need to thoroughly investigate the wages and benefits that factories around the world give workers and try to put them into practice. At the same time, the state must work to increase fairness in distribution through our tax laws and other legislation, and also actively promote producers' cooperatives and consumers' cooperatives so that from petty capitalists down to the poorest workers all have a legitimate weapon to protect their interests. And as for laborers' own spirit of self-governance, it should be cultivated in schools and factories. Enterprises, whether public or private, should all endeavor to foster a cooperative spirit. This is the bright prospect now before us. As for those too-clever and novel theories, we should take them as academic materials for liberating our thought, but as for putting them into practice, we should wait for now.

12. The Citizens' Movement

I think my readers will certainly challenge me: 'All your nattering on about politics and the people's livelihoods is completely beside the point. Our immediate problem is that the northern and southern warlords have ruthlessly seized the whole nation. Do you have a way to eliminate them? If you can't eliminate them, how can you carry out your plan?'

I reply: 'There is a solution, but it relies on you.'

'What is it?'

'Naturally it is the citizens' movement.'

'What is a citizens' movement?'

'First, it cannot be a movement of politicians. Second, it cannot be a movement of local bullies. Third, it cannot be a movement of secret society gangs. Rather, it must be an inclusive movement of the truly good people of the whole nation.'

'Ha! Ha! Your words are truly futile! Good people are content with their place and fear meddling in others' affairs – who wants to join your movement?'

'I take it that you are not a youth, for our youth would not be speaking like that.'

'What if I really am a youth? What's it to you? Are you telling me to boycott my classes and make your movement my profession? I could sacrifice my education without regrets, but what would it accomplish?'

'Oh, no! My dear youth! You are the treasure of the nation. Your nation will absolutely not allow you to sacrifice yourself in vain for such a useless movement. The first step is for you to uphold your present spirit to the end. Do not follow the youth of the past who fell into depravity in the blink of an eye. The second step is for you to find a way to share your strength with your generation to let more youths become like you. The third step, most importantly, is for you to truly liberate your thought, truly discipline your will, and truly cultivate your learning, and thus to hold onto your own individuality and seek complete self-fulfillment. Look! Aren't the elites of today about to make way for you? And then, won't the whole nation become ideal new citizens? Once the citizens' movement starts, no one can resist it.'

'That's easy for you to say, but it will take many years.'

'Of course – that's why I say you can't rush things. Facing the consequences of all the evil today's elites have wrought on the nation, do you think we can avoid three years or five years or seven years of disaster? After all, what is three years, or five years, or seven years? It took the French Revolution all the way from 1793 to France's great defeat in 1871 before we can say it established a republic. And hasn't it risen spectacularly to become one of the greatest countries in the world today? Broaden your horizons. Gather your strength. Then nothing in the world should leave you discouraged. Is it worth getting depressed over the dog-eat-dog machinations of the warlords and bureaucrats?

13. The Great Responsibility of the Chinese People for World Civilization

In the twelve sections above, I was writing spontaneously with no real order. But I reckon if we can examine our shortcomings and raise our spirits to face the future, it would not be difficult to engage in the great task of national salvation and reconstruction. Does this mean we have fulfilled our responsibilities? I don't think so. The most important goal in life is to contribute to the whole of humanity. Why is this? Because the whole of humanity is the 'self' at its greatest extent. If we want to develop this 'self', then we must work to improve the whole of humanity.

Why do we need countries? Because only when there is a country is it easy to unify, maintain and increase the cultural power of the people of that country so as to join the whole of humanity and help it develop. Therefore, nation-building is one way to promote the evolution of the whole of humanity, just as combining local self-government organs is a way to establish a nation. In other words, we cannot stop at making our country strong and prosperous. We want our country to contribute to the whole of humanity; otherwise, it is established in vain.

When you grasp this principle, you will understand that our country is facing a great responsibility. What responsibility? It is to take Western civilization to augment our civilization, and to take our civilization to enhance Western civilization, melding them into a new kind of civilization. When I was in Paris, I met the great philosopher Émile Boutroux (Henri Bergson's teacher), who told me, 'The most important job of a people is to advance and uphold their own national culture, just like descendants who inherit an ancestral legacy that they must preserve and make the best use of. Even if a country's civilization is not highly developed, as long as it is of use, that is all to the good. Because each country has its unique character, when it is melded with that of other countries they will form a third, better kind of character. You Chinese are indeed an amiable and reputable people. When my ancestors were dressed in deer skins hunting in the woods with stone knives, you had already produced so many philosophers. I have recently read some Chinese philosophical texts in translation, and I found them to be exceptionally broad and deep. Unfortunately, I am too old to learn Chinese. I sincerely hope the Chinese people will not lose their heritage.'

Upon hearing his words, I suddenly felt I was shouldering a very heavy responsibility. On another occasion I was chatting with some well-known socialists and I cited the words of Confucius – 'Within the four seas, all men are brothers' and 'We do not fear a small population, but unequal distribution' – and then I spoke of the well-field system.[20] I also cited Mozi's 'universal love' and 'laying down arms'. They all jumped up, saying, 'You have all these treasures – it is inexcusable that you have kept them all to yourself without sharing any with us.' I do not think we failed the foreigners so much as we have failed our own ancestors.

In recent years, many Western scholars have been wanting to adopt aspects of Oriental civilization to modify their own civilizations. After thinking it over, I concluded that we are certainly able to do this. Why is this? Past Western civilization inevitably separated the ideal from the real, taking the philosophies of

idealism and materialism to their extremes. Religion preached
the afterlife, while the philosophy of idealism centered on metaphysical matters all very far from the concerns of life. As science
emerged in reaction against these trends, the philosophy of
materialism swept across the world, rejecting all noble ideals.
Thus, as I have said before, 'The current fashion of socialism
has resulted in nothing more than fighting over crumbs.' Can
this be considered the highest goal of humanity? Therefore, the
recent philosophies of pragmatism and creative evolution are
both seeking to turn ideals into reality and to reconcile idealism
and materialism.

Actually, I think pre-Qin Chinese thought was developing precisely along these lines.[21] Although the doctrines of the sages
Confucius, Laozi and Mozi differ, they all share one common
goal: to seek the unity of ideals and reality. Examples include
Confucius's 'Develop one's individual nature to nourish humanity' and 'striving unceasingly'; Laozi's 'All return to their original
roots'; and Mozi's 'All must comply with Heaven'.[22] These three
sages perceived the oneness of the 'great self' or 'spiritual self' on
the one hand and the 'small self' or 'physical self' on the other,
realizing the great through the small and reaching the spiritual
from the physical.[23] If we follow the insights of the three sages in
order to seek a 'modern unity of ideals and reality', then I think
we will be able to open up uncountable new realms.

Although Buddhism first arose in India, it actually flourished
in China. The various schools of Mahayana have all become
extinct in India, while the dharma was sustained in China. More
and more Europeans are studying Buddhism, and nearly all the
Sanskrit sutras have been translated. But how much Mahayana
thought can one really grasp from Sanskrit texts, not to mention
from our own Chinese sects? China's Chan Buddhism, which
can indeed be considered applied Buddhism, precisely expresses
the Chinese character and shows that the worldly dharma and
the spiritual dharma are not in contradiction.[24] Such this-worldly
Buddhism could only develop outside India. Today, philosophers like Henri Bergson and Rudolf Christoph Eucken are
moving in this direction, but they haven't got very far. I often
think that if they could read Yogācāra texts, they would have

achieved more, and if they could understand the Chan school, their achievements would be even greater still.

You know that the rich legacy of the pre-Qin philosophers and all the masters of the Sui and Tang dynasties is what our wise and benevolent ancestors bequeathed us.[25] But we have failed our ancestors and neglected their legacy, and now our learning is depleted, although we are not inferior in literature and art and the like. At the same time, those backward and complacent members of the older generation who claim that Western Learning originated from China are completely ridiculous. And even more ridiculous are the people who are infatuated with the West and treat their own Chinese culture as worthless, as if we were a barbarian tribe that had created nothing over thousands of years.

We need to understand that all thought always reflects its period. What we want to learn is the essence of that thought, not the conditions that produced it, because those conditions are always shaped by the times. For example, Confucius spoke of many aristocratic ethical norms, which are assuredly of no use today; and yet we cannot dismiss Confucius because of this. Plato advocated preservation of the slave system; would you dismiss him because of this? When you study traditional Chinese learning with this point in mind, you can make a fair judgment, deciding what to keep and what to discard without making any mistakes.

Yet there is another very important matter. To further develop Chinese culture, we must learn from Western culture because its research methods are extremely accurate. As the proverb says, 'To do a good job, one must first sharpen one's tools.' Lacking such tools, everyone in the old society read Confucius and Li Bai and the like, but why did no one make good use of them?[26] Thus I hope our dear youth will proceed as follows. First, sincerely respect and cherish our country's culture. Second, adopt Western research methods to study and grasp its true essence. Third, systematize our own culture and then fuse it with other cultures to complement it and thereby produce a new cultural system. And fourth, disseminate this new cultural system around the world so that all humanity may benefit from it. Our population accounts for a quarter of the world's population, and so we have a quarter of the responsibility for the happiness of humanity. If we do not fulfill this responsibility, we will have failed our ancestors and failed all humanity, which is to say we will have failed ourselves.

Ah! My dear youth, stand to attention! March forward! Across the sea are millions of people anxiously facing the bankruptcy of their material civilization, desperately calling for help and waiting for you to save them. Our ancestors, the three great sages and many other elders in Heaven are eagerly hoping you can complete their great task and are giving you the blessing of their spirit.

14. Final Note

I am writing a travelogue, but now I have unceasingly prattled on and on without a word about my actual travels. I am only afraid that I might have bored you, by actually making myself a laughing stock like the fable of the Erudite who wrote out three highfalutin pages for a contract to buy a mule without ever specifying that he was buying a 'mule'.[27] The heavens have been acting up and it has been heavily snowing for three straight days, which at least has magnificently cleared out all our old stale air. I'm going out for a stroll now. I will write more tomorrow. Here I copy the commonplace of old novels as my final note: 'Let us pass over this small talk and return to the main story.'[28]

18

Human Rights and Women's Rights[1]

This is the transcript of a talk Liang delivered at the Nanjing Women's Normal School on 6 November 1922. In the 1890s Liang had made a then-radical plea for girls' education. More than twenty years later such a plea was not so radical but could be seen as an effort to tamp down the women's movement. Yet clearly Liang was looking forward to the day of gender equality. By the 1920s, talk of 'human rights' had become fairly common, although Chinese Marxists were soon to dismiss it as a bourgeois trick. Much human rights talk can be seen as a way of talking about citizenship, but in a universal sense not limited to a particular nation-state. For Liang, at this point, clearly the way to think about rights was in the global context. It should be noted that the Chinese language is not gendered in the way Western languages are; thus it is common to speak literally of 'person', 'human' and 'humankind' (ren) rather than cognates of 'man', as has been the practice in English until recently. Nonetheless, Liang was aware that the default gender of 'person' was indeed the male of the species. First published in Chenbao fukan, *16 November 1924.*

Upon seeing my talk's title, you would certainly say, 'Mr Liang doesn't make any sense. Of course, human rights include women's rights since women are also human. How can you set up human rights and women's rights as two separate things?'

Hahaha! Yes, it certainly doesn't make any sense, but the non-sensical title is not something concocted by this Mr Liang. I am simply pointing out the truth of our present social conditions, and I just want to find a way to make the nonsense make sense. I want to pose a question to test you: 'What is a human?'

When you hear this question, you will want to say again, 'I'm afraid that Mr Liang must have gone crazy. What is difficult about this question? Between Heaven and Earth all the animals with "round heads, square feet, horizontal eyes and bright minds" are of course human.'

Hahaha! No, your answer is wrong. Your answer can only explain the meaning of 'human' in nature, not the meaning of 'human' in history. In the earliest stages of history, very few animals with 'round heads, square feet, horizontal eyes and bright minds' counted as human – at most three out of a hundred qualified as 'human', while the rest did not qualify. In other words, previously there were very few people who possessed the moral character of the human, but as history slowly unfolded, the number of such humans gradually increased.

I'm afraid you might be even more confused by what I just said, but bear with me. Wait for me to analyze the question step by step. We are all the same species with 'round heads, square feet, horizontal eyes and bright minds' – naturally you can do whatever I can do, while I have the same rights as you. Isn't this the case? Exactly! Yes, it should be, but what we see from history is that this is not the case at all. In the history of every single country, in the beginning, a portion of the population was always classified as 'slaves'. Didn't slaves also have 'round heads, square feet, horizontal eyes and bright minds'? But those who were not slaves regarded them only as chattels, not as humans. You have studied Western history, so presumably you all know that in ancient Greece, Athens was called a 'polity of the whole people' which claimed everyone was equal and free. And you should also know that there was a great philosopher, Plato, who was a forefather of republicanism. That's right! Plato said that everyone should participate in politics, but slaves were not allowed to. Why was this? Because slaves weren't human! Athens had a population of several tens of thousands, but in fact there were only a few thousand people who could participate in politics. Then why was it called a polity of the whole people? Because those who were recognized as 'human' all participated, while the rest – the majority – were slaves who were fundamentally regarded as chattels, not humans.

This was true not only for slaves. When we compare nobles and commoners, only the nobles counted as full, complete humans. The commoners were at most mere semi-humans. Most education was reserved for nobles and not allowed to commoners; most professions were reserved for nobles and not allowed to commoners; and most property was reserved for nobles and not allowed to commoners. This was what China was like from Yao and Shun and the Three Dynasties down to the time of Confucius; this was also what Europe was like from the Roman Empire down to the eighteenth century.[2]

Under the system of slavery, those who were not slaves did not regard slaves as human, and even the slaves themselves did not know that they were 'human'. Under the system of aristocracy, the nobles regarded commoners as semi-human, and even the commoners themselves felt different from the nobles. This confusion lasted for several thousand years.

Humans are intelligent and aspiring animals. They slowly woke up from their dreams. They constantly pondered on this question: 'You have two eyes and one nose. I also have one nose and two eyes. So why do you get to live that way while I have to live this way?' After untold years of distress and sorrow, all of a sudden they realized a strange truth: 'Ahhhh! After all, I am a human!' To what degree the Chinese have realized this strange truth, I will not say for the moment, but when did the Europeans realize it? That was about the time of the Renaissance, in the fifteenth and sixteenth centuries.

Once they realized that they themselves were human, they instinctively united around one resolution: on the one hand to prepare themselves to become fully developed humans, and on the other to fully develop their rights as humans. The first step was to make sure that all people had the same opportunity to receive education, eliminating the monopoly that the nobility and the Church held over learning. The second step was to make sure all people found appropriate employment according to their talents, prohibiting the claims of particular classes to monopolize certain professions. And the third step was to make sure that all people had the right to participate in the nation's politics in order to ensure that the above two rights were upheld. In sum, once people experienced 'self-awakening', the human rights movement emerged. Equal rights to education, equal rights to employment and equal rights to political participation are thus the three stages of the evolution of the human rights movement.

What an extraordinary thing that once the human mind was liberated, there was no stopping it. 'Go, go, go, let's go! One, two, three' – step by step the human race finally arrived at the last years of the eighteenth century and in Paris, France, they fired a great cannon shot, 'The Declaration of Human Rights'.[3] Right on! Everybody, let's join forces to fight for self-government for the colonies, to abolish the class system, to make suffrage universal and to liberate slaves and serfs. In the nineteenth century it was precisely these struggles for human rights that threw the whole of Europe and the Americas into turmoil for a hundred years. Then success! Triumph! Sound the trumpets! Set off firecrackers! Celebrate with toasts! Long live human rights! Previously, only the emperors were human, only the nobles were human, only the priests and monks were human, but now we are all equal to them; those who didn't count as human now count as human, and whoever counts as human in the whole world has now recovered their humanity. Long live human rights!

Yet, amid this cheering, there was still a large portion of the animals with 'round heads, square feet, horizontal eyes and bright minds' who were quietly shedding tears. Although this portion of the animals composed half their species, they were never admitted into the human race. Who were they? They were women. The human rights movement fought for the rights of those who were human, but they were *women*, not *human*. The movement wildly boasted that it advocated human rights, yet it ignored women.

Tears are the most sacred things. They seep out from the self-awakened heart. No doubt all men have two eyes and one nose – this is equally true for nobles, commoners and slaves. Are you telling me that women only have one eye and half a nose? When the human rights movement reached its zenith, it discovered an even stranger truth: 'Oh! It turns out there are a

lot more humans in the world!' With this discovery, the movement for women's rights was born. We can call it a new 'broadly
defined human rights movement'.

The broadly defined human rights movement (encompass-
ing the women's rights movement) and the narrowly defined
human rights movement (the democracy movement) have one
thing in common: the need to meet two key conditions – first,
self-agency, and second, development through stages. What is
'self-agency'? For example, the American abolitionist movement didn't consist of black slaves liberating themselves, but of
a number of charitable whites liberating the black slaves. This
was a case of the agency of others, not self-agency. Even though
they were liberated, since it was not based on self-agency, it
didn't have much value. Furthermore, all movements work
through the mutual efforts of the majority, not through a com-
mandeering of the movement by a minority. This requires the
collective self-agency of the majority. For example, only a tiny
group of people participated in the establishment of the Chinese republic, while the majority remained uninvolved. This was
another case of agency of others rather than self-agency. In the
case of the democracy movement in Europe in the nineteenth
century, it truly emerged from the self-awakening and the self-
agency of the whole or the majority of commoners. This is the
sole reason they were able to successfully achieve democracy
and do so thoroughly. The first task in determining whether
the women's movement has significance or value is to evaluate
the true degree of women's self-awakening and self-agency.

What are 'stages of development'? Previously, I said that the
human rights movement possesses three aspects: first, equal
rights to education; second, equal rights to employment; and
third, equal rights to political participation. They formed a unified system, but this system was naturally built in separate
stages. During the age of aristocracy, the only weapon the
nobles had to defend their monopoly of rights was: 'You commoners have none of the learning and knowledge that we
nobles have; you commoners have none of the abilities to carry
out affairs that we nobles have.' Were their words correct? Yes,
they were. The social conditions in Europe during the Middle

Ages were exactly like this. If these conditions had continued unchanged into the eighteenth and nineteenth centuries, I can guarantee you that 'The Declaration of Human Rights' would never have been written and, if it had, it would have been nothing but idle phrases.

Thus, ever since the Renaissance, the most pressing demand of the commoners was for opportunities to receive the same education as the nobles. As they continued to grab those opportunities, they devoted 120 percent of their efforts to increasing their knowledge and abilities. By the eighteenth and nineteenth centuries, the knowledge and abilities of the commoners were always superior to those of the nobles and never inferior. Without ever letting up, the commoners then pressed on with the democracy movement until final victory. In other words, they first prepared themselves to become fully developed humans, and only then could they fully develop their rights as humans.

Right now, their women's rights movement is going in the same direction. Yet although it began to take shape quite a few decades ago, its influence remains rather weak. Why is its influence rather weak? It is because women have lagged behind men in knowledge and ability. Why have women lagged behind men? It is because women did not have the same opportunities as men to receive an education. But they used all their strength to break through this barrier; then they resorted to tougher and tougher confrontations to fight for their rights to equal employment and then for their rights to political participation. Gradually, these movements in the West have achieved a degree of success.

And what about us? Ah! Just thinking about it, we are shameful and pitiful. Even most of our men have not realized they are human, much less our women. We haven't even carried out the narrowly defined human rights movement, not to mention the broadly defined movement. That's why some people promote the 'too-early-for-women's-rights thesis', saying we should wait until the democracy movement is complete before working on the women's rights movement. Is this kind of talk correct? Not at all! When Europeans built their railways, they started with narrow-gauge railways before they gradually switched over to wide-gauge. But when we built our railways, we started with wide-gauge as a matter of course. Why wouldn't we? Europeans achieved human rights by moving from the narrowly defined movement to the broadly defined movement in two separate steps, but it is certainly possible for us to do it in one go. However, there is one thing we absolutely cannot forget: it doesn't really matter whether the railroad is narrow-gauge or wide-gauge, but you certainly must lay down the tracks before you can run the train.

There is something else I want to say that you may not like. In China today the knowledge and abilities of its men of course remain extremely weak and immature, but the knowledge and abilities of its women are far weaker and less mature. If you want to talk about women's rights, the first requirement is that you claim your independence by not relying on men. In other words, you need to have employment. For example, if a school is looking for a teacher and ten women and ten men are competing for the job, who do you think is going to get it? Or if a company or an individual is looking for a secretary, and ten women and ten men are competing for the job, who do you think is going to get it? Or a further case: if women's political participation is affirmed in the constitution, and women have the freedom to compete in elections by making public speeches, who do you think is going to win? Given current social conditions, I dare say that nine times out of ten the woman will be defeated. Why is this? Because in their knowledge and abilities, the women of today are truly inferior to men.

Yet are women born inferior to men? Not at all! Not at all! It is simply because their education is insufficient. Why is their education insufficient? It is because previously women did not have the same opportunities to pursue education as men. Of course, it is not the fault of today's women that they lacked the same opportunities for education, but we still have to face the fact that their education is simply inadequate. I presume that you have all read in your English textbooks the aphorism 'knowledge is power'. There is no way you can acquire power other than on the basis of knowledge, and if you do happen to get it by sheer luck, you won't be able to keep it. This principle is true for individuals; it is also true for social classes; and it is true for the two sexes as well.

At this point in my talk, we can come up with a rough conclusion. In principle I support the women's rights movement, whether for education, employment or political participation – and not only do I very much support it, but also consider it to be necessary. If I have to choose in terms of their order, I think education comes first, employment second and political participation third. Recent advocates of women's rights focus on the issue of political participation, but I think they are putting the cart before the horse. Let me be frank. Do Chinese men today have the right of political participation? If you say 'no', you can't be right, as our constitution clearly affirms it. But if you say 'yes', in the eleven years since the founding of our republic, when have you ever seen any men actually asserting their right to political participation? Is it not the case that the electoral rolls are simply a tool full of fake names for 'political hoodlums' to buy and sell votes?

Given this kind of popular political consciousness, even if you women win the right to political participation, it will amount to nothing more than adding a few thousand Miss So-and-Sos to the electoral rolls to help those political hoodlums get more business. I truly do not wish for our women of high aspirations and irreproachable virtue to be gratuitously defiled by such practices. But frankly speaking, in politics you cannot give up just because of one setback and I don't want to agitate you further. In the final analysis, whatever your movement is, you need to cultivate your power and avoid empty talk. The true significance of the women's rights movement lies in the painstaking self-awakening of women seeking equality with men by developing their knowledge and abilities. Once this is done, then women's employment and political participation will not be a problem. But if you fail to do this, even if you stir up a storm, it will all end up as idle talk.

Ah, ladies! In the whole country today, the only places producing knowledge for women are just some ten-odd women's normal schools. Ladies, you are the main army of the women's rights movement. Zhuangzi put it well: 'If water is too shallow, it lacks the capacity to bear a large ship.'[4] Ladies, you must know that you bear a great responsibility. You must also know that, if you want to fulfill this responsibility, you have no alternative to studying well and increasing your knowledge and abilities. I hope you and all the women of China will come to a thorough understanding that you yourselves are 'human' and that you will redouble your efforts to fulfill your individual humanity and one day join forces with women around the world to carry out the broadly defined human rights movement. And when the movement succeeds this time, we can truly shout for joy, 'Long live human rights!'

19

The Proletariat Class and the Idler Class[1]

By the 1920s, Marxism was becoming increasingly popular, the latest of various 'isms' such as socialism, anarchism, liberalism and the like. Liang was the first Chinese writer to introduce Marx to China, in 1902, though only with the briefest of summaries. Although the 1911 revolutionaries sometimes advocated socialism, they displayed relatively little interest in Marx. The success of the Russian Revolution and the founding of the Chinese Communist Party in 1921, however, brought Marxist historical materialism and class struggle to the fore. Liang's short May Day piece here fits into the genre of zawen ('jottings'), a term that came to describe short, sharply satirical essays, often playing on words – Liang could move with the times. To make sense of Liang's wordplay it is necessary to know that 'proletariat' was translated into Chinese as wuchan jieji ('property-less class' – true to its Latin origins and in line with a tendency to think of the peasantry as proletarian, though orthodox Marxists of course understood it referred to the still-tiny industrial labor force). Liang then contrasts this wuchan jieji to what he calls the 'propertied class' or youchan jieji – changing just the first character in this four-character term. He then creates two other terms by shifting the second character in parallel fashion: the 'idler class' (wuye jieji, literally the 'unemployed', but that is not Liang's meaning) and the 'employed class' (youye jieji, by which Liang means people doing useful jobs). First published in the International Workers' Day supplement of Chenbao, 1 May 1925.

Recently I have become utterly tired of hearing people referring to everything as an 'ism', because every 'ism' that gets into the hands of the Chinese becomes nothing but a big swindle.

Today is the world-renowned International Workers' Day. In Western societies, it truly has enormous significance. What is its significance? It represents the proletariat, or 'property-less class' – that is, the interests of the working class. It signifies the struggle against the classes that exploit the workers.

Whether class struggle is good for society is another question, which I put aside for the moment. What we need to keep in mind is that Western societies are divided into two distinct classes, the proletariat and the propertied classes. The proletariat are people who have regular employment, working every day in factories and markets. Because they are fighting to protect their hard-earned livelihoods and to provide relief for the unemployed, their struggle is justified and meaningful.

In the final analysis, does China have class divisions or not? I would rather not say, but if I were absolutely obliged to, then I consider that the 'propertied class' and the 'proletariat' are not terms in binary opposition, but that the 'employed class' and the 'idler class' are such binary opposites. What is the employed class? It is people such as farmers (including both small landlords and tenant-farmers), merchants (including both shop-owners and clerks), schoolteachers, minor officials and the various kinds of day laborers. Some of these people own property and some do not, so it is difficult to classify them into a separate class on the basis of whether or not they are 'propertied'. What is the idler class? It is people such as wealthy officials, wealthy militarists, party leaders and members, local hoodlums, gangsters in the foreign concessions, students in the pay of foreign propaganda organs, bandits (including those wearing military uniforms), beggars (including those wearing scholars' gowns) and various lazy types. Some of these people also own property and some do not, so it is difficult to classify them into a separate class on the basis of whether or not they are 'propertied'.

Another question is, does China have class struggle? I can say that if the employed class defeats the idler class, the world will be at peace, but if the idler class conquers the employed class, our country will be lost and our race exterminated. Alas! How sad! How unfortunate! It seems we are drifting down a road that will lead to the victory of the idlers.

This idler class is utterly shameless and its stratagems are effective – they are always proclaiming themselves to be acting as representatives of some portion of the people. Louis XIV said, 'L'état, c'est moi'; they say, 'We are the people.' They live off 'isms' – always flashing the latest fashionable 'ism'. I remember that a news item from a Shanghai newspaper last year said that a young man wearing a Western suit and metal filigree glasses took a rickshaw to the Longhua district. He was beating the rickshaw-puller with his cane, kicking him and cursing him the whole way, 'I'm in a hurry to get to the workers' rally, and you're delaying me. Damn you, scum!' Perhaps this was a story made up to satirize today's society, but in fact such grotesque things happen all the time.

A few years ago, I was giving a lecture somewhere. A joint reception was held by the farmers' associations, the chamber of commerce and the labor unions, attended by several dozen of their representatives, but none of them looked like farmers or businessmen or workers to me. To me, they all looked as if they basically came from the highest of our traditional 'four classes', the scholars.[2] After I formally expressed my gratitude, I added a comment: 'I hope that I can visit your organizations again in a few more years and get to see farmers wearing straw raincoats and carrying hoes, and workers with their faces covered in dust coming straight from their factories.' Alas! How long will it be before this dream can become reality?

How pitiful! How pitiful! I don't know how many honest and decent members of our employed class are fast asleep when actually they are being exploited by their representatives.

How pitiful! How pitiful! All the new 'isms' that the scholars of the world are sweating blood to develop turn out to be just their way to make a living.

International Workers' Day? Of course it should be commemorated. But we absolutely cannot allow non-workers to intrude on it. If actual workers do not understand its meaning, or if they do not see its necessity, then I think we had better not commemorate it at all, lest some people pretending to be workers steal it for themselves.

The movements in the West today nearly all fly the banner, 'At the hands of the proletariat, down with the propertied class!' But I don't think this banner is appropriate for China. We should change it to: 'At the hands of the employed class, down with the idler class!'

Notes

1. Preface to the *General Discussion of Institutional Reform* (August 1896)

1. 變法通議自序，《時務報》no. 1, GX 22-7-14 (August 1896).
2. 'Single whip', an annual land tax to be paid in silver.
3. Liang is referring to different dynasties' systems of choosing officials.
4. This is not a direct quote; Liang is taking phrases from the *Analects* (*Lunyu*) or classified 'sayings' of Confucius, a work perhaps compiled by his followers starting in the fifth or fourth century BCE.
5. Liang is referring to a standard historiographical category of the recovery of a dynasty after a near-death experience such as a major rebellion, coup or civil war. The Han Restoration refers to the establishment of the Eastern Han dynasty in 25 CE; the Tang Restoration refers to a recentralization of power in the early ninth century.
6. *The Book of Odes* is one of the Confucian classics: a compilation of ritual hymns, poems and folksongs from the eleventh to the seventh century BCE.
7. *The Book of Changes*, one of the Confucian classics, was an ancient text originally used for divination but later expanded and interpreted philosophically.
8. Yi Yin (seventeenth to sixteenth century BCE?) was an advisor to the founder of the Shang dynasty (trad. 1766–1122 BCE).

2. Essay on Grouping (May 1897)

1. 說群自序，《時務報》no. 26, GX 23-4-7 (May 1897); 說群序，說群一群理一，《知新報》no. 18, GX 23-4-16 (May 1897).
2. *On Evolution* was a translation with commentary of Thomas Huxley's *Evolution and Ethics* that Yan Fu published between

1897 and 1898. Liang and Yan exchanged letters. *On Benevolence* was written by Tan Sitong between 1896 and 1897; see Sin-wai Chan, *An Exposition of Benevolence: The* Jen-hsüeh *of T'an Ssu-t'ung* (Hong Kong: The Chinese University Press, 1984).

3. Liang did not complete this project. This Preface and the first chapter here are all that Liang wrote, though he continued to discuss grouping in other contexts (see the essays below).

4. This idea was actually expressed by the philosopher and political thinker Xunzi (third century BCE).

5. *The Book of Rites* was a Han dynasty compilation detailing pre-Qin dynasty ethics and ceremonial practices (Liang is eliding separate passages here).

6. Liang is referring to a three-stage theory of the development of civilization taught by Kang Youwei, from the Age of Chaos to the Age of Lesser Peace, and finally to the Age of Great Peace or Datong.

7. According to the *Zhuangzi*, Xi Shi was a beautiful woman from the state of Yue during the late Spring and Autumn period. When Xi Shi was upset and knit her brow, she became all the more lovely. Dong Shi was an unattractive woman; she tried to imitate Xi Shi knitting her brow to appear more beautiful but failed miserably.

8. *The Spring and Autumn Annals* is a chronicle of Confucius's state of Lu from 722 to 481 BCE, often attributed to Confucius.

9. Some sixty chemical elements were known by the mid-nineteenth century. Liang's reference to sixty-four may come from the sixty-four hexagrams (seen as representations of basic elements of the universe) of *The Book of Changes*.

10. 'Nobler' for Liang means displaying higher levels of grouping and thus of development.

11. That is, by gravity.

12. According to traditional Chinese medicine.

13. Liang's references are derived from accounts of the legendary Emperor Shun (twenty-third to twenty-second century BCE) and the historical King Wu (eleventh century BCE), both models of good rulers.

14. The kingdom (or ducal state) of Liang was one of over a dozen relatively small states in the early Spring and Autumn period; it was conquered by the kingdom of Qin in 641 BCE. *Gongyang zhuan* (Gongyang commentary on *The Spring and Autumn Annals*) was a Han dynasty text that emphasized the cosmological principles behind the political order, allegedly based on Confucius's

personal teachings; it was a key text of the New Text Confucianism which Liang was following at the time he wrote this essay.

Part Two: Radicalism: Exile 1, 1899–1903

1. *The Great Learning*, a chapter from *The Book of Rites*, promoted by Zhu Xi (1130–1200) as one of the Four Books to be studied as an introduction to Confucianism.

2. 'Baojiao fei suoyi zun Kong lun' [Preserving the Teaching is not the way to honor Confucius], *Yinbingshi heji* (Beijing: Zhonghua shuju, 1995), wenji 9:59.

3. The Similarities and Differences in the State Structures of China and Europe (September 1899)

1. 論中國與歐洲國體異同,《清議報》no. 26, GX 25-8-1 (September 1899).

2. From the *Daode jing* (chapter 80), attributed to Laozi (legendary dates sixth century BCE).

3. Dong Zhongshu (179–104 BCE), a Han dynasty official and philosopher.

4. According to myth, Gonggong was variously a water god or a kind of hydraulic engineer who fought for control of the empire. The Nine Provinces is an ancient way to refer to the territory of China. Chiyou was a god-king, sometimes seen as ancestor of the Miao (Hmong), who lost an epic battle to the Yellow Emperor, often regarded as the ancestor of the Han Chinese. Banquan is in present-day Hebei.

5. San-Miao was one tribe of Miao, adjacent to the Central Plains. 'Central Plains' refers to China or north China.

6. Three Dynasties: Xia (legendary dates 2070–1600 BCE), Shang (c. 1600–1046 BCE) and Zhou (1046–256 BCE).

7. According to tradition, Yu the Great founded the Xia dynasty. Mount Tu was perhaps in today's Jiangxi or Anhui. 'Jades and silks' might refer to sacrificial objects offered to Heaven or gifts symbolizing the tribes' surrender to Yu.

8. Tribal states in north China.

9. Zhou dynasty: founded in 1046 or 1045 BCE, declined in power between the eighth and fifth centuries BCE.

10. Aristocratic leaders of the various dukedoms or states originally enfeoffed by the Zhou but which gradually become de facto independent.

11. Zhou Li wang (877–841 BCE); Zhi: in today's Shanxi.

12. Teng Wen gong (fourth century BCE); Mencius (372–289 BCE, a pre-eminent follower of the Confucian school) told Duke Wen that one should mourn the death of a parent for three years.

13. Cao Mo and Xian Gao were commoners of the Zhou period who saved their states from enemy attack, while the ruler of Zheng was acting to protect a humble merchant. Liang assumed his readers would be familiar with the classical texts and so able to recall the original stories.

14. Spring and Autumn: 771–476 BCE, associated with the gradual decline of the Zhou dynasty. Warring States: 475–221 BCE. Qin Shihuang, the First Qin Emperor, unified China in 221 BCE, which formed the empire that was basically inherited and then expanded by the Han dynasty (202 BCE to 220 CE). 'Lesser Peace' refers to Kang Youwei's theory of human progress through the three stages of Chaos, Lesser Peace and final Datong (Great Peace). Today, in the early twenty-first century, the term is used to describe China's age of 'moderate prosperity'.

15. Jin dynasty (266–420): the so-called eight princes were descendants of the founding emperor who rebelled against the sitting emperor. The Ming Prince of Yan seized the throne in 1402 to become the Yongle Emperor; the Prince of Ning failed in an attempt to seize the throne in 1519.

16. Three Kingdoms: 220–280; Southern and Northern dynasties: 420–589; the Liao (916–1125) and Jin (1115–1234) coexisted in the traditional territory of China with the Song (960–1279).

17. Sixteen Kingdoms: short-lived dynastic states in northern China (304–439); Ten Kingdoms (907–960).

18. Han Wudi (r. 141–87 BCE) officially recognized Confucianism as a kind of state ideology. The Six Arts that marked (symbolically) the gentleman were rites, music, archery, charioteering, calligraphy and mathematics. The Hundred Schools refers to the various and contending schools of thought that had emerged over the previous centuries.

19. That is, various tribes mentioned in the Classics living around but not fully within the Central Plains.

20. Bu Shi (dates unknown) was said to have been granted various titles after making large donations to the court of Han Wudi (r. 141–87 BCE). Gongsun Hong (200–121 BCE) was said to be a pig-herder who studied the Classics and eventually made his way into government through the Han examination system.

21. Warring States thinkers and strategists.

22. Mozi (*c.* fifth to fourth century BCE) advocated 'universal love'.

23. Han Gaozu (Liu Bang, 256–195 BCE) founded the Han dynasty.

24. Song Taizu (927–976) founded the Song dynasty (960–1279); the basic phrase is usually attributed to Tang Taizong (598–649).

4. The General Trend of Struggles of Citizenries in Recent Times and the Future of China (October 1899)

1. 論近世國民競爭之大勢及中國前途，《清議報》 no. 30 (October 1899).

2. According to Mencius, '*The Spring and Autumn Annals* [thought to be compiled by Confucius] acknowledges no just wars' (*Mencius* 7B:2). *Mozi*, Book 5; *Mencius* 4A:14.

3. Jiaozhi (Giao Chỉ), present-day northern Vietnam (Annan), at various points under Chinese rule, though never under the Qing.

4. The Meiji government established the *ri* as 3.927 kilometers or 2.44 miles.

5. *Li*, approximately one-third of a mile.

6. 'Mourning for his times' was one of Liang's own epithets.

7. Thanks to various treaties signed since 1842, the foreign powers had the right to build railways (including developmental rights along their corridors) and set up mining operations in China. The foreign-dominated Chinese Maritime Customs Service collected tariffs at China's ports, turning some funds over to the Beijing government, but making sure indemnities and loan payments were first made to the foreign powers. 'Concessions' refers to the foreign-run enclaves in China's major cities. By the 1860s all of China was open to missionary activities.

5. Preface to *The New Citizen* (February 1902)

1. 第一節：敘論，新民說一，《新民叢報》 no. 1, GX 28-1-1 (February 1902).

2. 'Round heads and square feet': that is, people, humanity.

6. Renewing the People is China's Most Urgent Task Today (February 1902)

1. 論新民為今日中國第一急務，《新民叢報》 no. 1, GX 28-1-1 (February 1902).

2. Li Lou was a mythical figure with extraordinary vision.
3. Shi Kuang (sixth century CE) was a famous musician.
4. Wu Huo (fourth century BCE) possessed enormous strength.
5. 'Green Standard' refers to divisions of the Qing's military, mostly used for policing.
6. Yao, Shun: legendary sage-kings.
7. In the original context, Mencius was urging renewal of the state through educational reform. *Mencius* 3A:3.
8. In traditional Chinese medicine, the six conditions are wind, cold, dryness, heat, damp and fire (and are often associated with particular seasons such as winter cold, summer heat, etc.).
9. *Mencius* 4A:9; mugwort-related plants were used for moxibustion.

7. The Definition of the New Citizen (February 1902)

1. 釋新民之義,《新民叢報》no. 1, GX 28-1-1 (February 1902).

8. The New Citizen as Vindicated by the Law of the Survival of the Fittest (February 1902)

1. 優勝劣敗之理以證新民之結果而論及取法之所宜,《新民叢報》 no. 2, GX 28-1-15 (February 1902).

9. Public Morality (March 1902)

1. 論公德,《新民叢報》 no. 3, GX 28-2-1 (March 1902).
2. 'The Counsels of Gao Yao' is a chapter in *The Book of Documents* that speaks to virtues or methods of rule: affability combined with dignity; mildness combined with firmness; bluntness combined with respectfulness; aptness for government combined with reverent caution; docility combined with boldness; straightforwardness combined with gentleness; an easy negligence combined with discrimination; boldness combined with sincerity; and valor combined with righteousness. (Following James Legge, *The Shoo King, or The Book of Historical Documents*, one of the Confucian classics, containing ancient Zhou dynasty texts, but later texts or later versions of purported Zhou dynasty texts as well.)
3. 'The Hongfan' ('Great Plan') is a chapter in *The Book of Documents* that speaks to virtues or methods of rule: uprightness, resolution and flexibility.

4. *The Great Learning* is one of the Four Books that formed the basis of the Confucian educational program after the thirteenth century along with *The Doctrine of the Mean* (both were originally chapters in *The Book of Rites*, sometimes attributed to Confucius), the *Analects* and the *Mencius*.

5. This is generally interpreted to mean that meticulous observation of small matters may give rise to ultimate sincerity that can transform the world. *The Doctrine of the Mean* was one of the Four Books that formed the basis of the Confucian educational program after the thirteenth century, originally a chapter in *The Book of Rites*.

6. Figures in the *Analects* and the *Mencius*.

7. The Song (960–1279) and Yuan (1271–1368) dynasties saw the rise of Neo-Confucianism and its Cheng-Zhu orthodox branch, which was later criticized as overly scholastic and conservative.

10. State Consciousness (March 1902)

1. 國家思想,《新民叢報》 no. 4, GX 28-2-15 (March 1902).

2. Liang brings together a traditional opposition: the term 'universal love' is associated with Mozi (c. 470–391 BCE), and the term 'self-benefit' with Yang Zhu (c. 440–360 BCE).

3. This refers roughly to Christianity, Confucianism and Buddhism.

4. See the previous essay in this volume for chapter 5 of *The New Citizen*.

5. These ellipses imply Liang's own Qing dynasty, 1644–. Naming the Qing here would have explicitly labeled it a 'foreign race'. This would have raised sensitive issues both in regard to Liang's interest in relationships with reform-minded Qing officials and other reformers in China, and to his views on the growing revolutionary movement. That Liang regarded the Qing as a foreign dynasty is implied by his calculation that the 'whole of China' has been under foreign domination for 358 years. However, as a supporter of turning the Qing into a constitutional monarchy, and opposed to the revolutionary movement to overthrow the Qing, Liang wanted to fudge the issue of the Qing's foreignness and accept them as Chinese for political purposes.

6. Yellow Emperor: legendary ancestor (third millennium BCE) of the Han Chinese people.

7. This poem was commonly misattributed to Chen Baisha (Xianzhang, 1428–1500), a Confucian scholar, poet and calligrapher who did write on Mount Ya. Zhang Hongfan (1238–1280) was a

northern Chinese military leader who fought for the Mongol Empire and defeated the last Song (Chinese) resistance at the Battle of Mount Ya in 1279. Although Han in ethnicity, Zhang was born under Mongol rule in the north and he was never a subject of the Song; by the standards of his own times, Zhang did not necessarily owe loyalty to the Song.

8. Jin–Song: dynasties of limited territory of the third to fifth centuries. Liang's exact reasoning is not clear to me, but the point must be the importance of distinguishing between Chinese and foreign, or more precisely the failure to recognize that importance. Perhaps Liang thought Chen was confusing ethnicity with national (state) identity.

9. Dong Zhongshu (179–104 BCE) was a founder of official Confucianism; the *Luxuriant Dew of the Spring and Autumn Annals* attributed to him is a lengthy work which spoke to questions of politics, morality, epistemology and cosmology. Zhang Zai (1020–1077) was an early Neo-Confucian; his 'Western Inscription' is best known for its vision of cosmic harmony: all creatures, born from Heaven and Earth, form a single body.

10. Warring States period, 476–221 BCE; 'unification' was accomplished by the Qin kingdom, which defeated the remaining kingdoms of the Chinese plains and founded the Qin dynasty in 221 BCE.

11. That is, the statism of each individual kingdom. (This cannot be called nationalism since it was based on personalized loyalty to superiors.)

12. *Mencius* 1A:6.

13. Liu Bang established the Han dynasty in 202 BCE after the fall of the Qin.

14. Liu Yuan (d. 310): Xiongnu noble, founder of the Han Zhao dynasty during China's chaotic fourth century. Shi Le (274–333): Han Zhao general who broke away from the Han Zhao to found the Later Zhao dynasty and conquer the Han Zhao. Han Zhao and Later Zhao were both short-lived polities in northern China.

15. Ji Shao (253–304): died in battle protecting the Jin emperor. The Jin dynasty (266–420) briefly conquered most of territorial China.

16. The Boxer Uprising began in rural northern China in the late 1890s with attacks on missionaries and Chinese Christians; Boxers moved on to Beijing in June 1900, threatening the foreign legations and winning the support of the Qing court. A twenty-thousand-strong 'Eight-Nation' allied army was rapidly organized with British, Japanese, French, German, Italian, Russian, Austrian

and American troops, which took Beijing in August, looted the city and punished Chinese officials and suspected Boxers.

17. A traditional custom in many places was to honor virtuous local officials, especially when they might be retiring or leaving for a new post, by giving them a large 'myriad-persons umbrella', which symbolized how the official sheltered the people from adversity as an umbrella shelters one person from the elements. Tassels might be attached around the umbrella with the names of its sponsors.

18. *Ershier shi zhaji* by Zhao Yi (1727–1814), based on the official dynastic histories.

11. Limiting the Powers of the Government and the People (March 1902)

1. 論政府與人民之權限,《新民叢報》no. 3, GX 28-2-1 (March 1902).

2. Liang is making metaphorical use of Kang Youwei's theory of linear progress through three ages: from Chaos to the Lesser (or Approaching) Peace, and finally to the Great Peace (or Datong).

3. Yao (trad. *c.* 2356–2255 BCE) and Shun (trad. *c.* 2294–2184 BCE) were mythical sage-kings, so described by Confucius; Laozi also spoke of 'actionless rule' – meaning, variously, rule that works through moral principles rather than laws and punishments, a laissez-faire approach to rule that simply leaves the people alone, and principles of rule that are in accord with natural processes, etc.

4. While kings are of course not elected, Liang may have been thinking of constitutional monarchies such as Britain where elections determined political outcomes ultimately represented by the head of state (the king).

5. In these passages, Liang is not quoting, but rather freely paraphrasing from Mill's introduction to *On Liberty*.

6. The precise quotations come from the *Xinxu* compilation of Liu Xiang (77–76 BCE), though they are not unlike some of the statements in the mostly older *Book of Rites*.

7. *Mencius* 5A:5.

8. *Mencius* 6A:17. Zhao Meng (sixth or fifth century BCE?), founder of the Zhao lineage of the Jin kingdom.

9. Liang's term is *taiping*, which could also refer to the utopia (Great Peace or Datong) predicted by Kang Youwei as the third stage of his outline of historical progress.

12. Liberty (May 1902)

1. 論自由‧《新民叢報》no. 7, GX 28-4-1, and no. 8, GX 28-4-15 (May 1902).

2. The traditional four classes or status groups: scholar, farmer, worker and merchant.

3. In the *Sutra of the Fundamental Vows of the Bodhisattva Kṣitigarbha* (Sanskrit *Kṣitigarbha Bodhisattva Pūrvapraṇidhāna Sūtra*), the Kṣitigarbha bodhisattva (Ch. Dizangwang pusa) vows not to achieve Buddhahood until all the hells are emptied of all sentient beings.

4. Liang was alluding to a story from the *Strategies of the Warring States* (third century BCE?) which depicted a man who left home to study for three years. On his return, he called his mother by her personal name, a very improper act. When she questioned him about this violation of propriety, he said that he had learned to refer to the great sage-emperors Yao and Shun by their names, and Heaven-and-Earth by its name, and told his mother that since she was not as great as Yao or Shun or as vast as Heaven-and-Earth, he had concluded it was appropriate to treat his mother the same.

5. Liang is citing a passage in the *Mencius* (fourth to third century BCE, section 6A:14–15) which discusses human nature and morality (I have enlarged the quotation for the reader's convenience – many of Liang's readers would have memorized the whole passage and needed only the briefest reference to recall the context. Here, Mencius answers the question why some people are greater than others, positing that people within themselves possess both 'greater' qualities and 'lesser' qualities, and their personal greatness or smallness depends on what parts of themselves they follow. Skeptical of hedonism (*exclusive* gratification of the senses or the lesser parts of oneself), Mencius argues that it is our Heaven-bestowed 'mind' that thinks and understands and can thus make moral choices, based on the greater parts of oneself.

6. From chapter 21, 'Tian Zifang', of the *Zhuangzi*.

7. Some Boxers practiced spirit possession and invulnerability rituals. Although supported by elements in the Qing government, some Boxers did not maintain the legally required fashion of shaving their foreheads and keeping their hair in a queue.

8. Liang is referencing concepts central to Neo-Confucian epistemology: 'Principle' refers to something like the inherent organization of the cosmos. The specific allusion is to *The Great Learning*, the

same text from which the concept of 'renewing the people' is derived.

9. Liang is quoting a poem from the Eastern Han (c. first century CE) meant to convey a warning that wasteful fashions in the capital would spread to the populace at large.

10. Learning of the Heart-and-Mind was an influential school of Neo-Confucianism associated with the Ming statesman and scholar Wang Yangming (1472–1529) which stressed 'innate knowledge of the good' and intuitionism.

11. The Evidential Learning movement emphasized textual criticism and developed philological techniques in order to rediscover the true meaning of the Classics, while tending to reject earlier interest in metaphysics and other more philosophical questions.

12. Saigō Takamori (1828–1877) was a leader of Japan's Meiji Restoration of 1868 who, although (or because) he turned against the Restoration government in the 1870s, was remembered as a great hero. Giuseppe Mazzini (1805–1872) was a leader of the revolutionary movement to create a unified and republican Italy in the mid-nineteenth century.

13. Mozi (c. fifth to fourth century BCE), philosopher opposed to Confucianism, known for his theories of universal love and the will of Heaven.

14. Liang was using the translation of T. H. Huxley's *Evolution and Ethics* of 1893 by Yan Fu (1854–1921), which Yan finished in 1898. The original passage reads: '[T]he ethical progress of society depends not on imitating the cosmic process, still less in running away from it, but in combating it ... We are grown men, and must play the man "strong in will / To strive, to seek, to find, and not to yield", cherishing the good that falls in our way, and bearing the evil, in and around us, with stout hearts set on diminishing it.' James G. Pardis and George Christopher Williams (eds), *Evolution and Ethics: T. H. Huxley's Evolution and Ethics, with New Essays on Its Victorian and Sociobiological Context* (Princeton, NJ: Princeton University Press, 1989) pp. 141, 144 (quoting Tennyson).

15. Lu Xiangshan (Lu Jiuyuan, 1139–1192), a leading Neo-Confucian thinker influenced by Buddhism (as in this quotation).

16. Shao Yong (1012–1077), one of the direct ancestors of the Neo-Confucian school (poetic lines here modified by Liang).

17. Most of Liang's readers at the time would have recognized this as a passage in which Mencius (6A:10) discusses how the original goodness of human nature may be lost.

18. From Buddhist epistemology. The reference is to the six sensory organs: eyes, ears, nose, tongue, body and the mind (as understanding objects), which essentially correspond to the six fields of perception: the fields of form, sound, odor, taste, touch and concept-formation – which are regarded as sources of contamination.

19. Zeng Guofan (1811–1872), leading statesman and general pivotal to the defeat of the Taiping Rebellion (1850–1865) which had threatened the very survival of the Qing dynasty; noted also for his conservative Confucianism.

20. *Analects* 12:1.

13. Self-Government (June 1902)

1. 論自治,《新民叢報》no. 9, GX 28-5-1 (June 1902).

2. Yang Liang (*fl.* 818 CE), author of the oldest extant commentary on the *Xunzi* (third century BCE).

3. 'The Canon of Yao', opening chapter of *The Book of Documents*; Liang is citing a passage that describes virtues (of rulers). Its description of social relations (which Liang truncates but which would have been recognized by most of his readers) is generally understood to refer to the relationships of ruler–minister, husband–wife, parent–child, younger–older brother, and friends, while proper ritual behavior is determined by one's position or class: specifically, Son of Heaven, lords, state ministers, scholars and commoners.

4. Hu Linyi (1812–1861): governor of Hubei who coordinated his armies with those of Zeng Guofan against the Taipings. *The Comprehensive Mirror in Aid of Governance*: by Sima Guang, a history of China from the ancient Zhou dynasty to the tenth century, published in 1084.

5. Li Hongzhang (1821–1901) worked with Zeng Guofan against the Taipings and later became China's leading statesman. The *Lantingji xu* (Preface to the Poems Collected from the Orchid Pavilion) is valued for its calligraphy by Wang Xizhi (fourth century CE).

6. Chen Fan was a political figure of the second century CE. According to historical lore, at the age of fourteen or fifteen Chen was living away from his family. When his father came to visit with a friend, they found Chen's living quarters a mess and asked why he had failed to clean them up for guests. Chen replied that he saw no point in cleaning his rooms when it was the evils of the world that needed cleaning up.

7. Guanzi was a statesman of the seventh century BCE; the *Guanzi* text was mostly compiled in *c.* fourth to third century BCE.

8. The original version of this essay concluded with an author's note: 'I have been ill for several weeks and wrote this draft in a hurry. Some points are not conveyed completely, which I will address and explain in the future.'

14. The Relationship between Buddhism and the Social Order (December 1902)

1. 論佛教與群治之關係,《新民叢報》 no. 23, GX 28-12-1 (30 December 1902).

2. *Analects* 2:17, 9:8; *Zhongyong* 12; *Analects* 11:12.

3. World-honored-one: one of the ten epithets for the Buddha.

4. From the *Śūraṅgama Sūtra* (Ch. *Dafo dingshou lengyanjing*).

5. Liang is drawing on the distinction between the Mahayana and Hinayana schools of Buddhism; in Mahayana especially, bodhisattvas are persons on the path of enlightenment who are driven by compassion to help and awaken others. Chinese commentators, whose tradition Liang reflects, tended to regard themselves as followers of Mahayana ('greater vehicle') as opposed to Hinayana ('lesser vehicle'; Theravada Buddhism). Liang here is associating Hinayana with a kind of selfishness – with those who seek their personal escape from the cycle of transmigration (by achieving nirvana), rather than acting out of compassion for the salvation of all beings – that is, the Mahayana bodhisattva.

6. In Theravada/Hinayana Buddhism, an Arhat is one who has eliminated all fetters and defilements, achieving nirvana; a Non-returner has eliminated some fetters and will be reborn into a heaven where they can seek further enlightenment; a Once-returner has eliminated a number of fetters and will be reincarnated only one more time; and a Self-enlightened one has achieved nirvana without the help of others, such as teachers, and does not teach others.

7. Liang is misleading here; actually, disciples (Śrāvaka) and Self-enlightened ones (Pratyekabuddha) are together called the Two Vehicles in Theravada.

8. The Neo-Confucian school of the Song dynasty (960–1279) was influenced by, and also harshly critical of, Buddhism.

9. From the *Sutra of Perfect Enlightenment* (*Yuanjue jing*); this is a description of bodhisattvas.

10. Kalpa, in Buddhism, is an eon, the time between the creation and recreation of a universe, or simply an extremely long time.

11. Passages from Tan Sitong's *Renxue*; cf. Sin-wai Chan (trans.),
    An Exposition of Benevolence: The Jen-hsüeh *of T'an Ssu-t'ung*
    (Hong Kong: Chinese University Press, 1984), pp. 92–3 (modi-
    fied). Tan (1865–1898) was well known to Liang; by the late
    1890s, Tan was advocating extensive and radical reforms based
    on a synthesis of Buddhism and Western science.

12. The three ages of human development postulated by Liang's
    teacher Kang Youwei.

13. The 'three vehicles' to reach nirvana or enlightenment refer to
    the vehicles of the disciples and Self-enlightened ones (of Hina-
    yana, see above), and the vehicle of the bodhisattva (of Mahayana;
    while further in Mayahana thought it is presumed that all three
    vehicles are eventually subsumed by the One Vehicle). The 'three
    canons' may refer to the scriptures associated with each vehicle
    or to the three basic divisions of the Buddhist canon: teachings,
    rules and treatises.

14. Both these texts are associated with the Yogācāra school of Bud-
    dhism, which was undergoing a revival in the late Qing.
    Ālayavijñāna is generally translated into English as 'storehouse
    consciousness', referring to the storehouse of all karmic seeds,
    which ripen into karmic consequences.

15. The exact quote is from *The Book of Rites*; Mencius made very
    similar remarks as well.

16. This is an idiom derived from *The Book of Odes*; Liang's quote
    is from the *Shuo yuan*, a collection from the first century BCE,
    which includes a brief account of the refusal of Prince Hu of
    Zheng to marry into the more powerful royal family of the state
    of Qi in the late eighth century BCE.

15. Personal Morality (October 1903–February 1904)

1. 論私德,《新民叢報》 no. 38–39, GX 29-8-14 (October 1903);
   no. 40–41, GX 29-9-14 (November 1903); and no. 46–48, GX
   29-12-29 (February 1904).

2. This passage, which is not an exact quote, is here translated back
   from Liang's Chinese. See Yan Fu's paraphrastic translation of
   Herbert Spencer's *The Study of Sociology* (1873): *Qunxue yiyan*
   (Shanghai: Shangwu yinshuguan, 1915 [1903]), pp. 39–40; for
   this passage, cf. Herbert Spencer, *The Study of Sociology* (New
   York: D. Appleton & Co., 1924), pp. 43–7.

3. Li Lou was a mythical figure with extraordinary vision.

4. Shi Kuang (sixth century CE) was a famous musician.

5. Wu Huo (*c.* fourth century BCE) possessed enormous strength.
6. *Mencius* 1A:7.
7. This passage here is translated back from the Chinese; it is not a direct quote from Montesquieu but adapted from various observations found in Books 1–8 of *The Spirit of the Laws*.
8. Gu Yanwu (1613–1682): a pre-eminent thinker of the seventeenth century, much admired throughout the Qing period. Eastern or Later Han (25–220 CE) was the successor dynasty to the Western or Former Han (202 BCE to 9 CE), bringing a branch of the Former Han imperial family back to the throne after a brief interregnum. Song dynasty, 960–1279.
9. Wang Mang (45 BCE to 23 CE) established the Xin dynasty (9–23 CE), usurping the Western Han, and was generally regarded as an illegitimate ruler.
10. From *The Book of Odes*.
11. Gu Yanwu, *Record of Daily Knowledge and Collected Poems and Essays: Selections*, Ian Johnston (trans. and ed.) (New York: Columbia University Press, 2017), pp. 99–100 (modified). The Three Dynasties refers to the Xia–Shang–Zhou golden age of the second millennium BCE. Eastern Han, 25–220 CE.
12. Five Dynasties: major states of the period of division in the tenth century, lasting about fifty years between the Tang and Song dynasties; also more completely referred to as the period of the Five Dynasties and Ten Kingdoms.
13. Song Taizu (r. 960–976): founder of the Song dynasty; Han Tong (908–960): a leading – and loyal – general of the Later Zhou dynasty, defeated by Song Taizu who ordered his death and the death of his entire family; Wei Rong (dates unknown): chancellor of the Northern Han dynasty who went over to the Song in 960 and is said to have later died of drink.
14. Famous scholars of the late tenth and the eleventh centuries.
15. Jingkang Incident: in 1127 attacks by the Jurchen Jin dynasty of the northeast, abetted by Song court corruption, led to the capture of the Song emperor and his father, the abdicated emperor, and to the collapse of the Northern Song dynasty, though the imperial family was able to re-establish its rule in the south.
16. That is, from the decadence of the late Western Han to the moral revival of the Eastern Han. Ai (r. 7–1 BCE); Ping (r. 1 BCE to 6 CE).
17. Spring and Autumn period (770–476 BCE), marking the decline of the Zhou royal house.

18. Warring States period, 475–221 BCE; Qin dynasty ('unification'), 221 BCE to 206 BCE; Western Han dynasty, 202 BCE to 9 CE.

19. Famous 'roving swordsmen', sometimes pictured as righteous outlaws.

20. Cao Cao (155–220): powerful Eastern Han official who became leader of one of the three major kingdoms that arose during the collapse of the Han in northern China (Jizhou), posthumously named Emperor Wu of the Wei dynasty.

21. Ming Taizu (1328–1398): founder of the Ming dynasty (1368–1644).

22. The Donglin Academy was established in 1604 with the goal of reforming official corruption through a return to fundamentalist Confucian values; in Ming court infighting, some of its supporters were tortured, exiled and executed. The Revival Society (Fushe) was founded in 1628 as a literary society, but many of its members were interested in social and political reform and became caught up in dangerous factional battles.

23. In addition to maintaining the regular examination system – which some men born under the Ming boycotted – the early Qing held special examinations by imperial invitation to attract greater support or at least defuse opposition. 'Twice-serving': i.e., having served the Ming, they disloyally went on to serve the Qing. The *Biographies* (*Erchen zhuan*) was compiled according to an imperial edict of 1777, marking a change from earlier imperial praise of Ming officials who went over to the Qing to condemnation of them.

24. Yongzheng (r. 1722–1735); Qianlong (r. 1735–1796). Liang is referring to the 'literary inquisitions' that had begun under the first Qing emperors but reached a climax under Qianlong in the second half of the eighteenth century (and see the following note).

25. Liang is referring to the Confucian Way, not the Way of Daoism. *The Complete Library of the Four Treasuries* is a massive collection of Chinese texts in four sections (classics, historiography, philosophy and literary works) that Qianlong ordered to be compiled in 1772. It contains nearly 3,500 works, while the Qing destroyed roughly 3,000 allegedly anti-Manchu works during the collection process, part of Qianlong's literary inquisition. Its *Annotated Catalog*, in 200 volumes, was completed in 1798. The *Combined Overview of Comprehensive Mirrors to*

Aid in Government is a history of China that Qianlong ordered to be compiled, based on *The Comprehensive Mirror to Aid in Government* (1084) and its continuations, earlier universal histories.

26. Legalism was one of the ancient 'schools' or intellectual traditions most associated with unsentimental methods of strengthening the state and its rulers. Liang cites two of its leading thinkers, Shang Yang (390–338 BCE) and Han Feizi (280–233 BCE), and a reference in *The Book of Shang Yang* to six 'parasitic affairs' that could weaken the state (namely 'end-of-year', 'food', 'beauty', 'likes', 'aspirations' and 'conduct'). Cf. Yuri Pines (trans. and ed.), *The Book of Shang: Apologetics of State Power in Early China* (New York: Columbia University Press, 2019).

27. The final lines of a well-known poem by the Jin dynasty general Liu Kun (270–318), written when he was captured and facing execution. If Liu was referring to himself, Liang is perhaps referring to the literati tradition or to China as a whole.

28. Henri Jean Baptiste Anatole Leroy-Beaulieu (1842–1912).

29. Yan and Zhao were major kingdoms of the Warring States period (fifth to third century BCE); both fell to the Qin in 222 BCE.

30. Liang is referring to so-called 'foreign conquest dynasties'. The Wu Hu, or 'five barbarians', refers to nomadic peoples from the north and northwest (greater Mongolia and Xinjiang) who established relatively short-lived regimes in China proper in the wake of the fall of the Han dynasty (third to fourth century). The Northern Wei (386–535) came to control much of northern China under the Tuoba clan of the Xianbei, originally a nomadic people of greater Mongolia. An Lushan (703–757) and Shi Siming (703?–761) were Tang dynasty military leaders of Turkic origins who established the rebel state of Yan (756–763). The Khitans were a Mongolian people who established the Liao dynasty (916–1125) which stretched across much of Central Asia to Manchuria and Siberia and the far Chinese north (including today's Beijing). The Jurchens were a Manchurian tribal people who established the Jin dynasty (1115–1234) in north China. The Mongols had established their vast Eurasian empire by the beginning of the thirteenth century and went on to complete the conquest of China to establish the Yuan dynasty (1271–1368). The Manchus, a people evidently descended from the Jurchens, replaced the Han Chinese Ming dynasty to establish Liang Qichao's own Qing dynasty in 1644.

234   NOTES

31. The Taiping Rebellion was a massive civil war that began in about 1850 and lasted to 1865; at one point the Taiping Heavenly Kingdom controlled most of China's richest provinces and directly threatened the Qing.

32. Cf. William H. Nienhauser (ed.), *The Grand Scribe's Records* (Bloomington: Indiana University Press, 1994), vol. 7, p. 11, for a more precise translation.

33. *Mencius* 1A:7.

34. Uchida Ryōhei, *Roshia bōkoku ron* (Tokyo: Kokuryūkai, 1901).

35. 7.1 jiao is 0.71 Chinese yuan (dollar).

36. Yokoyama Masao (1861–1943): professor of statistics at Rikugun Daigakkō; 7 yen was worth approximately USD3.5 in 1904. I am grateful to Professor Lin Man-houng for guidance here.

37. The Haikwan tael was the monetary value used in the Chinese customs service, a little over an ounce of fine silver.

38. Wei–Jin–Six Dynasties: the dynasties or kingdoms that came to power during the political disunity following the collapse of the Han dynasty, from the early third century to the sixth century. The Pure Discussion school originated at this time among apolitical Daoist scholars interested in metaphysics and the arts, and later expanded to include Confucian and Buddhist topics.

39. The school of Wang Yangming (1472–1529) read Confucianism in a way that emphasized intuition and activism.

40. That is, they let themselves be coopted by the Qing dynasty. Kangxi (r. 1661–1722) sponsored the most notable of these special examinations in 1679.

41. Wang Fuzhi (1619–1692), Huang Zongxi (1610–1695), Sun Qifeng (1583–1675), Li Yong (1627–1705): famous literati whose careers began under the Ming and who refused to serve the Qing.

42. The Cheng-Zhu school, originating in the Song dynasty, was a branch of Neo-Confucianism treated as orthodox by both the Ming and Qing imperial courts, to some extent at the expense of Wang Learning. It is named after Zhu Xi (1130–1200) and the brothers Cheng Hao (1032–1085) and Cheng Yi (1033–1107). Li Guangdi (1642–1718) and Tang Bin (1627–1687) were both high officials in the Kangxi court who promoted Cheng-Zhu orthodoxy.

43. The imperial court ultimately determined which persons would be enshrined as sages or worthy men to receive sacrifices along with Confucius. The court thus shaped the official orthodoxy, but independent intellectual trends could be equally important.

44. Koxinga (Zheng Chenggong, 1624–1662): Ming loyalist general; Quan Zuwang (1705–1755): historian; Gongsun Hong (200–121 BCE): Han dynasty philosopher and prime minister.

45. Lu Longqi (1630–1692), Lu Shiyi (1611–1672), Zhang Lüxiang (1611–1674), Fang Bao (1668–1749) and Xu Qianxue (1631–1694): orthodox Confucians and officials of the early Qing.

46. Xu Heng (1209–1281) and Wu Deng (1249–1333) also promoted Song Learning (i.e., Cheng-Zhu Neo-Confucianism); for Liang, they were also Han Chinese working for a foreign dynasty.

47. A late eighteenth-century, somewhat idiosyncratic collection of short biographies of philosophers. 'Song Learning' in the Qing dynasty referred to a metaphysical turn and a new emphasis on ethics associated with Zhu Xi and the Cheng brothers. The 'Han Learning' movement rejected much, though not all, of Song Learning and sought to return to more precise readings of the ancient classics through philological research.

48. Yan Ruoqu (1636–1704), Wang Niansun (1744–1832), Duan Yucai (1735–1815) and Dai Zhen (1724–1777): pioneering philologists, less known for any philosophical work properly speaking, with the exception of Dai Zhen. For Han Learning, see the note above.

49. Qianlong (r. 1735–1796); the Inner Court was the preserve of the imperial family, reserved primarily for the emperor, his wives, concubines and children, and the eunuchs.

50. Wang Mingsheng (1722–1797): Qing official and classicist. *Final Notes on the 'Book of Documents'* was a compilation of commentaries on the ancient *Book of Documents*, and *A Discussion of the Seventeen Histories* was a study of the official dynastic histories.

51. The 'eight-legged essay' was the prescribed style of answers to the civil service examinations, which were key to defining the governing class.

52. China's loss in the Sino-Japanese War of 1894–1895 was a shock to the system and a spur to radical reform efforts.

53. By 'destruction', Liang is implying revolutionism. 'National essence', a popular term at the time, referred not to some unchanging core of identity but to China as a complex and evolving culture, including ancient thinkers neglected in the mainstream tradition.

54. Cf. Herbert Spencer, *The Study of Sociology*, pp. 19–20: 'Given an average defect of nature among the units of a society, and no

skillful manipulation of them will prevent that defect from producing its equivalent of bad results . . . For suppose that by some
official instrumentality you actually suppress an evil, instead of
thrusting it from one spot into another – suppose you successfully deal with a number of such evils by a number of such
instrumentalities; do you think these evils have disappeared
absolutely? To see that they have not, you have but to ask –
Whence comes the official apparatus? . . .'

55. The second quote is actually from the *Yanzi chunqiu* which, like
The Book of Rites, is dated to roughly the fourth to the third
century BCE.

56. That is, 'we can see that national calamity is approaching'. For
Xin You, unbound hair was a mark of the barbarians. According
to an account in the *Zuo zhuan* (a fourth-century BCE account
of ancient history), in the ninth century BCE Xin You had predicted the political events of the following century.

57. Hong Xiuquan (1814–1864): leader of the Taiping Rebellion
(1850–1865) which came close to overthrowing the Qing dynasty.
Zhang Xianzhong (1606–1647): Ming soldier who rebelled
against the dynasty, tried to found his own dynasty and was
eventually defeated by the new Qing dynasty. Both men were
Han who fought the Manchus.

58. Wang Mang (45 BCE to 23 CE) seized the Han throne, unlike Yi
Yin and the Duke of Zhou, who served as loyal regents of the
ancient Shang and Zhou dynasties, respectively. Cao Pi (187–
226) proclaimed himself emperor of one of the kingdoms that
emerged during the fall of the Han dynasty in the early third
century; Shun and Yu were legendary sage-kings.

59. Han Tuozhou (1152–1207): statesman of the (Han) Southern
Song dynasty who pursued a disastrous policy of trying to retake
the north from the Jurchen (Manchu) Jin dynasty (1115–1234).

60. Wang Meng (325–375): a Han who was prime minister to the
foreign (Di) ruler Fu Jian (337–385) as he expanded the territories of the Former Qin, one of the short-lived kingdoms that
arose in the post-Han period of political struggle.

61. That is, for Liang, the political disunity and barbarian invasions
of the third to fifth centuries.

62. The mythical Yellow Emperor was regarded as the ancestor of
the Han people and founder of the first Chinese kingdom. (Other
peoples, from the Toba to the Manchus, sometimes claimed des-
cent from the Yellow Emperor as well.)

63. *Daode jing*, chapter 69.

64. Zeng Guofan (1811–1872): (Han) Chinese military leader and master strategist of the Qing dynasty's victory over the Taipings (1850–1865) and postwar recovery.

65. Wang and Li were high-ranking subordinates of Zeng, who found their performances wanting.

66. The *Scholarly Annals of the Song and Yuan Periods*: a historical work on Confucian thinkers, compiled over the seventeenth and eighteenth centuries and achieving its final form in the early nineteenth century.

67. Monkeys represent wickedness and should not be encouraged in their natural propensities; conversely, the verse continues, if the ruler has good plans, the common people will submit to him. Centuries of attempts to illuminate these ancient verses have not always succeeded. The lines Liang quotes here are from a section of the *Odes* called 'lesser court hymns' and were long associated with political lessons. 'Teach a monkey to climb trees' became an idiom meaning to encourage a wicked person to carry out evil deeds.

68. Cf. Daniel K. Gardner, *Chu Hsi and the* Ta-hsueh: *Neo-Confucian Reflection on the Confucian Canon* (Cambridge, MA: CEAS, Harvard University Press, 1986), pp. 111–12.

69. From Laozi, *Daode jing, c.* fifth century BCE. Cf. Moss Roberts (trans.), *Dao De Jing: The Book of the Way* (Berkeley: University of California Press, 2001), p. 128. Whatever Laozi may have meant, Liang imbues 'Way' with a sense of righteousness or morality; the ancient Chinese term 'Way' or *dao* became part of the modern term 'morality' (*daode*), which is the title of the Laozi text, generally translated as something like 'The Way and Its Power'). As is his wont, Liang is playing with words to make a point.

70. Cf. Julia Ching (ed.), *The Records of Ming Scholars by Huang Tsung-hsi* (Honolulu: University of Hawaii Press, 1987), pp. 46, 45.

71. Cf. Wing-tsit Chan (trans.), *Instructions for Practical Living and Other Neo-Confucian Writings by Wang Yang-ming* (New York: Columbia University Press, 1963), pp. 123–4. The 'Sage' refers to Confucius.

72. Cf. Julia Ching (trans.), *The Philosophical Letters of Wang Yang-ming* (Canberra: Australian National University Press, 1972), p. 28.

73. Chapters of the ancient *Book of Rites*, part of the elementary educational curriculum from the Song through the Qing dynasties.

74. 'Innate-knowing': i.e., *good* knowledge is inherent to human beings. Cf. Julia Ching (trans.), *Philosophical Letters*, p. 90.

75. Cf. Wing-tsit Chan (trans.), *Instructions for Practical Living*, p. 193.
76. Qian Xushan (Qian Dehong, 1496–1574); Liang took this quote from Huang Zongxi's *Mingru xuean*, Huang's systematic survey of Ming dynasty thinkers.
77. Cf. Julia Ching (trans.), *Philosophical Letters*, p. 102.
78. Zhezhong School: one of the major schools of Wang Learning, based on the teachings of Wang's disciples from his native prefecture.
79. Liu Zongzhou (1578–1645): sharp critic of later schools of Wang Learning and to some extent of Wang Yangming himself.
80. *Shijing*, no. 236, no. 256.
81. *Analects* 19:11.
82. From the *Shuo Yuan* (a collection of short texts compiled by Liu Xiang, 77–76 BCE) and *Kongzi jiayu* (*School Sayings of Confucius*, third to second century BCE?). Liang has truncated; the full quote should be: 'If trickles of water are not stopped, they will become a great river. If thread is woven continuously, it will become a net [laws]. If green buds are not chopped down, you will need to use an ax [reins of government].'
83. In the Neo-Confucian worldview that Liang is citing here, 'Principle' refers to something like the inherent organization of the cosmos.
84. The original quote is from the advice of the Song philosopher Zhu Xi (1130–1200) on how to study properly: with full and complete attention in order to reach true understanding.
85. The quote is an unacknowledged citation from *Mencius* 4A:10.
86. Liang modifies *Mencius* 7B:31; while Liang metaphorically refers to moral boundaries, most interpretations of the original passage take there to be a literal wall, as between houses or neighboring courtyards, that it would be wrong to bore through or jump over.
87. *Mencius* 4B:30.

16. Defects of the Chinese People (February 1904)

1. Chapter 40 of *New World Travel Notes* (新大陸遊記). First published by 新民叢報社 as a supplement to *Xinmin congbao*, distributed free to subscribers. Liang did not title the chapter; the title given here comes from the chapter's first sentence.
2. Cf. the partial translation in R. David Arkush and Leo O. Lee (eds), *Land without Ghosts: Chinese Impressions of America*

from the Mid-Nineteenth Century to the Present (Berkeley: University of California Press, 1989), pp.92–5.

3.   From *The Great Learning*, a Confucian text long central to the school curriculum.

4.   Zhou dynasty, 1046–256 BCE.

5.   Lian Po (*c.* 327–243 BCE): a famous general of the Warring States period; after being forced to leave the kingdom of Zhao for the kingdom of Chu, he still thought Zhao soldiers were superior. Zifang (Zhang Liang, *c.* 251–186 BCE): an early Han dynasty statesman originally from the kingdom of Hán (unrelated to the Han dynasty); he sought to assassinate Qin Shihuang in revenge for his conquest of the kingdom of Hán and never forgot his home even while working for the Han dynasty.

6.   Zuo Geng: San Francisco consul between 1889 and 1901.

7.   Gustave Le Bon (1841–1931): French psychologist and social thinker, deeply skeptical of democracy.

8.   Most Chinese immigrants to America came from Guangdong Province (Cantonese region), as did Liang.

9.   Guanzi (Guan Zhong, seventh century BCE) and Shang Yang (*c.* 390–338 BCE): statesmen associated with strong authoritarian government and the School of Legalism. Lycurgus (ninth century BCE): legendary 'law-giver' of Sparta. Oliver Cromwell (1599–1658): English leader of the Parliamentary forces against the monarchy, Lord Protector in the 1650s.

10. Shao music was said to have been composed by Emperor Shun (trad. dates late third century BCE); Liang is further extrapolating from *Mencius* 14B:71.

11. Xu Qin (1873–1945): a reformer and fellow student of Kang Youwei.

17. The Self-Awakening of the Chinese People (March–July 1920)

1.   中國人之自覺, from *Impressions from My European Travels* (歐 遊心影錄). First published in 1920 in the *Shishi xinbao* 時事新報 (Shanghai) serially from March to July; and in the *Chenbao* 晨報 (Beijing) from March through August. I have largely followed the version in *Yinbingshi heji*, which is slightly revised.

2.   Liang may be referring to the late Qing political movements of the 'constitutionalists' (of which he was a leader) who wished to reform the Qing dynasty by turning it into a constitutional monarchy, and the 'revolutionaries' who wished to overthrow the

Qing and replace it with the republic. That is to say, Liang is looking back to the 1911 Revolution, which created the Republic of China that soon fell into the hands of competing warlords, but he also seems to be thinking of a similar split between reformers and radicals in the 1910s.

3. Du Fu (712–770): Tang dynasty poet writing in another era of political disintegration.

4. *Zhongyong* 23; this text was one of the Four Books that formed the basis of Confucian education.

5. The original sentence in full: 'Even if you are illiterate, you must try to be a righteous person.'

6. Han Yu (768–824): literary and political figure of the Tang dynasty. The 'Sage' refers to Confucius.

7. Legendary sage-kings and dynastic founders, traditionally held to be models of virtue and wisdom.

8. Qin Shihuang (259–210 BCE) conquered the 'warring states' to unify China by founding the Qin dynasty in 221 BCE. He was remembered as a tyrant who killed Confucian scholars and burned classical texts such as the *Odes* and the *History*.

9. The Cheng brothers, Cheng Hao (1032–1085) and Cheng Yi (1033–1107), and Zhu Xi (1130–1200) were leading figures of the Song school of Neo-Confucianism.

10. Liang is borrowing the term 'true self' (*zhenwo*) from Mahayana Buddhism with connotations of autonomy and freedom.

11. The original version of this section was titled 'Organizational abilities and rules of collective life', a term that in the body of this section is sometimes replaced and sometimes retained.

12. Geographical constituencies refer to popular voting in a given district; functional constituencies consist of government-recognized professional or other groups or juridical persons.

13. Liang is presumably referring to Switzerland's system of direct democracy.

14. Ongoing conflicts between loose alliances of warlords from southern and northern China led to several efforts at reconciliation, including a 'peace conference' in 1919 that Liang regarded as the result of public pressure.

15. 'Local self-government' became a major topic in Chinese reformist discourse in the 1890s, sometimes seen as a route toward democratization; however, in practice it came to mean either top-down state intervention or rule by local elites.

16. Since the *Kangxi Dictionary* was published in 1716, a Song dynasty (960–1279) edition would be quite remarkable.

17. *Analects* 16:1.
18. *Mencius* 1A:7.
19. This paragraph was expanded from the original version, which simply classified three schools of socialism as the communist, the collectivist (in apparent reference to Marxism) and the distributionist.
20. According to ancient classics, the well-field system was a method of land distribution and taxation, so named because the Chinese character for 'well' (井) expressed the layout of nine fields.
21. Pre-Qin, i.e., before the founding of the Qin dynasty in 221 BC.
22. *Zhongyong* 23, and *Yijing*, Qian hexagram; *Daode jing*, chapter 16; *Mozi* 3:1.
23. 'Great self' refers to community and 'small self' to the individual.
24. Chan ('school of meditation'), or Zen in Japanese.
25. Sui dynasty (581–618); Tang dynasty (618–907).
26. Li Bai (Li Po, 701–762): Tang dynasty poet.
27. Erudites were officials recognized for their broad learning or their knowledge of ritual. The story of the Erudite and the mule was first written down in the Northern Qi (550–577).
28. This short 'final note' was omitted from the revised version when the chapter was published as a stand-alone essay.

18. Human Rights and Women's Rights
(November 1924)

1. 人權與女權,《晨報副刊》, 16 November 1924.
2. Legendary sage-kings Yao (2324–2255 BCE) and Shun (2294–2184 BCE); Three Dynasties (golden age): Xia (*c.* 2070–1600 BCE), Shang (*c.* 1600–1045 BCE), Zhou (1045–256 BCE).
3. That is, *Déclaration des droits de l'homme et du citoyen* (Declaration of the Rights of Man and of the Citizen), 1789.
4. Zhuangzi (trad. late fourth century BCE); cf. trans. Brook Ziporyn, *Zhuangzi*, p. 4.

19. The Proletariat Class and the Idler Class (May 1925)

1. 無產階級與無業階級,《晨報副刊》no. 96, 1 May 1925.
2. That is, scholar, farmer, artisan, merchant.

Acknowledgments

I am grateful to a large number of people who helped me select essays to translate and sort out several knotty questions. These include Stephen Angle, Ke-wu (Max) Huang 黃克武, Philip J. Ivanhoe, Theresa M. Lee, Xianglin (Sean) Lei 雷祥麟, Man-houng Lin 林滿紅, Sarah Paine, Jean Tsui, Sebastien Veg, Fansen Wang 王汎森, Wen Yu 于文 and not least Mr Google. I am further grateful for the advice and patience of my editor at Penguin, Simon Winder; and also for early work with Qilin Cao, Bu Chen, Jeremy James, Yingqi Tang, Yuji Xu, Yongyan Ye and Anli Zhang. I alone am responsible for remaining errors. As Liang remarked of one of his own works, 'there are doubtless quite a number of mistakes and omissions, which I hope my readers will correct'.